Maya® Studio Projects
Dynamics

TODD PALAMAR

WILEY
Wiley Publishing, Inc.

Acquisitions Editor: Mariann Barsolo
Development Editor: Jim Compton
Technical Editor: Campbell Strong
Production Editor: Angela Smith
Copy Editor: Sharon Wilkey
Editorial Manager: Pete Gaughan
Production Manager: Tim Tate
Vice President and Executive Group Publisher: Richard Swadley
Vice President and Publisher: Neil Edde
Media Assistant Project Manager: Jenny Swisher
Media Associate Producer: Josh Frank
Media Quality Assurance: Shawn Patrick
Book Designers: Caryl Gorska, Maureen Forys, Kate Kaminski
Compositor: Kate Kaminski, Happenstance Type-O-Rama
Proofreader: Carrie Hunter, Word One New York
Indexer: Ted Laux
Project Coordinator, Cover: Lynsey Stanford
Cover Designer: Ryan Sneed
Cover Image: Todd Palamar

Library of Congress Cataloging-in-Publication Data:

Palamar, Todd.
  Maya studio projects : dynamics / Todd Palamar.
    p. cm.
  ISBN-13: 978-0-470-48776-1 (paper/DVD)
  ISBN-10: 0-470-48776-3 (paper/DVD)
  1. Science—Computer simulation. 2. Science—Experiments—Data processing. 3. Computer graphics. 4. Three-dimensional display systems. 5. Maya (Computer file) I. Title.
  Q183.9.P355 2010
  006.6'9—dc22
                    2009035818

Dear Reader,

Thank you for choosing *Maya Studio Projects: Dynamics*. This book is part of a family of premium-quality Sybex books, all of which are written by outstanding authors who combine practical experience with a gift for teaching.

Sybex was founded in 1976. More than 30 years later, we're still committed to producing consistently exceptional books. With each of our titles, we're working hard to set a new standard for the industry. From the paper we print on, to the authors we work with, our goal is to bring you the best books available.

I hope you see all that reflected in these pages. I'd be very interested to hear your comments and get your feedback on how we're doing. Feel free to let me know what you think about this or any other Sybex book by sending me an email at nedde@wiley.com. If you think you've found a technical error in this book, please visit http://sybex.custhelp.com. Customer feedback is critical to our efforts at Sybex.

Best regards,

Neil Edde
Vice President and Publisher
Sybex, an Imprint of Wiley

Acknowledgments

When I set out to write a book on dynamic simulations using Maya, I prepared myself for the largest undertaking of my career. I had several powerful computers at my disposal. I allotted a large chunk of time from my daily routine, and I bottled up a ton of energy and motivation. A few weeks into the project, none of this would matter. Like a heavy downpour of rain and hail, so were the misfortunate events. Blow after blow, my seemingly well-constructed plans were dismantled. Each week presented a new hurdle to jump, from personal loss to computer failure; it was a decade of challenges condensed into a few months. ■ Throughout this turbulent time, one thing remained constant: the support of the people around me. I am so grateful for my wife, Brindle. She keeps me balanced and whole; without her, I am nothing but a shell. I must thank my four kids who listened endlessly to my technobabble and somehow always had the answers. ■ I would like to thank the entire team at Wiley for their incredible patience and understanding in creating this book. Most important, I want to thank Mariann Barsolo. Her faith and guidance kept me motivated throughout the writing of this book. I'd also like to thank Jim Compton, Angela Smith, and Sharon Wilkey for all their editorial guidance, and Technical Editor Campbell Strong for lending his technical expertise.

About the Author

Todd Palamar is a 20-year veteran in the computer animation industry. Transitioning early in his career from traditional special effects to computer-generated imagery, Todd has done effects work for several direct-to-video movies. He later worked on numerous video games, including Sega of Japan's coin-operated title Behind Enemy Lines, as well as Dukes of Hazzard and Trophy Buck 2 for the Sony PlayStation console. For six years, Todd taught at Full Sail University. During this time, he received numerous accolades for outstanding educator. Additionally, Todd was a trainer at the DAVE School, bringing post-graduate students up to speed in Maya. Todd has written four books, including Maya Cloth for Characters and Maya Feature Creature Creations. His breadth of experience has allowed him to work in location-based entertainment, military simulation, television commercials, and corporate spots. Todd currently resides at Vcom3D as technical director, creating real-time characters capable of sign language and lip syncing.

CONTENTS AT A GLANCE

Contents

Introduction

Simulation: You hear the term a lot. It's used by the military to describe how they train, it teaches airline pilots how to fly, and it shows meteorologists what the weather will be. Even doctors are getting in on the game by doing virtual surgery. Simulation is everywhere; as computers get more powerful, so do the simulations.

Simulation is the action that results from established parameters describing a particular scenario. The hard part about understanding simulation is how each component influences the outcome. Take the weather, for example. Meteorologists look at the amount of moisture in the air, the direction of the wind, and even the position of the moon to try to predict what the weather will be. Each of these factors has as much influence on the other, as it does by itself. This interdependency has a seesaw effect. When one attribute rises, it causes another to fall. It is simple to visualize when comparing two values, but imagine 50 or 100. Juggling this information in your head is challenging to say the least. Computers can do the work for us; however, we must comprehend each value in order to create an accurate simulation.

Maya has an abundance of tools to handle simulation, including Inverse Kinematics and certain lighting effects. For the purpose of this book, only those tools related to creating natural and physical phenomena such as tornadoes, explosions, and the like are discussed. The tools include Particles, Rigid Bodies, Soft Bodies, Fluids, nParticles, nCloth, and Hair. Even with such a variety, there is commonality among them. Each has an influenced point that is simulated. Information is fed to the point, solving for its position, speed, and numerous other variables. The point may be a vertex or a particle, but in essence, is still a simulated point.

Who Should Read This Book

If you have ever been interested in creating visual effects or natural phenomena for films, television, games, or simulation, you should read this book. The book starts off with some basic principles of 3D simulation using particles and fluids. If you are an experienced user, you can skim over the first two chapters. They are designed to bring you up to speed and familiarize you with the techniques and conventions of the book.

The book is designed for the intermediate Maya user. It is assumed that you have a thorough working knowledge of Maya's interface and have at least dabbled in each module. The dynamic simulations presented in this book use more than the menus and tools related to Maya dynamics. Working knowledge of modeling, animating, texturing, and rendering is extremely beneficial.

What You Will Learn

In this book, you will learn how to work with Maya Dynamics to create natural phenomena. The principal focus is on using Fluids, nParticles, Rigid Bodies, and to a lesser degree, Particles. Each project teaches you which tools to use and how to use the attributes to get the desired results. Most of the projects are accomplished through the Maya settings only; no scripts are used and only a minimal number of expressions are employed. This was done intentionally, to focus on maximizing Maya's out-of-the-box capabilities. When you are finished with this book, you will be able to use a combination of Maya's simulation tools to produce desired results.

Hardware and Software Requirements

When dealing with visual effects and reproducing natural phenomena, there's no such thing as too much computer power. All of these effects are computationally expensive and eat as much computer power as you can feed them. At a minimum, you should have nothing less than a 2.8GHz CPU and 2GB of RAM.

It is also recommended that you run only Maya-certified graphics cards. Although most graphics cards can run Maya, they do not support every feature; icons may be missing, and software may crash.

For more specific information on system requirements and certified graphics cards, go to

`www.autodesk.com/maya`

Finally, to access all of Maya's dynamic tools and to complete the projects in this book, you need to be using Maya 2010 or Maya 2009 Unlimited. Maya 2009 Complete does not give you access to Fluids or nDynamics, the principal tools used in this book.

How to Use This Book

The projects in this book follow a sequence from least to most difficult and processor-intensive. The further you go, the harder and more in-depth the projects become. The projects also become more taxing on your computer. I recommend that you complete each chapter in order, because some tools are explained incrementally. Following along gives you a better understanding of the tool as the demand on it increases. The material covered in each chapter is as follows:

Chapter 1, "Exploring Particles," starts you off with basic particle simulation. By building a solar system, you learn how to add per particle attributes and expressions. You are also introduced to using fields to control dynamic motion.

Chapter 2, "Fluid Mechanics," introduces you to fluid simulation. You start by doing a practical experiment and translating the results into a 3D Fluid simulation. The chapter finishes by creating a sun with Fluid dynamics.

Chapter 3, "Breaking Ground," takes a look at nParticles and nCloth and the features they offer. Using the two, you first build a virtual sandbox. When you're finished playing in the sand, it's time to create a sinkhole in the middle of a city street.

Chapter 4, "Volcanic Activity," focuses on creating volcanoes and the lava they produce. Your first project is to re-create a Plinian-style eruption by using a combination of fluids and nCloth. The next task is to build a rolling wall of lava. By the end of the chapter, you will understand how to make fluids look gaseous or solid as rock.

Chapter 5, "Tornadoes," utilizes the power of nParticles, and the rendered look of fluids, to destroy a cabin in seconds. Learning about the massive destructive power of a real tornado helps you to simulate its look and effects. This chapter teaches you how to gain control over fluids by using dynamic fields.

Chapter 6, "Playing with Fire," uses fluid effects to create fire. After building a flame from scratch, you'll save it as a preset to be used in the next project to create a much bigger fire. The simple flame is transformed into a large-scale fire and used to burn down a house.

Chapter 7, "Explosions," takes fire to the next level by simulating a combustible material. Once again, using the versatile power of fluids, you create a small explosion. The explosion becomes the basis for the chapter's second large-scale project, destroying a gas station. Employing nCloth to destroy the building's geometry, you'll also use fluids to provide the spectacular finishing touches of a huge fireball and burning columns of gasoline.

Chapter 8, "Floods," tackles the ultimate natural phenomenon for simulation: water. Pushing nParticles and your computer to the limit, you'll create an enormous body of gushing water through the middle of a city.

When you start a project, it is best to copy the files from the DVD to your local hard drive. In Maya, set the project directory to the root of the copied files. Doing this ensures that all of the scenes and other referenced files will be mapped properly.

It is also worth mentioning that I set the precision of my Channel Box to 15 for greater accuracy. You may notice the extended decimal value in some of the illustrations that show input fields for various settings. This is not a requirement, only a personal preference.

The Companion DVD

The DVD included with this book contains incrementally saved Maya scene files, all of the figures shown in the book, and incrementally created movies of each project. All of the Maya scene files are called out in the text of the book. Use these to confirm your settings or test new ideas. The figures are useful to scrutinize detail that doesn't show up in print. Some can also be used for reference, to match color and shapes.

When creating a simulation in a production environment, after you are happy with the results, you typically create a *cache file*. Cache files store all of the necessary data to play back the simulation without having to reprocess it. Cache files can be extremely large. Most of the simulations included with this book are not cached, because the finished cache files are simply too large to include on the DVD.

Contacting the Author

I welcome any and all feedback you might have about this book and the simulations within it. You can contact me at `tap@speffects.com`. To see my latest endeavors, please visit `www.speffects.com`.

Sybex strives to keep you supplied with the latest tools and information you need for your work. Please check the book's website at `www.sybex.com/go/mayastudioprojectsdynamics`, where we'll post additional content and updates that supplement this book should the need arise.

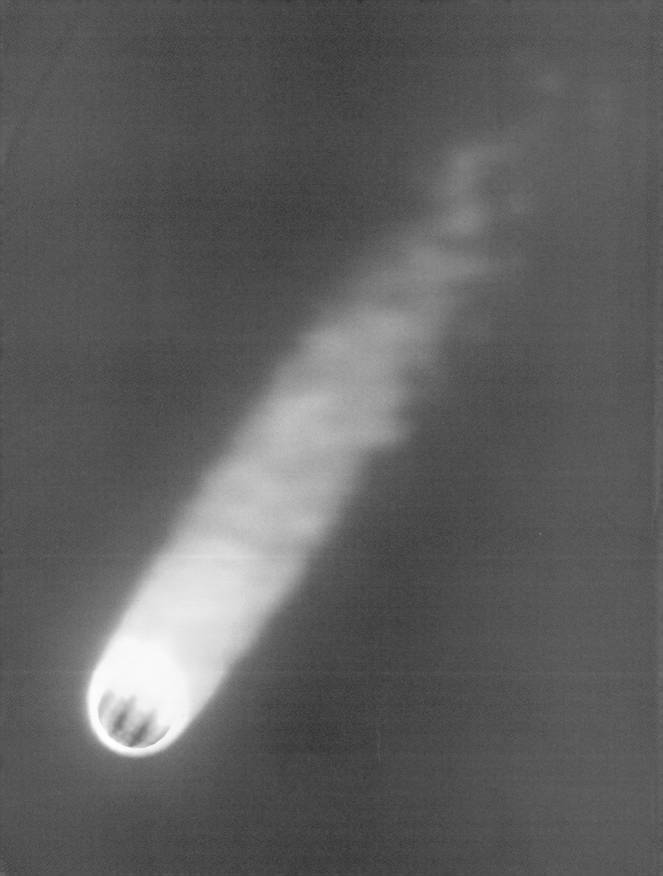

CHAPTER 1

Exploring Particles

In the beginning, 3D computer graphics consisted of triangles with colored vertices. People laughed and said it would never be useful for film-quality work. A select few could see the future of the technology. Then an explosive, cataclysmic event occurred. In an ironic twist of art and science, an extinct animal brought life to computer graphics. *Jurassic Park* (1993) would change filmmaking forever. No longer limited to shiny, reflective surfaces, computer-generated imagery was utilized in all aspects of the movie. The dinosaurs were only the beginning. Their interaction with the world around them was just as challenging. Trees needed to break and shatter. Rain had to splash and pour off the tyrannosaur's back. To make these things happen, particle simulation was put into action. The work done on *Jurassic Park* gave life to new technologies and rise to worlds unseen.

Particle Simulation

Particles are versatile and can be rendered in a multitude of ways. Relatively inexpensive to simulate, they can look like sparks or a splash of water. Particles can also be used to drive geometry or be driven by other simulations. Their adaptability makes them a powerful and resourceful tool.

Simple points in space, these objects exemplify the law of inertia: An object in motion tends to stay in motion unless acted upon. Particles are calculated with no understanding of the world around them. A particle simulation does not solve for atmospheric factors such as air density, pressure, and temperature. Particles are allowed to move unencumbered through space. It's possible to impose restrictions on them through fields and expressions, but once a particle, always a particle. You can't change what it was born to do.

Many scientists accredit the creation of the universe to a cosmic explosion. Referred to as the Big Bang, it is the idea that the universe exploded from a central point in space and is still expanding today. Millions of particles were fired into the blackness, all at different velocities. The farther from Earth they are today, the faster their initial speed. Whether you believe this theory or not, computer-generated particles operate in the same manner.

To understand particle simulation, in this chapter you'll look at what it takes to create a big bang explosion. The point isn't to create something realistic or perfectly crafted. The goal of this chapter is to show you the anatomy and functionality of particle simulation. Even if you have worked with simulation before, it's important to work through this chapter. Simplistic on the surface, it addresses key nodes usually hidden from view.

Following Newton's laws of motion, simulated particles have very little inherent motion. They are the simplest form of simulation. You could say they can't think for themselves. They must be told what to do. That's fine as long as you want to simulate stuff in outer space, where air and friction don't exist. If you are simulating under Earthlike conditions, then it is up to you to direct every aspect of the particle simulation. This typically requires extensive use of fields and expressions.

Project: Building a Solar System

The following exercise takes you through the creation of a particle solar system. It teaches you how to emit a variety of particles and use fields to control their motion. The purpose is to familiarize you with the basic workflow and common attributes of particle simulation. This exercise covers core attributes for manipulating particles. When finished, you will have simulated a small explosion.

1. Before starting any project, it is essential to establish its parameters. First, create a new project and name it **SolarSystem**. Next, set the proper frame rate by choosing Window → Settings/Preferences → Preferences. Within the Settings category, Maya sets the rate to be 24fps by default. This is fine as long as you plan on outputting your final results to film. For this book, all simulations are done at 30fps, making it easy to output to DVD. The simulation will now be solved at the proper frame rate. However, by itself the frame rate doesn't guarantee the simulation will always simulate properly.

    In the Preferences window, choose Time Slider. Set the Playback Speed to Play Every Frame. Without this setting, the simulation can skip, like a scratched record. (Maya does this so that it can maintain the set frame rate.) If this happens, you get unpredictable results, from failed collision detection to erratic speeds. Playing every frame ensures a smooth simulation, but it does have a drawback. As the simulation gets more complex, your computer slows down, in turn slowing the playback speed. This does not adversely impact the simulation. It only makes it difficult to judge the proper speed. You can overcome this problem by storing the data into a cache file, a technique I cover later in the chapter. Once created, the simulation can play directly from the cache file.

2. Switch to the Dynamics module. Choose the Particles → Create Emitter tool options. Reset the settings and create the emitter. Change the range of the time slider to go from 1 to 5,000 and click Play. The emitter sprays particles in every direction, as shown in Figure 1.1.

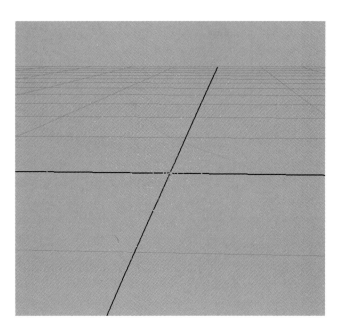

Figure 1.1

The particles are emitted in every direction.

3. The particle simulation is reset every time you return to frame 1. This doesn't happen because you went to the beginning of the time slider; it happens because the Start Frame of the simulation is set to 1. Select the particles. Look in the Channel Box under particleShape1. Find the Start Frame attribute. Change the value to 30. Play the simulation again. The particles are not emitted until frame 30.

The particle simulation has an explosive look but lacks chaos. To help, use the Speed Random attribute, which varies the speed at which the particles are emitted. Remember, objects in motion tend to stay in motion. This is true for the speed as well. When a particle is emitted at a speed of 1, it continues at that speed until acted upon by another force. The Speed Random attribute alters the speed of each particle. The particles retain the speed they were assigned at emission. As a result, the distance between each particle increases over time. Change the Speed Random attribute to 1. Play the simulation.

Figure 1.2

The number of particles is displayed in the Attribute Editor.

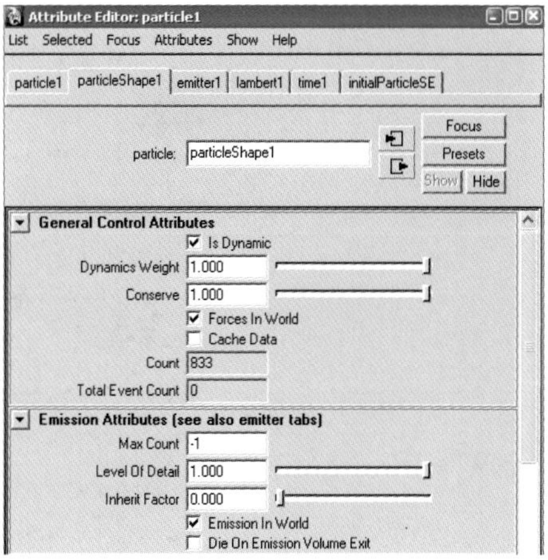

4. Select the emitter. In the Channel Box, change the Rate value to 50,000. Click the Play button to see the particles emit at a rate of 50,000 points per second. Remember, they won't start until frame 30. Go to frame 30. Set a keyframe for the Rate. Go to frame 32, change the Rate to 0, and keyframe the value. Return to frame 1 and play the simulation.

The particles explode out in one quick burst. Because the emitter has a fraction of a second to respond, only 833 particles are emitted. Counting particles can be tedious. Fortunately, Maya feeds this information into the particles' attributes. Select the particles and open the Attribute Editor. Click on the particleShape1 tab. Under General Control Attributes, the Count field displays the number of particles contained within the node. Figure 1.2 illustrates.

5. In this simulation, the particles represent orbiting satellites, such as space debris and moons. Rename emitter1 to **satelliteEmitter**. Change particle1 to **satellites**. Let's add some large planets.

Obviously, this isn't a scientifically accurate simulation. We'll add a sun for our planets to orbit in the next chapter.

Select satelliteEmitter and open the tool options for Duplicate Special. Select the Duplicate Input Graph check box to replicate the emitter's emissions and animation applied in the previous steps. Choose Duplicate Special. Change the new particle type for this emitter to Spheres and name it **planets**. Select emitter2 and name it **planetEmitter**. Open the Attribute Editor. Find the Rate under the Basic Emitter Attributes tab. Right-click on the keyed value and choose emitter1_rate1.output from the pop-up menu. Set the value of frame 30 to 800. Play the simulation. Figure 1.3 shows simulated frame 300. I've changed the background color of the viewport to a dark blue for added effect.

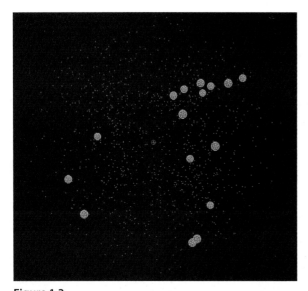

Figure 1.3

The spheres and particle points explode out from a single point in space.

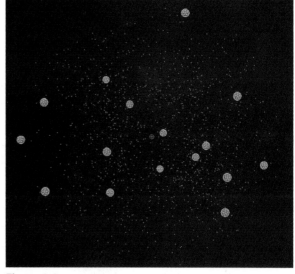

Figure 1.4

The planets' distribution is more spread out after changing the Random Stream Seeds setting.

The points and spheres emit in unison. If the two emitters discharged the same number of particles, they would all overlap. This won't matter for this example, but the way the spheres are clumped together in the top-right corner does. You want the spheres to have an even distribution. Select the planet particles. Open the Attribute Editor and choose the planetsShape tab. Under Emission Random Stream Seeds, change the planetEmitter value to 34. This setting varies the particle emission. It doesn't add or take away particles; it only changes their initial starting positions. Figure 1.4 shows the new results for frame 300. Compare it to Figure 1.3.

6. The satellites need to orbit the planets. To accomplish this, it is only fitting to use a Newton field. Based on Newton's law of universal gravitation, this field is the same as the Earth's pull on the Moon. The only difference is that you set the value of the force. In the real world, the force is generated by the product of the two objects' masses pulling on one another. The pull is also directly affected by the distance between the two objects. In Maya, if the force or Magnitude of one object is set higher than the force of the object's mass it is influencing, and the second object is close enough, the first object pulls the second object into the field. This is similar to a black hole.

   Select the satellite particles and choose Fields → Newton. The field is automatically applied to the particles. Playing the simulation reveals the particles orbiting the origin of the field like a swarm of bees. To make them orbit the planets, select the sphere particles, hold Shift, and select the Newton field. Next, choose Fields → Use Selected as Source of Field. The field is parented to the planets. Play the simulation. The satellites still swarm around the Newton field, but as the planets move farther away, the swarm gets larger.

7. To get the satellites to orbit the planets closely, you need to alter a few of the Newton field attributes. Select the field. In the Channel Box, set Apply Per Vertex to On. Each particle now emanates a Newton field. Play the simulation to check the results. Figure 1.5 demonstrates.

   The particles are a little closer to responding in the desired fashion. Because all of the particles originate from the same location, you must keyframe the Magnitude of the field. Set the Magnitude to 0 at frame 100 and set a key. Move to frame 101 and

Figure 1.5
The satellite particles have latched on to a single planet.

key a value of 1. You also need to limit the amount of influence each field has on the particles. Turn on Use Max Distance. Change the Max Distance to 3. Try out the simulation. Figure 1.6 shows the result.

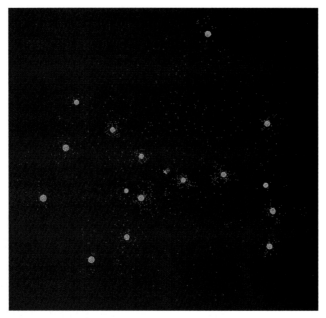

8. Our solar system is forming nicely, but it needs some variety. First, let's add some color to the planets. Select the planet particles and open the Attribute Editor. Click the Color button under Add Dynamic Attributes and select the Add Per Particle Attribute check box. The RGB PP parameter is added to the Per Particle (Array) Attributes. Right-click next to it and add a Creation Expression. Use the following expression:

```
planetsShape.rgbPP=rand (<<1,1,1>>);
```

The expression takes the red, green, and blue channels for each particle and assigns a random value between 0 and 1. Zero is assumed as the minimum when not explicitly defined. Play the simulation. Each planet gets its own color as it is created.

9. Each planet should also be a different size. This time, click the General button under Add Dynamic Attributes. The Add Attribute window pops up. Choose the Particle tab from across the top and scroll down to find radiusPP. Use Figure 1.7 for reference.

Click OK and add a creation expression. The expression is similar to the one used for color, except that instead of a vector for the randomize value, there are two floating points:

```
planetsShape.radiusPP=rand (.5,3);
```

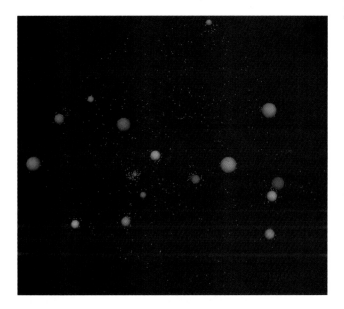

Figure 1.7
Add a radiusPP
attribute.

The first number indicates the minimum radius, and the second is the maximum radius. The minimum is needed to ensure that the planets won't be too small and become obscured by their own satellites. Figure 1.8 shows the progress of the simulation at frame 700.

Figure 1.8
The result of the
simulation at
frame 700

10. An interesting problem arises from changing the radius of each planet. The Max Distance of the Newton field is no longer appropriate. The smaller planets have numerous orbiting satellites, while the larger planets swallow theirs. Change the Max Distance to 6 to accommodate the new radius.

To check your work, you can compare it to solarSystem.ma on the DVD.

You just created a solar system with particle simulation. You used a few expressions along the way to accomplish this. Expressions play a vital role in simulation. Their power and importance will increase with every project.

Particle Emitters

Emitters are not necessary for particle simulation, but they play an essential part in the creation of many types of effects. Being in charge of particle distribution, they control speed, spread, and direction. Particles can be painted into a scene or attached to geometry, but emitters are the easiest way to control varying amounts of particle emission.

Emitter icons function like any other node. They can be animated or placed into a hierarchy. The only exception is that scale has no influence. Even though emitters have internal directional controls, you can still rotate them and alter particle bearing.

Particle emitters have a simple function: to emit particles into a scene. Although the concept is basic, your control over particle emission goes far beyond that. A lot is determined before the particle ever leaves the emitter. From birth, particles begin to age. Even if a particle lives forever, it still has an age, and this age can be called upon to influence other properties.

Surface Emitters

The essential function of an emitter is to control emission. Besides the rate at which particles flow, your control extends into where they flow from. Surface emission is controlled by the surface's control vertices or by its U and V direction. The added advantage is that textures can be used to control emission.

When connected, geoConnector nodes are inserted between the object and the emitter. One of the functions of these nodes is to handle collisions between the particle and object. Figure 1.9 displays the structure in the Hypergraph.

Figure 1.9

The structure for objects that emit particles

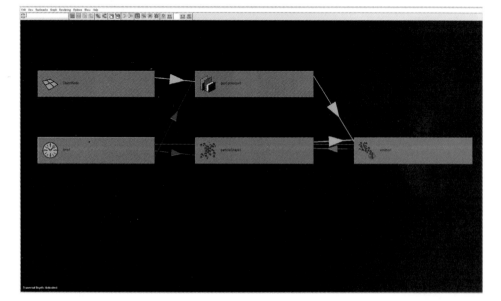

Using objects to emit particles offers a few extra options over standard emitter icons. The first is that particles can be emitted from the points of the object. This instantly creates multiple emitters from one node. Second, an object's properties, such as texture values, can be used to influence emission. Surfaces can also be deformed by other nodes, directly altering particle emission. Also, unlike emitter icons, surfaces can be scaled.

Project: Creating a Comet

This project has you build a flaming comet. Particles are emitted from a primitive sphere and made to trail behind it. Per particle attributes and expressions are added to give the comet's tail its appearance. Your objective for this project is to understand how a particle's age can be used to control the particle's look and feel over time.

1. Open the scene file comet1.ma. The scene contains a polygon sphere traveling on a curve. The animation runs from 1 to 500. The geometry has been named *comet* and added to a layer of the same name. It is also textured.

    Select the comet node and choose Particles → Emit from Object. Change the Emitter Type to Directional and make sure the direction is 1 in the X axis. Change the Spread to 1 and make sure the Rate is 100.

2. Play the animation. A lot of particles accumulate onscreen during playback. The particles should eventually die off. Select the particles. In the Attribute Editor, set the Lifespan Mode to lifespanPP only. Add the following Creation Expression to the lifespanPP attribute listed under the Per Particle (Array) Attribute tab:

    ```
    particleShape1.radiusPP=rand(1,2)
    ```

    Play the animation again. The particles die off randomly but abruptly. The look should be slower and more drawn out. Instead of using the random expression, change it to Gaussian:

    ```
    particleShape1.radiusPP=gauss(1,2)
    ```

    Using the Random function is like rolling dice to get a value. The Gaussian option pulls numbers from a bell curve. Although still random, the Gaussian values have a greater chance of being closer together, giving a more rhythmic look. Play the simulation again to observe the difference between Random and Gaussian.

3. Add an rgbPP attribute by clicking the Color button in the Attribute Editor. Choose Add Per Particle Attribute. Right-click in the new attribute's field and open the creation options for Create Ramp. Use the particle's age for the Input V. Change the ramp's colors to represent a white-hot burning flame that fades to dark smoke. Use Figure 1.10 to color the ramp. Figure 1.11 shows the progress of the ramp.

Figure 1.10

Create a ramp for a flaming comet.

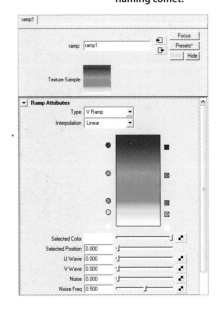

If you are new to ramps, the start of the ramp is at the bottom. The particle reads from bottom to top or, using the default ramp colors, from red to blue.

4. As a finishing touch, add an opacityPP attribute to make the tail of the comet dissolve over the life span of the particle. Create a ramp by using the default ramp for one-dimensional attributes, white (opaque) for the start and black (transparent) for the end.

5. Test other particle types to see what makes the comet look the best. Figure 1.12 shows the comet with particle clouds.

   To check your work, you can compare it to comet2.ma on the DVD.

Figure 1.11

The comet is burning through space.

Figure 1.12

Particle clouds used in place of the points in the comet

Curve Emitters

The power of particle simulation is in the tools you use to manipulate the particles. Curves provide an interesting set of tools. Surface emitters can do all of the same things that curves can do, but curves can do them more simply. It is easy to extract data from curves, such as the distance between each point along the length of the curve. These values can be used to control particles in exotic ways.

Curves have other advantages over surfaces. Curves can be fitted to specific parts of a surface for particle emission. This is a lot easier than painting a texture map or isolating certain vertices on the surface. Because curves aren't rendered, they save you the overhead and trouble of making them invisible. They are also cheaper and faster in every aspect, because you don't have to deal with geometry.

Project: Creating an Asteroid Belt

In this project, you use a curve as a particle emitter. The particles are then controlled through a volume curve field.

1. Open the scene file `asteroidBelt1.ma`. The scene contains a texture-mapped NURBS sphere (representing a planet) and a NURBS circle. A 3D texture is also in the scene. It is used in step 6. The sphere has an expression driving its rotation. The NURBS circle represents the asteroid belt circling the planet.

   Select the circle and emit particles from it. Change the Particle Render Type to Spheres. The spheres need to be emitted for only the first couple of seconds, just enough to generate a sufficient number of asteroids. Keyframe the default rate of 100 to turn emission off from frame 100 to 101. This gives you 412 emitted spheres. Figure 1.13 shows the results.

Figure 1.13

Emit spheres from the curve for 30 frames.

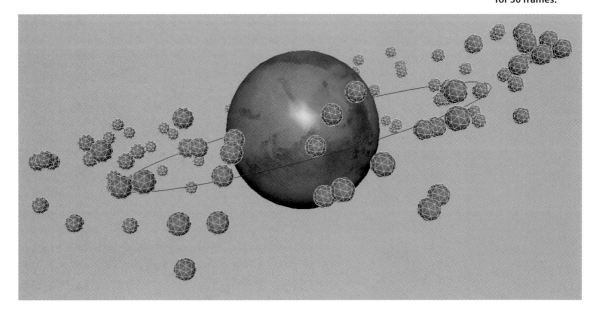

2. The spheres are too large, and they all have the same radius. With the particles selected, open the Attribute Editor. Add the General Particle attribute radiusPP. Right-click on the new attribute and choose Create Expression. Use the following expression:

```
particleShape1.radiusPP=rand(.01,.1)
```

The expression calculates a radius for each particle being emitted. Each sphere is assigned a random radius between the set values.

3. The asteroids shoot off in all directions. The goal is to have them circle the planet. To make full use of the curve emitter, you will add a volume curve emitter. Select the NURBS circle and choose Fields → Volume Curve. Next, select the particle spheres and the new Volume Axis Field and choose Fields → Affect Selected Objects.

If you play back the simulation, you will see that the particles still fly away from the curve. To contain the particles within the volume, set the Trap Inside value to 1. The particles rapidly shake around the planet, contained within the circular volume.

4. The particles are still out of control. Select the particles and change Conserve to 0. Conserve scales the velocity of the particles at each frame. At a value of 1, the particles retain their original velocity and add any forces being applied. In this case, the volume curve causes their speed to increase over time. The asteroids should not retain any of their original velocity values. By changing Conserve to 0, we have killed the particles' original velocity. The only force pushing the asteroids now is the volume curve.

The particles almost come to a dead stop. Their speed is close to what you are looking for, but they need better distribution. They are huddled on top of one another. To have them disperse, animate the Conserve value to go from 1 at frame 200 to 0 at frame 201. The particles now emit in a frenetic state. At frame 201, the field takes over, calming them down. Figure 1.14 shows the progress.

Figure 1.14

The volume curve takes complete control over the particles at frame 201.

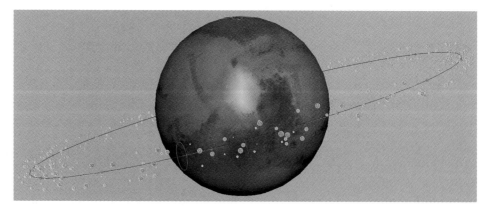

5. Add some turbulence to the asteroids' motion. Select the volume curve and set the Turbulence to 0.01. This adds a little modulation to the asteroids' path. Adding too much turbulence makes them look like they are the wrong scale.

6. For the final look, change the color of each asteroid. The color values need to be added at creation, similar to how the radius values were added. Add the rgbPP attribute by clicking the Color button in the Attribute Editor. Choose Add Per Particle Attribute. Right-click in the new attribute's field and open the tool options for Create Ramp. Change the Input V to radiusPP. This makes the color dependent on the size of each particle. Edit the ramp, changing the colors to match those of the planet. Additionally, add 1 to the V wave and 1 to both Noise attributes. This helps create more of a variety in the particles' colors. Figure 1.15 shows the finished ramp texture.

7. The asteroid belt is finished. You can further explore the power of the curve emitter by changing the shape of the curve. You can scale it or hand-edit each control vertex. The volume field and particles automatically update to the new shape. Figure 1.16 shows the finished results.

To check your work, you can compare it to `asteroidBelt2.ma` on the DVD.

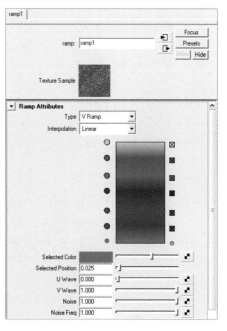

Figure 1.15

A ramp texture is created from the colors of the planet.

Figure 1.16

The asteroids circle the planet.

Particle Rendering

After you finish a particle simulation, it's time to render it. In addition to caching and playblasting, which give you a quick but accurate look at your simulation before rendering, Maya has three renderers to choose for particle rendering: Maya Hardware, Maya Software, and Mental Ray. Not all particle types can be rendered through software or hardware rendering, but all of them can be rendered through Mental Ray. Table 1.1 compares the renderers in terms of which particle types can be rendered.

| | | MAYA | MAYA | |
TYPE	PLAYBLAST*	HARDWARE	SOFTWARE	MENTAL RAY
MultiPoint	×	×		×
MultiStreak	×	×		×
Numeric	×	×		×
Points	×	×		×
Spheres	×	×		×
Sprites	×	×		×
Streak	×	×		×
Blobby Surface	×		×	×
Cloud	×		×	×
Tube	×		×	×

Table 1.1

Particle Types

*Screen capture only

This section gives you a quick look at each of these options, with an overview of the process for using software rendering and Mental Ray. In-depth rendering techniques are addressed in later chapters on a per project basis. Note that rendering is a subject unto itself and beyond the scope of this book. Only the factors surrounding a specific project are addressed. To learn more, read *mental ray for Maya, 3ds max,* and *XSI: A 3D Artist's Guide to Rendering*, by Boaz Livny (Sybex, 2007).

Playblast and Caching

Arguably, using Maya's Playblast tool and caching are also forms of rendering. Both of these methods compile information into a finished result, enabling you to play back and watch the simulations without flaw, prior to rendering.

Playblast rendering is limited to what your graphics card can produce in real time. Playblast performs a screen capture at every frame. When it's finished, the playblast can be viewed as a movie. This option is located under Window → Playblast.

The second technique is to cache the simulation. Caching simulations is similar to a playblast in that the particle output—its position, color, and other properties—is captured per frame. When it's finished, the cache is used instead of resimulating. This provides consistent results. If you change any of the particle parameters, you must delete the cache and repeat the process. Cache files are usually created after the simulation is finalized. Because the simulation is still small, you can continue using the playback from the time slider to evaluate the results.

Hardware Rendering

Rendering through your computer's hardware can be likened to taking a screen capture at every frame. Although a hardware render is more complex, it produces essentially the same results as those you see during a playblast. Some extra features enable you to add motion blur as well as some texture support. For instance, you can render bump maps and high-resolution images, particularly useful for sprite particles.

Even though hardware rendering is seemingly simple, very complex results can be achieved. Take a look at Figure 1.17. It shows particle points in a viewport window. Figure 1.18 shows the same particles rendered with motion blur, demonstrating what can be done in hardware rendering.

Through multiple passes and motion blur, high-quality results can be achieved. Figure 1.19 shows the comet created with hardware rendering. The benefit of hardware rendering is speed. You can rapidly produce finished animations by utilizing most of the features used in software rendering.

Figure 1.17
Particles as seen in Maya's viewport

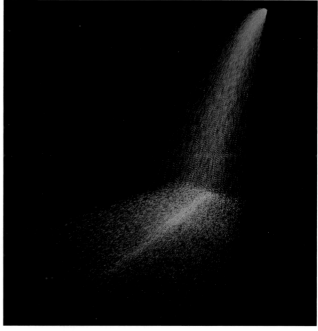

Figure 1.18
Particles rendered with the Maya Hardware renderer

Figure 1.19

The comet rendered with hardware rendering

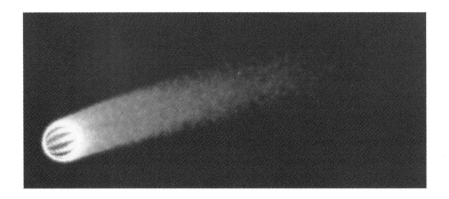

Software Rendering

Some types of particles can be rendered through Maya's software renderer. Maya flags these with a (s/w) under the Particle Render Type options. This opens the door to attributes and quality not accessible through hardware rendering. Software-rendered particles require a shader or material in order to be rendered properly. The following exercise takes you through the process.

Project: Software-Rendered Comet

Our first comet project used a sphere to emit particle points. Using that project as a base, this project replaces the particle points for clouds. In order to render the cloud particle type we must add a shader.

1. Open the scene file cometSoftware1.ma. The scene picks up where comet2.ma left off. The animation runs from 1 to 200. In the previous comet project, you added per particle ramps to describe color and transparency. These same techniques are used in software rendering, but are applied through a particle cloud shader.

   The Cloud particle type was added at the end of the comet exercise. Clouds have a more noticeable and detailed radius than particle points. To take advantage of this, create a radiusPP attribute. Add a ramp by using the Particles Age for the Input V. Change the start grayscale value to 0.373 and the last to pure white. The middle color is not necessary. Use Figure 1.20 as a guide.

2. Open the Hypershader. Assign the particles to the particle cloud shader called comet_Mat. Select the shader and the emitted particle. Graph the input and output connections in the Hypershader. The ramps from the particle can be transferred to the particle cloud. There are many ways to accomplish this. Perhaps the easiest way is to open the particle cloud shader in the Attribute Editor and drag the ramps onto the desired attributes. Drop the ramps into the Life Color and Life Transparency channels. The normal Color and Transparency channels are automatically connected as a result. Figure 1.21 demonstrates.

Notice that Particle Sampler Info nodes are created when the ramps are added to the particle cloud. These nodes enable you to drive shader attributes with per particle attributes. You can also control how the shader values are mapped to the particle attributes. The Life Transparency map we pulled from the previous project is actually backward. The particles are transparent at the beginning of their life and not at the end. Instead of altering the map, open the Particle Sample node and select the Inverse Out UV check box. This effectively flips the way the ramps' values are mapped.

3. A major benefit to using a particle cloud is the extra attributes. To improve the look of the comet, add a ramp to the Life Incandescence channel. Make the ramp go from red to black. Move the black position to 0.4. This limits the self-illuminating look of incandescence to the flaming part of the comet, keeping it away from the smoke trail. Use Figure 1.22 as a guide.

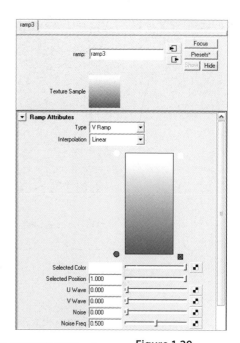

Figure 1.20
Create a ramp for the radiusPP.

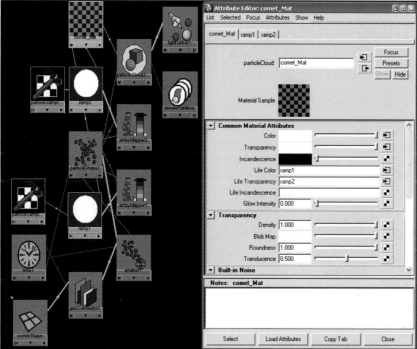

Figure 1.21
Drag and drop the particle ramps onto the corresponding particle cloud attributes.

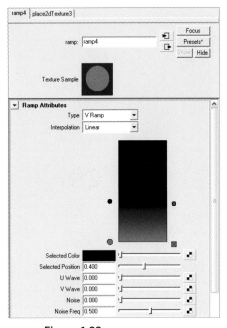

Figure 1.22

Create a ramp for the Life Incandescence.

4. In addition to self-illumination, the comet needs a glow. Add a white-to-black ramp for the Glow Intensity attribute. Move the black position to 0.21, once again to separate its effects from the smoke trail. Set the white color value to 1.5 to increase the glow's intensity.

5. The Transparency section offers several great attributes for creating complex effects. To keep things simple, adjust only the following settings:

   Density: 0.719

   Blob Map: 0.5

   Roundness: 0.107

   Translucency: 0.5

6. The shader is finished. The particle cloud shader creates a smooth dissipating smoke trail. As the smoke fades away, it should also lose speed. Change the Conserve attribute of the particle to 0.95. Play back the simulation and observe the differences. A little less Conserve goes a long way.

7. Open the Render Settings window and use the Production Quality preset. Render the animation. Figure 1.23 shows the results from frame 100.

   To check your work, you can compare it to `cometSoftware2.ma` on the DVD.

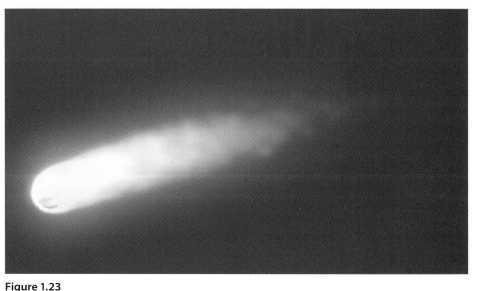

Figure 1.23

The results of the software render at frame 100

Mental Ray Rendering

Mental Ray is the only renderer in Maya capable of rendering every particle type. It is also the most robust renderer included with Maya. It offers numerous indirect lighting capabilities to heighten the photorealism of particle simulation.

Just as in Maya software rendering, a shader group must be applied to the particles in order to be rendered.

Project: Mental Ray Asteroids

Mental Ray has the ability to use an image to light a scene. In this project, image based lighting is employed to illuminate the asteroid belt.

1. Open the scene file `asteroidBeltMR1.ma`. The scene picks up where `asteroidBelt2.ma` left off. A shader for the asteroids is included in the Hypershader. Assign it to the sphere particles. Open the Render Settings window and make sure Mental Ray is the current renderer. Figure 1.24 shows the render with Mental Ray's Draft preset.

2. By default, Maya enables a light if one is not in the scene. It is important to turn off this light. A lot of tools and features of Mental Ray are not recognized as light sources. If you leave the default light on, it could interfere with your rendering. Deselect the Enable Default Light check box under the Common → Render Options tab. A quick test render should render completely black. This is exactly where you want to start.

Figure 1.24

The scene is rendered by using the Draft preset for Mental Ray.

3. Click on the Indirect Lighting tab. Create an Image Based Lighting setup. An IBL node is generated. Load galaxy.iff for the Image Name. Figure 1.25 shows a snapshot of the galaxy image at this point.

The IBL node is an infinite light source. Its scale is predetermined by the size of your scene. You can rotate it to align the image in your scene.

4. Under Light Emissions, select the Emit Light option. This creates hybrid directional lights based on the loaded image. Each directional light takes on the color and intensity of the averaged pixels it is closest to.

5. The intensity of the image is too dark to make a difference in the scene. Under Image Based Lighting Attributes, increase the Color Gain to a value of 2. This effectively doubles the image intensity. Render the simulation. Figure 1.26 shows the results.

To check your work, you can compare it to asteroidBeltMR2.ma on the DVD. You can also watch the rendered movie comet.mov.

Figure 1.25

Use galaxy.iff with the Image Based Lighting node.

Figure 1.26
The asteroid field is rendered by using Mental Ray.

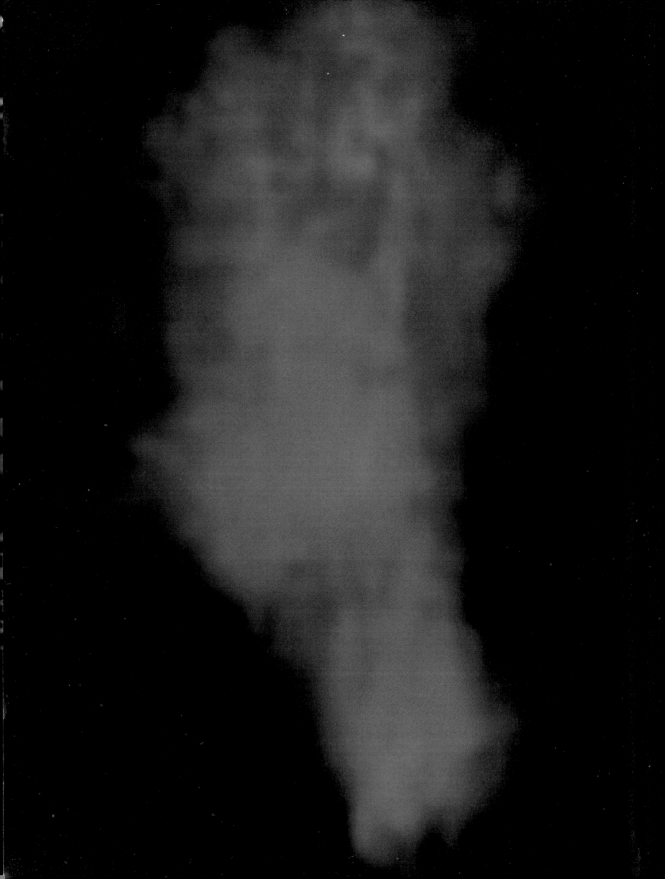

CHAPTER 2

Fluid Mechanics

The particle technology you explored in Chapter 1, "Particles," was considered the pinnacle of simulation when it was first introduced. And over several years, this technology found new uses in manipulating geometry. New techniques and better solvers quickly followed. However, particles lack the realism needed for certain film special effects. To answer this need, a new tool emerged based on an old science. The real-world study of fluid mechanics is the basis of Maya's 3D Fluids tool.

Fluids are challenging to work with. They are more mathematically intensive than other simulations, for both the computer and the creative artist. It is necessary to understand a little about how real-world fluids function to achieve desired results. This doesn't mean you have to become a mathematician yourself, only that you have a basic understanding of the principal concepts.

Understanding Fluids

Although the name implies watery substances, *fluids* are named after the mechanics of how substances flow, not their appearance. The science of *fluid dynamics* embraces liquids, gases, and the forces related to them. Fluid effects in Maya can readily produce vapor and viscous substances. Figure 2.1 shows fire created by fluids.

Keep in mind that fluids are completely different from particles; do not think of them in the same way. Instead of being emitted into open air, fluids must be emitted into a container. They cannot exist outside of the container. You manipulate fluids by adding values to sections of the container. To insert values, you can either paint them or use an emitter.

As an analogy, think of a clear glass of water. Left untouched, it appears to be empty. Squeeze red food coloring into it, and sections of the water turn red. As the food coloring dissipates, the water takes on a pinkish hue. It shouldn't come as a surprise that 3D fluids operate in the same way. Figure 2.2 and Figure 2.3 illustrate how fluids behave in the real world. Later in the chapter, you'll simulate the same effect in Maya.

Figure 2.1

Fluids were used to create a blast of fire.

Figure 2.2

Several drops of food coloring are dripped into a still glass of water.

Figure 2.3

After a minute, the red coloring dissipates in the water.

Fluids are located in the Dynamics module of Maya. Their menus are mixed with the particle menus. Fluids and particles use different solvers, but they can be connected to the same fields. There are two main menus for fluids: Fluid Effects and Fluid nCache. Fluids use the nCloth caching system (explained in Chapter 3, "Breaking Ground"), improving performance and storage of a cached fluid simulation. Figure 2.4 displays the Dynamics module menus and the two drop-down menus for fluids.

Figure 2.4

Fluids have two main drop-down menus: Fluid Effects and Fluid nCache.

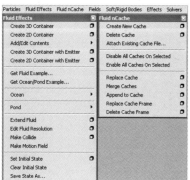

Containers

With Maya's 3D fluids, the fluid *container* is a world unto itself. It is the only dimension fluids can exist in. Containers come with their own coordinate system and a definable grid for fluid values. They can be scaled to any size. The resolution of the container is controlled separately. The larger the container, the more resolution it typically requires.

You always want to keep size and resolution values in sync. If you scale the container 10 units in the X axis, 20 units in the Y, and 5 units in the Z, the resolution should increase or decrease accordingly. For a high-resolution container, you might use 30 in the X, 60 in the Y, and 15 in the Z.

Unlike other simulation tools, fluids are generated through *volumetric pixels*, or *voxels*. A voxel is a cell within the container. Values are assigned to describe the look of the cell. All these cells put together create a three-dimensional grid. Figure 2.5 shows the anatomy of a container.

Maya fluid containers can also be 2D, and 2D fluids calculate significantly faster than 3D fluids. A 2D container is always 1 voxel thick. You can scale it to any size, but its resolution is always the same. Two-dimensional containers are often used instead of the more expensive 3D containers to produce similar results. A powerful use for a 2D fluid is surface generation, as illustrated in the pond seen in Figure 2.6. Even though 2D fluids are restricted to 1 voxel in the Y axis, multiple elevations can be described within that voxel. Thus, the points of a surface are allowed to move up and down in the Y axis.

A container is aligned to Maya's global coordinate system when first created. However, containers are transformable nodes, making it easy to change a container's orientation. This capability becomes tremendously important for making fluids move with attributes such as gravity and buoyancy, which are fixed to the container's Y axis. Therefore the fluid will always rise or fall in terms of the Y direction of the container, not its orientation to the world.

Figure 2.5

The coordinate system of a container reflects its scale and resolution, expressed in voxels.

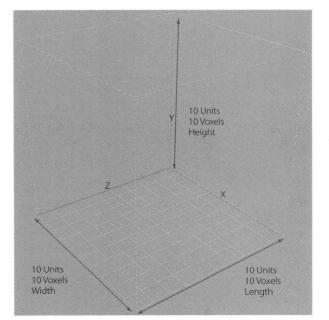
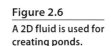

Figure 2.6

A 2D fluid is used for creating ponds.

Each container can house only one fluid. You can put multiple emitters in it, but they will emit the same fluid. Air, which is a gas, is also a fluid. Because fluids cannot interact with each other, you cannot combine air with other types of fluids. For example, it's impossible to create a fluid splash, because that is the interaction of two fluid phases: an air and a liquid one. Instead, to create a splash in Maya, you need to use nParticles, discussed in Chapter 8, "The Flood."

Fluids have multiple methods for delivering content into a container. These methods can be used all at once or individually. Two emitters using different methods can give the illusion of two fluids interacting with one another or can be used to create a reaction. Figure 2.7 shows two emitters in the same container emitting different-colored fluids, and Figure 2.8 shows the altered methods.

Figure 2.7

Two emitters in the same container were made to mix together.

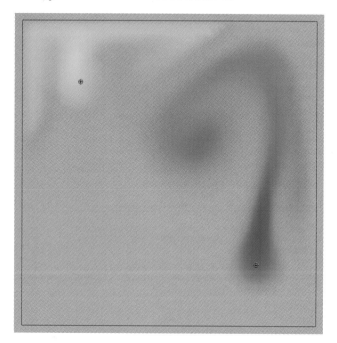

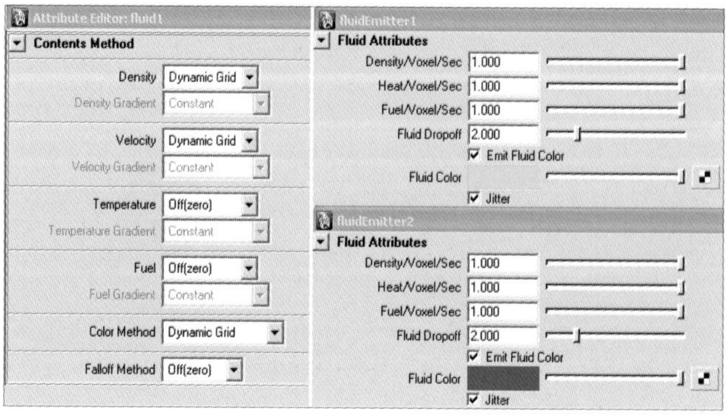

Figure 2.8

The color contents method was changed to a Dynamic Grid, enabling each emitter to produce a different color.

Content Details

You describe the contents of a container by modifying what Maya calls *content details*. The properties you control through the various Content Detail windows affect the way fluids act and react within their world, the container. Details primarily control fluid movement; they also drive shading values, such as opacity and color.

There are six content detail categories: Density, Velocity, Turbulence, Temperature, Fuel, and Color. Each has a section in the Attribute Editor. Even though their names imply a substantial degree of control, don't take them too literally. Details merely apply values to voxels and should be thought of as just values. Compared to their real-world counterparts, these properties are not as influential as their names suggest. Lowering the temperature, for example, will not in itself cause a fluid to freeze. It is possible to create this type of reaction, but numerous values have to be set to make it happen.

Density

Figure 2.9

The content details for Density

Density is arguably the most important property you specify about a fluid. Density gives a fluid its substance. Figure 2.9 shows its attributes.

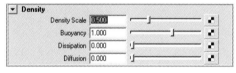

Most gases and liquids, regardless of how viscous, let some light pass through. By default, Density drives the fluid's opacity. A density scale of 1, coupled with opacity of 1, would block all light. Using a density of 1 is rarely suitable, unless of course for effect. A density of 0 doesn't necessarily mean fluids are not being emitted. Emission is still controlled by the emitter. You can emit other details about the fluid, such as its Temperature. You might do that, for example, to create hot air. Air is never visible. In the real world, water, debris, and other gases can cling to air molecules, giving air an appearance like fog or smog, but pure air cannot be seen. You could replicate pure air in Maya by setting the Density Scale to 0 and emit only Temperature, effectively creating an air current or wind.

To return to the example from the beginning of this chapter, emitting density into a Maya fluid container is like squeezing food coloring into water. Higher densities yield thicker fluids. Take a look at Figure 2.10 and Figure 2.11. The food coloring example is re-created in Maya. Note that Color is a separate detail, modified in this example to help you visualize the effects of density. In the next section, you'll try out this simulation.

Don't underestimate the power of physical scientific observation. Watching a movie always falls short of seeing the real thing. Performing an experiment multiple times enables you to see patterns and minor deviations in a process (such as food coloring dissolving in water) that a movie can't provide. In addition, you never know all of the conditions the movie was shot under. For instance, was the water cold or hot? Would that make a difference?

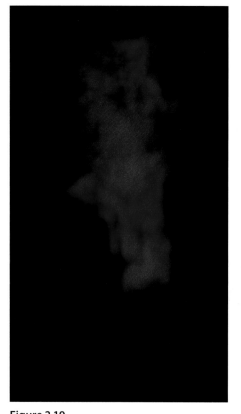

Figure 2.10
A 3D fluid made to look like food coloring is
emitted into a container.

Figure 2.11
The 3D food coloring dissipates after several
seconds.

Project: Food Coloring Density

The following exercise helps you better understand the role of density, by using the food
coloring example shown in the previous two figures. Nothing beats the real thing. Before
starting, get your own glass of water and food coloring. Figure 2.12 shows what you need
to create the experiment.

In case the materials are unavailable, two movies are provided on the DVD.

Observe what happens when you drop some coloring into the water. Try again, but
this time do not let the coloring drop into the water. Submerge the tip of the food coloring bottle and squeeze the dye into the water. The effect is very different.

After you've observed the real-world behavior enough to reproduce it in Maya, take
the following steps:

1. Open the tool options for Fluid Effects → Create 3D Container. Change the Y Resolution and Y Size to 20, as shown in Figure 2.13. Click the Apply and Close button. Add
   a default emitter. Set the range of the timeline to 2,000.

Figure 2.12

To perform the experiment, you need a clear glass of water, a squeezable bottle of food coloring, and preferably a white backdrop.

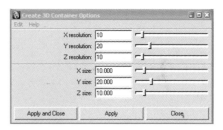

Figure 2.13

Change the Y Resolution and Y Size to 20.

2. Relocate the emitter to the very top of the container. Make sure the emitter stays within the boundaries of the container.

3. Under the Density content details, change the Buoyancy to –0.1. Upon playback, a solid stream of fluid density is emitted into the container. It acts a bit like mercury, falling straight to the bottom, and dispersing only when it comes in contact with the container's boundary. Figure 2.14 shows the results.

4. The fluid emitter has attributes to describe how much fluid is pushed into the voxels per second. When we increase the flow rate, the fluid accumulates, making the fluid denser.

   To replicate squeezing the food coloring into the water, increase the density per second to 150. Key it at frame 3 and again at frame 4 with a value of 0, effectively turning the emitter off. Add another squirt starting at frame 121 and ending at 124. Figure 2.15 shows the animation curve values.

   While you are modifying the emitter, check Emit Fluid Color and set the Emitter Color to red. Maya prompts you to change the color method to Dynamic; choose Set to Dynamic. This is necessary to have the color update throughout the container.

Figure 2.14

The fluid density at 1,000 frames into the simulation

Figure 2.15

The Attribute Editor
shows the keys and
values needed for
two drops of fluid
density.

Keys				
	Time	Value	InTan Type	OutTan Type
0	3	150	Clamped	Clamped
1	4	0	Clamped	Clamped
2	120	0	Clamped	Clamped
3	121	150	Clamped	Clamped
4	124	150	Clamped	Clamped
5	125	0	Clamped	Clamped

5. Even after the animation has turned off the emitter, the fluid emission still looks active. The density sits stagnant like a stain in space. To fix that, change the Dissipation to 0.1. Figure 2.16 shows the change.

You can compare your results with the final scene file, FoodColoringDensity1.ma.

The fluid now has a good, slow dissipation and fades out over time. This is where its behavior deviates from the actual food coloring example. In the real world, the color-

Figure 2.16

The fluid density at
500 frames into the
simulation

ing was dropped into water, another fluid. It dissipated, but not evenly. Maya does not support multiple fluids interacting with one another. In essence, our 3D fluid is dispersed into empty space, but not the emptiness of outer space. The container has gravity. Its atmosphere is artificially implied through other attributes such as Buoyancy and Dissipation. You must create the fluid's anticipated reaction to its surroundings. Understanding this concept is key to understanding how Maya fluids work.

If you squeezed out a drop of fluid coloring in outer space, the drop would stay whole. It would not separate or disperse. It would travel through space at the same speed it was emitted with. This is true for its shape as well. Even though Maya fluids behave with the natural laws of fluid dynamics, the world in which they live in is not natural. It is up to you to make it as natural as possible.

Velocity and Turbulence

Velocity and Turbulence are separate details. However, combining them has practicality. Figure 2.17 shows their properties from the Attribute Editor.

Figure 2.17

The Velocity
and Turbulence
properties

Velocity is the speed at which fluid attributes move from one voxel to another. Increasing the velocity in one axis causes it to move in that direction with increased speed. *Turbulence* alters the pattern in which fluids move. Turbulence is just like hitting an air pocket while flying on a plane. The direction the plane is traveling remains the same, but the path it was on is interrupted.

The Velocity Scale is a multiplier, speeding up or slowing down fluid motion. Velocity is not a constant driving force. As fluid progresses through its container, its speed diminishes based on its surroundings. Swirl is a detail of Velocity. Whereas the scale controls XYZ vectors, the swirl adds a circular pattern.

Project: Food Coloring Velocity

In this exercise, detailed motion is applied to the food coloring as it is emitted into the container. Identifying the differences between Velocity Swirl and Content Turbulence is the focus of this exercise. Used properly, these attributes add big visual impact and realism.

1. Open the scene file `foodColoringVelocity1.ma`. It picks up where the food coloring density exercise stopped. Change the Swirl to 5. The fluid disperses into a ball-like formation. Swirl has a huge impact on fluid movement. Figure 2.18 shows frame 300 of the simulation.

2. Try Turbulence next. Change the Strength to 0.1. Turbulence is not active until you add a strength value. Before running the simulation, set the Swirl back to 0 to compare the differences. Figure 2.19 shows frame 200 with only Turbulence. Look at how much the fluid has moved in a third of the time.

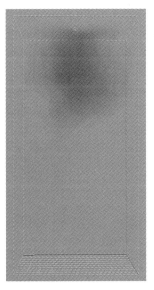

Figure 2.18
Velocity Swirl disperses the fluid into a ball.

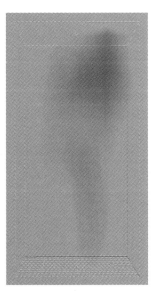

Figure 2.19
Turbulence adds a wavelike motion, propelling the fluid.

3. Combine both settings. Set the Swirl to 5 and the Turbulence Strength to 0.1. You can also increase the resolution of the container to see the results with greater detail. Figure 2.20 shows the results of using 40, 80, and 40 for the resolution at frame 75.

4. When using Swirl or Turbulence, you also have to consider using the High Detail Solve setting. It is located under the Dynamic Simulation Attributes. Turning it on enables the fluid to roll or have a boiling appearance. This is important, especially for balls of fire or rolling explosions. Turn on High Detail Solve for All Grids. Figure 2.21 illustrates the changes.

 You can compare your results with the final scene file, `FoodColoringVelocity2.ma`.

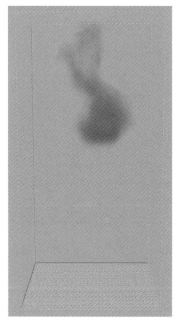 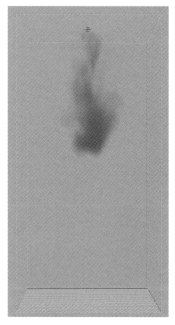

Figure 2.20
The fluid disperses quickly and randomly with Swirl and Turbulence values.

Figure 2.21
The High Detail Solve option adds the final touches to replicating the food coloring.

Temperature

Temperature is used to add or take away values when mixed with other details. By default, Temperature is turned off. To make full use of its attributes, you must set the fluid content method to Dynamic Grid. Figure 2.22 shows the content details related to Temperature.

Figure 2.22
Here are the Temperature properties.

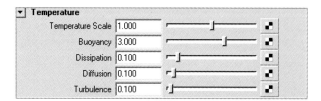

Temperature is used to drive the incandescence of a fluid by default. You can use this to help describe a fluid as being hot or cold. For instance, using a typical hot color such as red for the incandescence causes the fluid to have a red hue when Temperature is emitted. In the real world, however, color is not the defining factor of temperature. In both the real world and Maya simulations, fluids react extremely differently, comparatively speaking, based on their temperature. However, when simulating, the response is not automatic. Adding a negative temperature scale does not freeze the fluid. Instead, it causes the gases to fall instead of rise. Hot air rises; cold air falls. Temperature provides a set of values to alter the action of a fluid. Whether it is hot or cold is up to you. You must determine how a fluid reacts to temperature. Remember, temperature is merely a set of values that influence other values. You define what numbers constitute hot and cold based on the behavior you want to induce. Temperature is explored more thoroughly in the Lava project in Chapter 4, "Volcanic Activity."

Fuel

Fuel is purely reactive. Unlike other contents, Fuel cannot be static. Its purpose is to provide a catalyst necessary for a reaction. Figure 2.23 shows the content details related to Fuel.

Fuel does not have to be used in an explosive nature. It simply brings about a change. Examples include two paint colors mixing together, or the conversion of liquid to gas. Both of these are reactions. Fuel can be used to bring them about. A fuel reaction can release light and heat. When the reaction takes place, the values are added to the Incandescence as well as the Temperature. Just like Temperature, Fuel modifies existing values. Two values simply set up the condition; you control and define the outcome. The reaction created by mixing fuel and temperature can burn fuel away or cause it to freeze. You'll work with Fuel in Chapter 6, "Playing with Fire," when making fire.

Figure 2.23

Here are the Fuel properties.

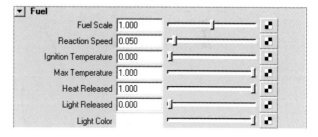

Color

Color functions similarly to the other details, but its only attributes are Color Dissipation and Color Diffusion. Figure 2.24 shows its details.

As most Maya users know, color is not just a content detail. Outside the context of delivering fluids into a container, there are a host of other color and shading attributes. They can be made to dynamically update by inputting content detail into them. Opacity, Color, and Incandescence are defined under the Shading tab. They have inputs to pipe in any dynamic attribute. Figure 2.25 shows the layout.

Figure 2.24

The Color properties

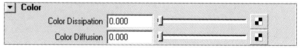

In the real world, food coloring is a dye. Its sole purpose is to change the color of things. To make our simulation as realistic as possible, it is important to retain the color of the dye. Figure 2.26 shows a rendered frame of the fluid. Notice the gray shading around the outskirts of the shape. In our next project, we will correct this unnatural effect.

Project: Food Coloring Color

To keep the red dye's integrity, you must use the opposite color setting for its transparency. The next exercise takes you through the steps to maintain the dye look. You will also implement Mental Ray to render the final simulation.

1. Open the scene file foodColoringColor1.ma. It picks up where the previous Velocity exercise left off. Select the fluid and find Transparency in the Attribute Editor. Make a note of the current Transparency value. It is set to 0.250.

2. Click the color square to open the Color Chooser. Use the Eye Dropper to select the red Fluid Color from the Emitter node.

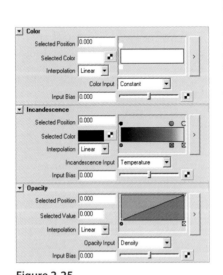

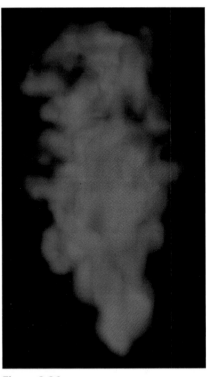

Figure 2.25

Color, Incandescence, and Opacity properties are found under the Shading tab.

Figure 2.26

The 3D food coloring is bordered with unnatural gray shading.

3. The color takes on a deeper red in the hardware view; however, rendering it with Mental Ray reveals the complete opposite. Figure 2.27 shows a side-by-side comparison. You need to use Mental Ray to observe this effect.

4. Change the color to the opposite side of the wheel, a shade of turquoise. To reclaim the original transparency of the fluid, change the Saturation. Decrease its value to 0.750, subtracting the original grayscale value. Figure 2.28 demonstrates.

The food coloring effect is finished. Figure 2.29 shows the final results, which you can find on the DVD as `foodColoringColor2.ma`. You can also watch a movie of the simulation.

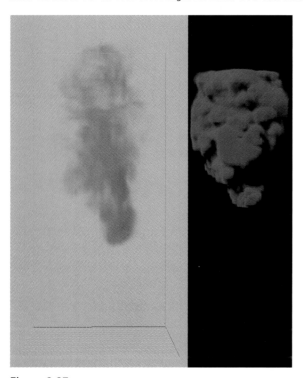

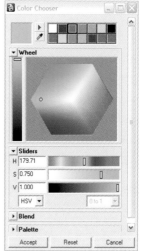

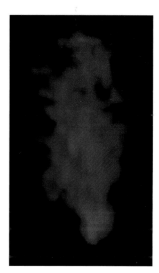

Figure 2.27
Rendering the fluid with its red-colored transparency makes the red transparent so only the blues show up.

Figure 2.28
Invert the color and subtract from the Saturation to make the fluid semitransparent.

Figure 2.29
The finished food coloring simulation is rendered with Mental Ray.

Building a Simulation

Simulation should be 60 percent research and 40 percent labor. The more you understand about the properties and physics behind your simulation, the easier it is to create. That does not mean your simulation will look cinematically better; it simply means it will be more scientifically accurate. Here is the dilemma: Most of the projects CG artists work on require a cinematic flare—huge explosions rolling at a fraction of their normal speed toward the camera, for example, or tidal waves taller than the Empire State Building. Based on Earth's gravity and the laws of physics, these things are impossible. The more accurate your simulation, the harder it becomes to create the impossible. Fortunately, it's possible to cheat gravity or turn it off completely. The downside is that there is no reference for these types of effects. After you leave the realm of possibility, you are on your own.

Simulation requires a lot of trial and error. Knowing how a natural phenomenon is created is only half the battle. A lot of additional work goes into translating research into usable values. As physically accurate as Maya is, its attribute names are tailored for general use and are not specific to a force of nature. It is up to you to decipher how to replicate a naturally occurring set of values. Everything can be described mathematically, but translating values into attributable natural phenomenon settings is difficult. In part, this is because these phenomena are difficult to study. Until recent years, capturing the full force of a tornado or an exploding star was as elusive as the Loch Ness monster. New technology and high-speed photography have greatly improved our references.

Simulations need to be built from the inside out. When you think of visual effects, the focus is often on the end product. The only way to achieve a convincing end product is to start with a solid foundation. Take a project like building the sun, for example. The temptation is to jump immediately to rendering the look of the sun, quickly establishing color and glow, and then fine-tuning those attributes. This skips the reactive nature of the sun, making for a flat, uninteresting, glowing orb. Developing a method for replicating nuclear fusion creates a convincing dynamic solution. Outwardly, it may seem to take a lot of extra time. However, in truth, you will spend the same amount of time and end up with a much better final result. This is because if you don't put in the research time up front, you may spend much more time tweaking the render. Don't misunderstand— taking the scientific path does not eliminate fine-tuning; it merely gets you closer to the final outcome quicker. It reduces the number of parameters you need to refine. As you build your simulation, you find which values are dependent on other values.

Project: The Sun

Picking up where Chapter 1 left off, our solar system is missing a sun. We'll use fluids to create one, because fluids can form primitive shapes by simply modifying fluid opacity. Before jumping into fluid creation, however, you need to gather information. The goal of the project is to create a yellow dwarf star viewable at close distances. The surface is a burning mass spewing large flares into space.

The sun is made of primarily hydrogen and helium. It is also composed of small amounts of numerous other heavier elements such as iron, nickel, and magnesium. Its temperature is about 5800 Kelvin, giving it its color.

The sun is powered by nuclear fusion, a release of energy that results from fusing hydrogen into helium. The energy is discharged as light and heat. The whole process takes billions of years to complete, the lifetime of the sun. Because of this slow reaction, the sun still shines today. If it happened faster, the sun would have used up all of its hydrogen a long time ago.

Creating the Sun

The sun is almost a perfect sphere. A simple way to create this would be to use an Opacity drop-off shape. This prevents the fluid from being visible beyond the spherical shape. The sun needs to be reactive, however. It must look like an infinitely evolving plasmatic surface. Using the National Aeronautics and Space Administration (NASA) photo shown in Figure 2.30 as reference, let's get started.

Figure 2.30

This photo was taken by an extreme ultraviolet imaging telescope.

1. Create a 3D container and add a fluid emitter. Change the end of the timeline to 1,000 frames. By default, Density is emitted into the container. It travels up and is deflected off the top.

   The first goal is to create a spherical surface. Change the Density Method to Gradient and use Center Gradient. Under the Shading tab, use Sphere for the Dropoff shape and change the Edge Dropoff to 0.1. Figure 2.31 shows the progress so far.

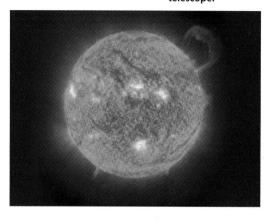

2. Make sure Velocity is set to Dynamics Grid. This eventually will provide the plasmatic surface.

3. Establishing some preliminary colors is next. Unless we do this, the fluid is solid white, making it difficult to establish any animation. The Sun leans toward the yellow end of the spectrum but is perceived as white light to us. You also have to take into account the location from which you are viewing the sun. Looking at the sun through the Earth's atmosphere alters its appearance. Mixing with atmospheric gases and debris can make the sun appear darker or orangish. For this project, you are viewing the sun from deep space. We want to see eruptions on the surface, so it should not be a solid color.

Figure 2.31

The Dropoff shape creates a sphere object within the fluid container.

   From our earlier research, we saw that the sun has deep orange and yellow hot spots. Change the color graph to represent those colors. Use Figure 2.32 for additional reference. The range of color is mapped from 0 to 1 by the Color Input channel. When you are finished, change the Color Input to Speed and the Input Bias to 0.28. This puts the primary color close to orange on the color graph.

The range sliders often feel like they are reversed, because they range from 0 to 1 and the fluid attribute is at 1 and typically fades to 0. The beginning value of the fluid is 1, which corresponds to the right side of the graph and moves to the left.

Figure 2.32

Use the sun reference image to create the colors of the sun.

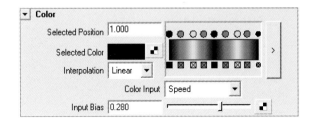

4. The range of colors represents the heating and cooling effect on the sun's surface. As fusion takes place, the fluid speeds up, changing its color. The color additions are not apparent yet. The fluid is emitting at the same speed and density throughout the simulation. To affect the speed and also give the sun a plasmatic look, set the Turbulence Strength to 0.1 and Frequency to 5.

5. The colors and speed undulate in the sphere. The low resolution of the container prevents any definition. Change it to 60, 60, and 60. You may need to cut this resolution in half based on your computer's speed. By frame 60, your sun should look like Figure 2.33.

Figure 2.33

Turbulence causes the fluid to shift and alter its speed, causing the color to change as well.

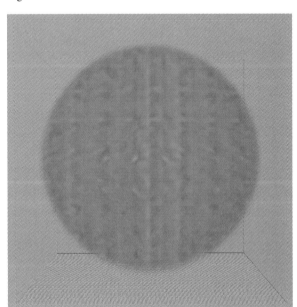

6. The sun still lacks detail. It is mainly missing turbulent motion. To contribute to the existing Turbulence settings, change the Velocity Swirl to 20. Figure 2.34 shows the result.

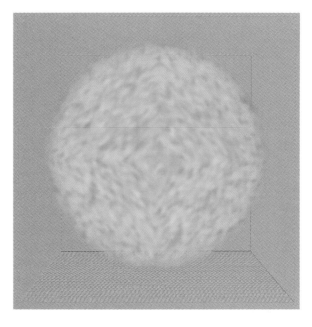

Figure 2.34

Swirl disrupts the pattern created by the Turbulence.

Congratulations—the shape and actions of our sun are complete. Make sure to save your scene. From a distance, the real sun appears to be nothing more than a glowing orb. Upon closer inspection, it has a lot of detail, which we'll add in the next phase of the project. Fluids can be textured by using built-in procedural attributes. This method is not as customizable as painting your own texture but offers a good amount of detail.

Adding Detail to the Sun

With the shape of the sun established, you can now move on to adding detail. Utilizing the built-in texture of a fluid object, this project adds the finishing touches to the sun.

1. Open the scene file sunDetails1.ma. It picks up at the last step of the previous project. To add more detail to the sun, it is a good idea to create an initial state. Waiting for the speed and colors to ramp up to full nuclear reaction is unnecessary. You can grab the reactive look of the sun and establish it as frame 1. Play through the simulation to frame 60.

2. Choose Fluid Effects → Set Initial State. Maya captures the values of the fluid and uses them as a starting position. Return to frame 1. The sun is in the same state as it was at frame 60. We can now modify the look of the sun at frame 1, instead of having to play through the simulation.

3. Select the Texture Color option under the Texture tab. Change the Amplitude to 2 and Frequency Ratio to 5. Increase the Frequency to 30. The texture provides more random detail to the existing colors. Figure 2.35 shows the results.

Figure 2.35

Add a Perlin texture to the color.

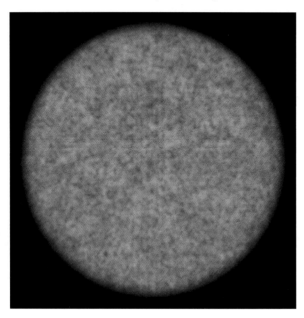

4. Some of the details are fuzzy. The Shading Opacity is making this happen. The Opacity is an extremely powerful attribute that aids in shaping or detailing a fluid. The opacity graph is not a one-dimensional slider; it has both a horizontal and a vertical value. Like the other range widgets, the opacity goes from 0 to 1 in both directions. The right side of the graph represents the core of the fluid, and the left side is the border. Do not think of this as a life span. Fluids do not really have a life span. The attribute causes the fluid to dissipate, but only because it is mixed with other attributes. It does not die, like a particle does. A good way to think about this is in terms of energy: Energy never dies; it only changes form.

   Raise the 0 value to 0.4. The result increases the amount of opacity in the Density attribute, ultimately giving the sun greater contrast. Changing the Input Bias to 0.4 would produce the same results. Compare Figure 2.36 with 2.35.

5. To finish the effect, add 0.6 to the Glow attribute. Figure 2.37 has the final rendered image of the sun.

   Make sure to save your scene. You can compare your results with the final scene file, sunDetails2.ma.

PROJECT: THE SUN   ■   41

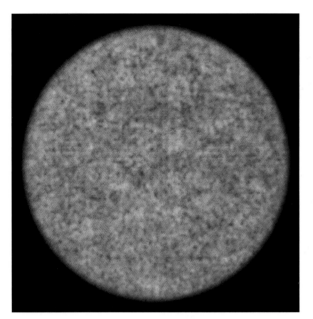

Figure 2.36
Change the Opacity to 0.4 to increase the contrast between the colors.

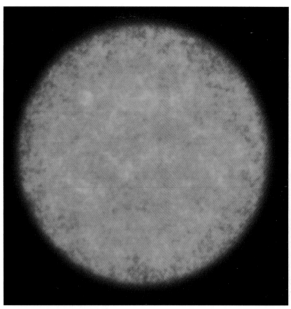

Figure 2.37
Add a glow to complete the look of the sun.

CHAPTER 3

Breaking Ground

The ground you walk on is in a constant state of flux. Every day it shifts by microscopic amounts, which over time add up to entire continents sliding against one another. The Earth is filled with marvels we take for granted. It filters and reuses everything and is the home of billions of organisms. It also harbors underground rivers, pockets of air, and rising molten rock. Sometimes we unknowingly live and build on top of these, not knowing if or when the ground may break.

Layers of the Earth

The focus of this chapter is manipulating the Earth's outer surface. Having an idea of what goes on underground is important for design purposes. The decisions you make early on are critical. Knowing how things work helps you develop reusable 3D systems instead of one-time effects. This chapter provides a brief background overview of the Earth's makeup and also sets the stage for Chapter 4, "Volcanic Activity," where you will build a volcano.

The Earth is not a solid sphere. It is made up of four layers: the solid crust, the liquid mantle, the outer core, and the solid inner core. The layers work together in recycling the Earth's material. The Earth is like an engine. It is fueled from within by the intense heat of the core. As the heat travels through every layer, numerous things happen, primarily expansion and contraction—when things heat up, they expand; when they cool, they contract. These processes churn the Earth's interior like a turbulent ocean, pushing materials to the surface and sucking other materials down.

The Core

The Earth's core is made up of an inner and outer layer. The inner core is a solid sphere about the size of the Moon. It is composed mainly of metals, particularly iron and nickel. Temperatures reach over 10,000 degrees Fahrenheit. Even at this heat, the metals do not melt, because of the intense pressure they are under. Amazingly, the core is also expanding, about 1 centimeter every millennium. This may seem insignificant, but consider the scale. The Earth is not getting larger, only its interior. This expansion contributes to the release of heat.

The outer core is less dense than the inner core. Therefore it remains a swirling mass of liquid metal. The expansion and release of heat from the inner core drives its motion. These two layers are grouped together because the combination of the moving outer core and solid inner core cause the Earth's magnetism. On a smaller, more identifiable scale, DC motors have similar behavior.

The Mantle

Surrounding the core is a liquid shell called the mantle. It is roughly 1,800 miles thick. The mantle is the largest layer of the earth. It consists mostly of liquid rock, which flows around the Earth by means of convection. Hotter temperatures cause streams and rivers throughout the layer. The currents cause all sorts of phenomena in the Earth's outermost layer, the crust. On a huge scale they cause *plate tectonics*, the movement of large land masses, or plates. From time to time, the plates rub, bump, and even slide over one another, causing tremors and earthquakes. When the currents hit weak spots in the crust, volcanoes emerge. The building pressure of the expanding heat pushes the ground up until it breaks open, spewing liquid rock from the mantle.

The Crust

The crust is the outermost layer of the Earth. It floats on the liquid ocean of the mantle. The crust is made up of all types of materials and varies based on location. Its thickness varies as well, ranging from 4 to 45 miles deep. The crust is where it all happens. The actions below eventually rise to the surface, forcing other parts of the crust to sink. The subterranean temperatures and movement have enormous ramifications on our daily life. You can think of it as the "pebble in the pond" or the "butterfly effect"—a centimeter or a few degrees change results in earthquakes, tsunamis, hurricanes, and volcanoes, and perhaps they contribute to global warming.

This chapter focuses on the uppermost 20 to 30 feet of the crust, just scratching its surface. Our goal is to move dirt or make lasting impressions in it by using Maya's Nucleus simulation system, which encompasses nParticles, nCloth, and nRigids. These versatile mechanisms can be made into solids, liquids, gases, and substances in-between. Learning to control them is a must, but understanding their potential is just as important. The next section sets the groundwork, using nParticles to create sections of earth that we will then build on.

Project: The Sandbox

The term *sandbox* is used loosely. Instead of the typical image of kids playing in a boxed section of dirt, your sandbox is large enough to build a house on. The point of this exercise is to provide a foundation to create other types of effects. The sandbox is the play area, a dynamically driven plot of land where you can execute numerous effects. Let's get started!

The purpose of the sandbox is analogous to the relationship between the Earth's crust and the mantle. The particles inside the box act as the liquid mantle. Layering geometry over the particles acts as the Earth's crust. By moving the particles around, we influence the geometry-based crust. Geometry is added over the top and allowed to float on the particle-based mantle. The underlying particles can be manipulated through any means, affecting the geometry above. All of this may seem excessive, but the benefits are overwhelming.

1. Create a cube with a scale of 10, 1, and 10 respectively for the XYZ. Move the object pivot to the base of the cube and set the object on the XZ plane. Delete the top face. Delete the box's history and freeze its transforms. Use Figure 3.1 for reference.

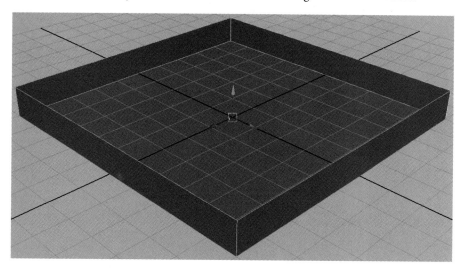

Figure 3.1

Create an empty box without a lid in the center of the world.

2. Switch to the nDynamics module. Choose the tool options for nParticles → Create nParticles →Fill Object. From the same menu, set the object type to water. In the tool options, change the resolution to 20 and select the Closely Packing check box.

3. Select the box and make it an nMesh → Passive Collider.

4. By default, water nParticles do not collide with themselves. Open the Attribute Editor and turn on Self Collide. Next, add some randomness to the particle radius. nParticles use the graph widget to control the radius scale. Set the first position to 0 and the last to 1 for a linear ramp. Because the nParticles were all born at the same time and have no movement, you need to change the input to Particle ID. Randomized ID works as well but provides a different range of values. Finally, change the Radius Scale Randomize to 0.1. Figure 3.2 shows the settings.

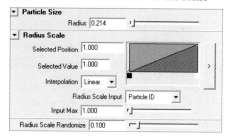

Figure 3.2

Use these settings for the Radius Scale.

5. Before making any performance modifications, add some color to give the nParticles the look of dirt. Under Shading, set the Opacity to 1. Make the color ramp go from brown to dark brown and change the Color Input to Randomized ID. Figure 3.3 shows the settings.

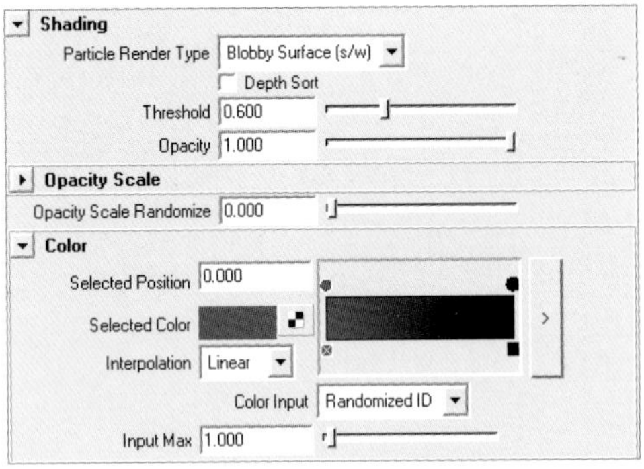

Figure 3.3

Use these settings to change the Opacity and Color.

6. Because the nParticles are supposed to represent dirt, deselect the Enable Liquid Simulation check box. Even though you are turning off Liquid Simulation, the rest of the settings are good. Play the simulation and observe what happens. Figure 3.4 shows a snapshot.

Figure 3.4

Playing the simulation launches several nParticles up in the air.

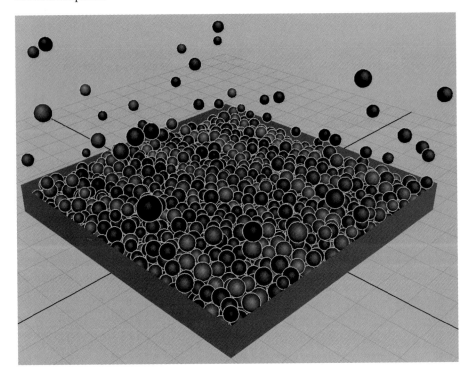

7. The scale of the scene needs to be toned down. Connected to the nParticles is the Nucleus Solver. Its calculations are done in meters by default. Change its Space Scale to 0.304, effectively converting the scale to feet. Figure 3.5 shows the settings. Play the simulation again.

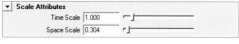

Figure 3.5

The settings for the nucleus's Scale Attributes

8. Notice that the nParticles are calmer, but a few still fall out. Set the Radius to 0.175 to prevent this.

9. Now we need to give it some earthlike properties. Set the Mass to 10 and the Friction and Bounce to 0.1. Play the simulation to around frame 200. The nParticles should have settled in. Choose nSolver → Initial State → Set from Current. This locks in their current position, allowing you to return to frame 1 without altering their rested state, as shown in Figure 3.6.

The Mass is labeled differently depending on where you set it. The Attribute Editor calls it Mass. However, in the Channel Box it is listed as Point Mass. Regardless of where you change it, the value and attribute are the same.

10. The sandbox is complete. It's time to play. Create a primitive cylinder and cut it in half lengthwise to create a rudimentary shovel. Animate it, scooping up some particles, and make it a Passive Collider. Figure 3.7 shows my results.

To animate objects, disable the Nucleus node. With it off, the nParticles do not update. This prevents errors and possibly crashing Maya.

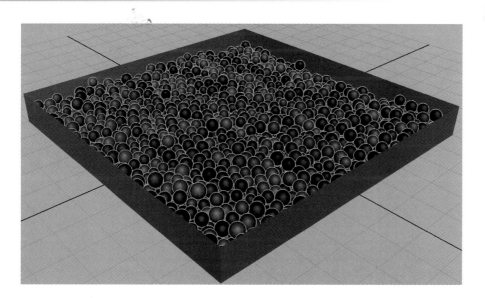

Figure 3.6

The nParticles are allowed to relax, and then their positions are set to the initial state.

Figure 3.7

Create a basic
shovel and scoop up
some nParticles.

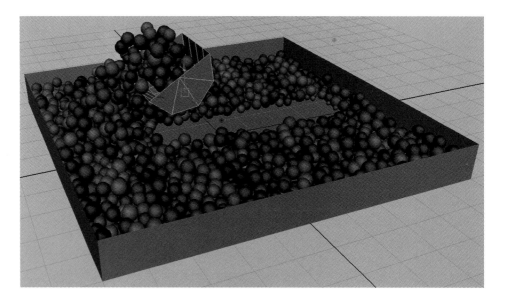

You can compare your finished work to the saved scene file, sandbox.ma.

Use the sandbox to test other attributes. Try raising the Friction value or add some stickiness. See what you come up with.

Natural Simulation

Our knee-jerk reaction is to start at the end of an effect, directly influencing rendered geometry. Doing that eliminates a lot of natural secondary motion. In the end, it forces us to add excessive handles, fields, and expressions to achieve desired results and often results in deliberate anticipated motion.

Natural phenomena are unpredictable. This doesn't mean your simulation has to be at the mercy of your solver; you still control the action, but you do it naturally. Of course, some projects will require every boulder, rock, and pebble to move precisely. Those cases are often best keyframed. True simulation is best left to its own devices, with as little post- or in-simulation influence as possible. You are not giving up control or eliminating cinematic drama. Instead, you control the outcome of the simulation the way nature had intended. For example, if you want to have lava flow past the right side of a tree, design the terrain with grooves, rocks, or mounds of dirt to guide it, instead of using a field or other tool to direct particle flow. The bottom line is to use natural elements to influence the outcome of the simulation. This may seem ridiculous or obvious, given that it's all artificial; but if it doesn't exist naturally, then it shouldn't be included in your simulation.

Another advantage to this natural approach is to capitalize on the use of layers. Just as the Earth has its mantle and crust, you create an *influencing mantle object* and an *influenced crust object*. The sandbox floor is your first layer. It can be used to drive particles in your second layer. Extra geometry can be added to the sandbox to help shape the particle layer. You can manipulate the geometry by using basic tools to provoke a reaction in the particle layer. The crust layer, or detailed geometry layer, inherits and reacts to the motion of the particles. Each element is modified independently and is built upon the previous layer. This approach enables you to modify each layer in a nondestructive manner. For instance, the crust could be changed from rigid body pieces, to nCloth, to a shattered surface held together by constraints. Regardless, the simulated bottom layers do not need to be changed. Think of it this way: If you put a stick of dynamite under water or underground, the force of the explosion is identical. Only the material being exploded changes. Therefore, you could simulate an explosive force and change out the top layer to be either water exploding or a city sidewalk. You could also create levels of detail, fine-tuning the lowest level and then applying it to your high-resolution version.

Destroying Geometry

Breaking apart geometry is a difficult and potentially time-consuming process. Numerous scripts and third-party tools are available to handle the chore automatically. Maya also comes with a Shatter tool, capable of dividing planar and 3D objects. It is limited in its abilities, however, and is often unreliable with detailed, dense objects. To this day, manually splitting your geometry is still the best way. There are several reasons for this. The first is that the results are guaranteed. You control what pieces of your geometry will crack apart and where. You also dictate the size of the shards, which is a huge concern for simulation. Too much geometry not only slows down the simulation, but can prevent the simulation from occurring at all. You can fracture your surface, simulate it, and then add thicknesses or additional detail. Finally, it's important to evaluate what you expect to see during simulation. Real-world objects break apart differently depending on their makeup. A piece of wood splinters, glass shatters, and concrete crumbles. They are all different and require geometry to match.

Regardless of how you split the geometry, the hard part of the process is getting the pieces to move properly. The following project uses the sandbox as a base to shatter a plane. The plane is not identified as being a known material, such as glass or concrete. The point of the project is to work through the process before realistically replicating a surface.

Project: Smashing the Ground

Breaking apart geometry is primarily a modeling process. nCloth, however, provides a constraint operation that splits vertices for you. In this project, we employ the Tearable Surface constraint as a means of separating faces on a polygon plane. A sphere is created and made into a solid ball capable of smashing the polygon plane.

1. Open the scene file smashingGround1.ma. The scene contains a sandbox and a sphere. Create a plane with 20 divisions in the X and Y axes. Scale the plane uniformly to 9.9.

The plane fits just inside the sandbox. Move the plane to 1.2 in the Y axis. Add the plane to a layer and hide it. Figure 3.8 shows the scene's progress prior to hiding the plane.

Figure 3.8

The progress of the scene

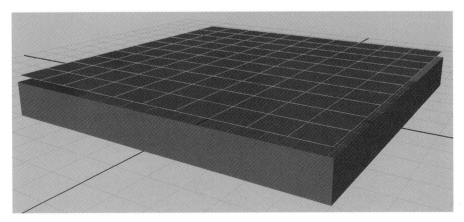

2. Make the sandbox an nCloth Passive Collider. Make the sphere an active nCloth mesh. To create the wrecking ball effect on the sphere, change the following attributes:

   Self Collide: Off

   Rigidity: 2

   Deform Resistance: 4

   nCloth is always flexible. Adding the preceding values does not prevent the surface from flexing, but does prevent it from losing its shape.

3. Run the simulation. The speed of the ball is too fast for the solver to calculate properly. The wrecking ball passes through the rigid sandbox, as shown in Figure 3.9.

   Higher-quality settings must be used for the solver to calculate properly. Change the Substeps to 12 and the Max Collision Iterations to 20 on the Nucleus node. Figure 3.10 shows the settings.

Figure 3.9

The wrecking ball deforms as it passes through the passive collider, because of the low quality of the Nucleus node.

4. The scale of the scene also needs to be established. Change the Space Scale to 0.304 to convert to feet. Play the simulation again. It now evaluates accurately.

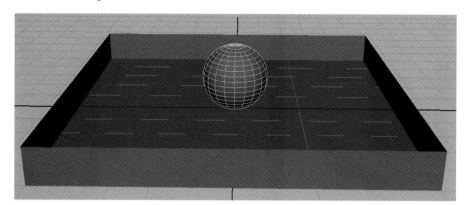

Figure 3.10

The settings for the Solver Attributes

5. The simulated wrecking ball bounces off the sandbox and quickly comes to a stop. Take a look at Figure 3.11.

Figure 3.11

The wrecking ball lands with a perfect vertical bounce and has no additional motion.

The ball remains in the same rotational position as it fell. Until another force or object acts upon it, its motion will remain linear. Fill the sandbox with a resolution of 20 water particles.

Figure 3.12

The settings for nParticle's collisions

6. Select the nParticles and select the Self Collide check box. Change the nParticles Friction to 0.1 and the Stickiness to 0.3. Figure 3.12 shows all of the collision settings.

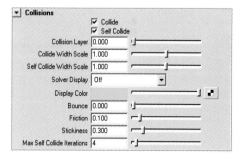

You can now continue simulating the wrecking ball. Run the simulation to test the attributes. Ignore the motion of the nParticles; focus only on the falling sphere. Figure 3.13 shows the wrecking ball's new final position. You can cache the wrecking ball.

You can compare your work to the saved scene file, smashingGround2.ma.

7. After the ball has been cached, the nParticles can be refined. This does take away from the realism of the simulation, because the wrecking ball will no longer be influenced by refinements made to the nParticles. The first task is to keep all of the particles in the sandbox. Change the Nucleus solver back to 3 for the Substeps and 4 for the Max Collision Iterations. The nParticles do not require the high values to solve properly.

Figure 3.13
The nParticles greatly contribute to the wrecking ball's motion.

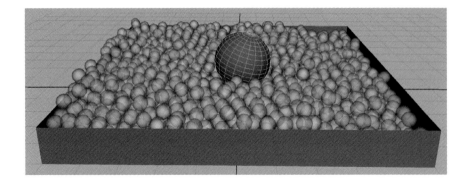

8. Next, change the nParticle radius to 0.220. This causes the nParticles to fit tightly in the sandbox. The tighter they're packed, the more impact a collision will have. It is best to get the nParticles as close as possible to ensure a strong reaction. The results can be tamed or increased through other attributes. However, if the nParticles are too loose, neither can be done. Run the simulation. Figure 3.14 shows the results.

Figure 3.14
The wrecking ball hits the nParticles, causing just a little noticeable damage.

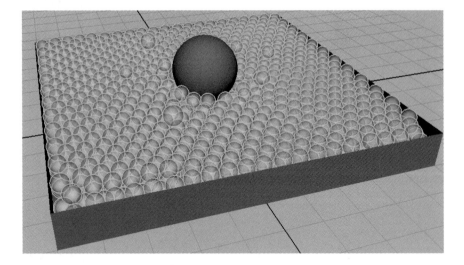

9. Add some random color to the nParticles, as you did in the sandbox exercise. The color does not play a part in the simulation. It is only for visual diversity, although the contrasting colors make it easier to evaluate. Also, change the Opacity to 1 to make the particles easier to see. You can use Figure 3.15 for reference.

10. The nParticles are almost ready to go. A critical step is to set their initial state. Disable the wrecking ball to facilitate this. Play through the timeline until the nParticles

stop moving, somewhere around 70 frames. Choose nSolver → Initial State → Set from Current.

At this point, you could increase the solver quality to achieve some different results. Make sure to re-enable the wrecking ball and then experiment with different values. Figure 3.16 and Figure 3.17 compare two different settings. When you're finished, make sure to save your scene.

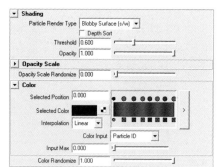

Figure 3.15

The color and opacity settings used for the nParticles

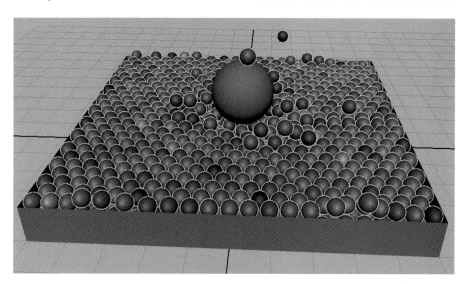

Figure 3.16

In this simulation, the Substeps were set to 8 and the Max Collision Iterations to 12.

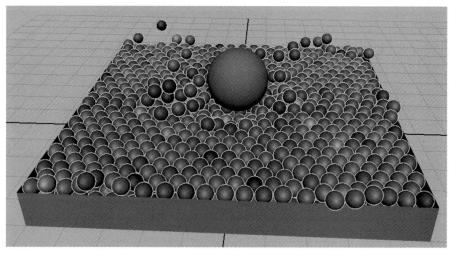

Figure 3.17

In this simulation, the Substeps were set to 12 and the Max Collision Iterations to 20.

You can compare your work to the saved scene file, smashingGround3.ma.

11. Let's see some damage. Unhide the plane. Raise the plane to 1.2 in the Y axis, just above the nParticles. Make it an nCloth object. Next, select all of the vertices, except for the two outside rows. Choose nConstraint → Tearable Surface. Select the other, boundary vertices and choose nConstraint → Transform. Use Figure 3.18 for reference.

Figure 3.18

Add a Tearable Surface constraint to the interior of the plane and a Transform to the outer.

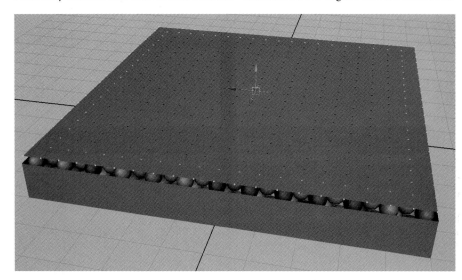

12. Change the Glue Strength on the Tearable Surface constraint to 0.03. Watch the simulation. The nCloth plane ripples briefly and then settles. Upon impact, the plane crumbles under the ball. Although effective, it's not very exciting. The results are shown in Figure 3.19.

Figure 3.19

The plane crumbles under the impact from the wrecking ball.

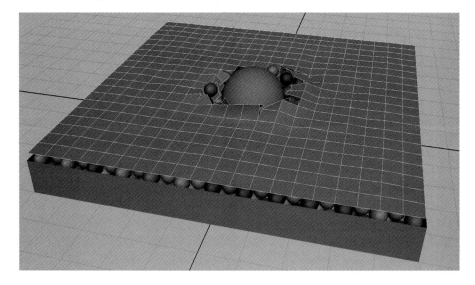

13. To make the impact more devastating, change the Mass of the nParticles to 50. The increased weight adds to the rippling effect through the density of the nParticles. Figure 3.20 shows the results.

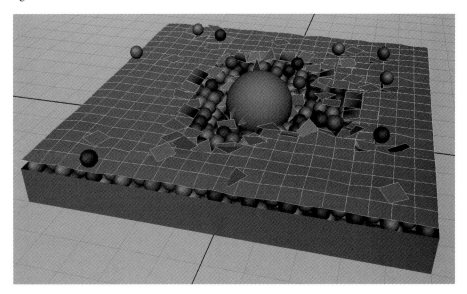

Figure 3.20

The plane explodes from the impact with the mass of the nParticles set to 50.

14. The nCloth object needs to be made into a concretelike substance. To prevent bending and allow some bounce, change the Stretch and Compression Resistance to 50. Set the Bend Resistance to 1 and its Mass to 5. Concrete is also rough, so change the Friction to 1. Figure 3.21 shows frame 50 of the final simulation.

You can compare your work to the saved scene file, smashingGround4.ma.

Figure 3.21

The results at frame 50

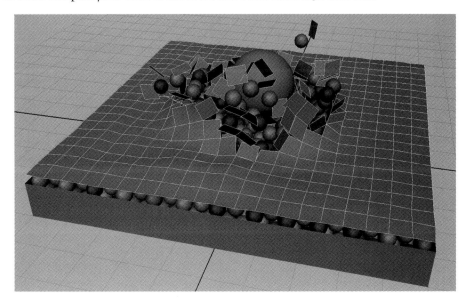

The wrecking ball used Rigidity and Deformation Resistance to increase its toughness. Using those attributes for an object that needs to dent or break causes them to re-form.

Use this project to experiment further. A lot can be changed to get a variety of effects. Following are a few ideas, explanations, and tips to help your research:

- You can relax the initial state of the geometry or nParticles at any time.
- Decrease the Stickiness and/or Friction for a more volatile reaction. Increasing them has the opposite effect.
- Sometimes faces from the plane may get caught inside the wrecking ball. Turn on Trapped Check to fix the problem.
- You can paint Glue Strength weight on the Tearable Surface constraint to get different shapes breaking away.
- Bend Resistance controls the folding or tumbling of the concrete. The higher the value, the slower the parts move. Keeping it low is ideal. Too high, and the pieces appear sluggish. Too low, and the faces bend.
- Compression Resistance enables the pieces to bounce. High compression values can also cause jitter.

Sinkholes

Throughout the Earth's crust are pockets of air and water. When the ground above these hollows can no longer support itself, the earth comes crumbling down. Sinkholes appear with little warning. After they begin, very little can be done to stop them. What makes them even more dangerous than their concealed location is their potential size. Sinkholes have been as large as 50 miles wide. Some have never stopped growing. Others have undetermined depths. They have opened up in the middle of cities, jungles, and even the ocean. They may not be as visually impressive as other natural disasters, but dollar for dollar their devastation is unparalleled.

Sinkholes are more common in certain parts of the world. Florida is notorious for sinkholes. Most are small and don't amount to much. Others have swallowed homes, cars, and numerous roads. Regardless of location, the process by which a sinkhole forms is generally the same. The earth erodes below the visible surface. Many things cause this, but in general the culprit is water, either too much or a sudden lack of it. Florida has thousands of underground aquifers. In times of drought, these subterranean oases become empty caverns. The worst case occurs when the ground is strong enough to maintain its stability, but the next time it rains, the ground becomes saturated. If not enough water fills the chamber, the wet earth, now twice as heavy with water, is loosened and gives way.

The next project creates a sinkhole that has been long in the making. The effect is similar to the smashing ground project, except that it relies on gravity instead of a wrecking ball to do the damage.

Project: Sinkhole

A city block is there one minute, gone the next. Some sinkholes can be predicted, or even noticed in the early stages as slight depressions. What would happen if a hole had been forming for years? Every day it grew a little more—some days just an inch, other days 2 inches. In the end it spells only one thing: certain destruction for whatever lies above. In this project, the techniques learned in the smashing ground project are employed to create a sinkhole in the middle of a city street.

1. Open the scene file sinkhole1.mb. As seen in Figure 3.22, the scene contains a city block and a cutaway curve that serves as a template for the sinkhole's shape and position. It's a good idea to use a pattern instead of cutting immediately into the geometry. The template gives you the opportunity to see the sinkhole's size in relation to the scene.

   After you approve the template, its time to cut the shape into the geometry. Make the cityBlock node a Live surface. Switch to an orthographic top view. Select the template curve and slightly move each CV with the Move tool. All you are doing is tapping each vertex just enough for it to snap to the Live surface. Use Figure 3.23 for reference.

Figure 3.22

The scene contains a city and a curve template.

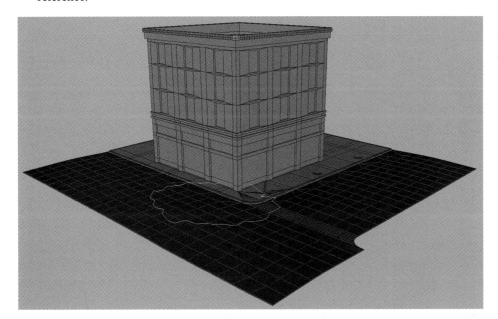

Figure 3.23

Slightly move each control vertex with the Move tool to get each to snap to the Live polygon surface below.

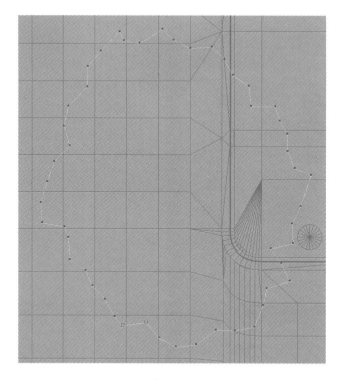

You may be tempted to use a Boolean to intersect the geometry. Typically, with this type of erratic shape, the Boolean fails. If you do manage to succeed, the resulting geometry undoubtedly contains bad topology. Manually cutting the shape is the safest way to go.

2. Display the CVs for the curve template by choosing Display → NURBS → CVs. Using the Split Polygon tool, cut the template into the geometry. Turn off Split Only From Edges and the Snapping Points feature in the tool options. Turn on Snap to Point in the interface. Starting on an edge, split faces by snapping to the curve. It's okay to skip over edges on the street geometry. The Split Polygon tool cuts through them all. This is especially useful at the sidewalk. Figure 3.24 shows how a single split has cut through the entire curb. Only two points were snapped on the curve.

When you get close to an existing edge, or have crossed a large distance on the city block model, accept the cut and start again. This helps eliminate potentially invalid cuts with the Split Polygon tool.

3. After the street and sidewalk are cut, detach the faces. Delete the history and unparent the models from the automatically generated group node. You now have two separate models for the city block. Rename them both and hide the breakaway section under a layer. Select all of the faces surrounding the newly formed hole and triangulate the geometry. This is done in preparation for a constraint that will be added later. Figure 3.25 highlights the progress so far.

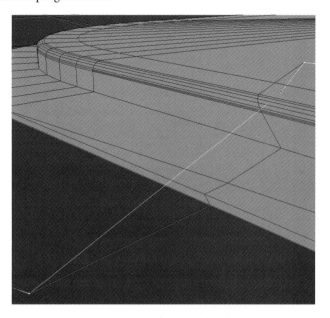

Figure 3.24

The Split Polygon tool cuts through multiple edges.

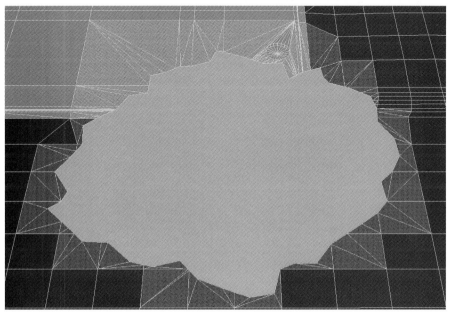

Figure 3.25

Triangulate the geometry surrounding the hole.

To select the bordering faces quickly, use the Select → Select Border Edge tool. Convert your selection by Ctrl+right-clicking and choosing To Faces → To Faces from the marking menu.

You can compare your work to the saved scene file, sinkhole2.ma.

4. Select the border edge of the hole. Extrude the edges in the World and translate Y to –20. Extrude a second time and translate another –20 units in the Y axis. Scale the bottom of the hole uniformly to about 4 units wide. Use the front orthographic view as a gauge. Figure 3.26 shows the final shape.

5. Select all the faces making up the sinkhole. Detach them from cityBlock. Delete the history and unparent the new nodes. Delete the group and rename the surfaces to **cityBlock** and **sinkhole**.

6. Select the faces from the first extrusion. Using Edit Mesh → Add Divisions, divide them eight times in the V. Figure 3.27 shows all of the settings.

Figure 3.26

Extrude the border edge and scale the bottom to create a funnel-like shape.

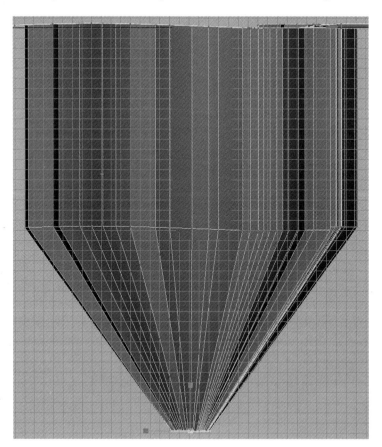

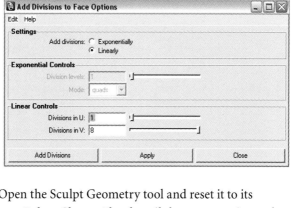

Figure 3.27
The settings used for Add Divisions

7. Deselect the top row of faces. Open the Sculpt Geometry tool and reset it to its defaults. Change the Operation to Relax. Choose Flood until the geometry is evenly displaced. It should take six or seven times. Go back over the faces with the Push and Pull operations and sculpt the surface to look more like an open pit in the Earth's crust. Figure 3.28 shows how the hole is shaping up.

   You can compare your work to the saved scene file, sinkhole3.mb.

8. It's time to fill the sinkhole with artificial earth. Open the tool options for nParticles → Create nParticles → Fill Object. Make sure Water is selected before applying the tool. You are actually going to turn off liquid simulations, but the other settings are good for our purpose. Change the Resolution to 15 and select the Close Packing option. Choose Particle Fill. Figure 3.29 shows the result.

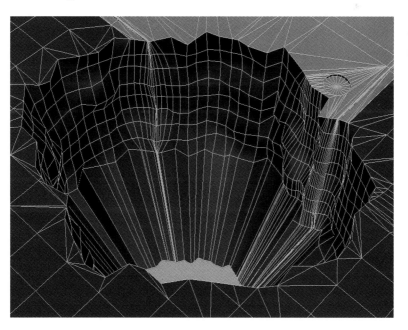

Figure 3.28
Sculpt the geometry to make the sides have grooves and outcroppings.

Figure 3.29

Fill the sinkhole
with water
nParticles.

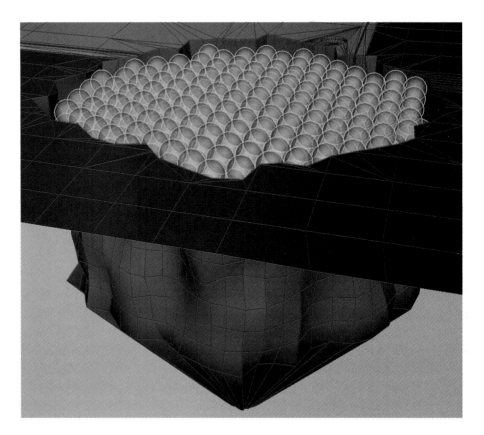

9. Select the Self Collide option for the nParticles. Set the Mass to 10. Deselect the Enable Liquid Simulation option. Having this on or off won't play a big part in the final outcome; however, shutting it down speeds up simulation time.

10. Change the Space Scale on the Nucleus node to 0.304 to match the scale of the scene. Also increase the Substeps and Max Collision Iterations to 6 and 8, respectively. Last, make the sinkhole geometry a passive collider. Watch the simulation play back. The nParticles trickle out the bottom of the sinkhole—an interesting effect, but not quite what you are looking for.

11. You want a domino effect with the draining of the particles. The strongest force should begin in the middle of the particle pool. It should start with a slow suction that quickly gains momentum, dragging other nParticles down with it. To achieve this, the nParticles need to act as one, almost like a sticky, gooey substance. The best way to achieve this is through springs.

    Open the tool options for nParticles → Create Springs. Set the defaults and change the Max Distance to 5 and the Damping to 1. Confirm your settings with Figure 3.30. Watch the simulation. There is no real difference at the top of the nParticle mass. At the end, however, the springs are clearly holding the nParticles together.

Another part of the solution is to add more weight to the center of the nParticle mass. Currently, its entire weight is being supported by the shape of the sinkhole. The culprit is the small opening at the bottom of the cavity. It isn't large enough to let the nParticles drain out sufficiently. This was intentionally done. In fact, by closing the aperture, you have created a funnel shape out of the nParticles. Adding springs keeps the shape, placing the bulk of the mass in the center of the pool. Take a look at Figure 3.31. The aperture was scaled wider, allowing the nParticles to slip out. Notice how they stay together.

You can use the shape of the hole to guide where you want your destruction to begin. If you want the nParticles to drain under the building first, you would move the bottom hole in line with it prior to filling. The nParticle's greatest mass would also be shifted.

12. Before opening the aperture, thus triggering the sinkhole, the nParticles need to be fitted to their new surroundings. Choose the sinkhole geometry. In the nRigidShape attributes, set the Friction and Stickiness to 0.4. Select the nParticles and change their Friction and Stickiness to 0.3. The combination causes the nParticles to slide down the walls of the chasm. Playing the simulation at this point reveals the nParticles freely collapsing to the bottom of the pit. Even though they were created by filling the geometry, the nParticles still are not the perfect size. Change their Radius to 1.26.

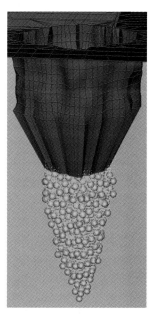

Figure 3.31
The springs are keeping the nParticles together as a solid mass.

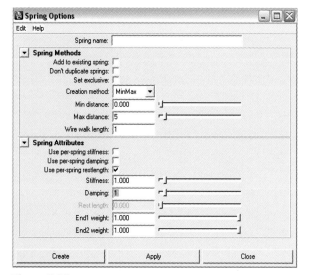

Figure 3.30
The settings used to create springs for the nParticles

You could increase the Collide Width Scale or the Self Collide Width Scale. They are just as effective but do give different results.

If you are using your own geometry, you will have to play with the numbers to get the right size. The effect should push the nParticles out against the walls, gaining only minimal height. It's important that the nParticles don't pop up and get pushed out. The nParticles pushing out happens within the first frame of the simulation. A few frames later, the center of the nParticles should start to sink, as shown in Figure 3.32.

Figure 3.32

The sticky, rough walls cling to the outside of the nParticle mass.

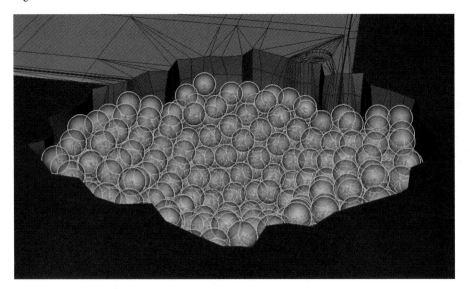

The effect can be slowed down by uniformly increasing the Friction and Stickiness of the nParticles. Increasing the Substeps and Max Collision Iterations also add to the effect.

13. With an established radius, turn on the breakaway geometry and make it a Passive Collider. The new radius causes the nParticles to pop into place, and the passive breakaway model forces them into the inverse of its shape. Advance one frame on the timeline and then set the initial state from the current position on the nParticles. They are now form-fitted to the sinkhole and street geometry. Choose nCloth → Remove nCloth to get rid of the passive collider properties on the breakaway geometry.

14. Select the last row of vertices on the sinkhole and uniformly scale them roughly 28 units wide. Use the front orthographic view as a gauge. Notice the shape of the nParticles in Figure 3.33. Make sure to save your scene.

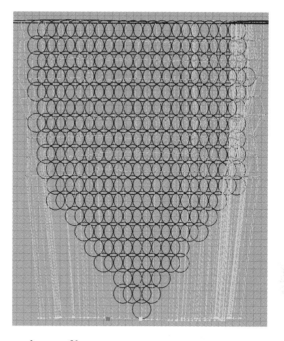

Figure 3.33
Scale the aperture
of the sinkhole to
28 units.

You can compare your work to the saved scene file, sinkhole4.mb.

15. You are almost ready to destroy the city street. The breakaway model needs some
work. First, try to remove all of the triangles. The goal is to balance the geometry or
edge spacing as much as possible without altering the surface shape or border edge.
Use Figure 3.34 for reference.

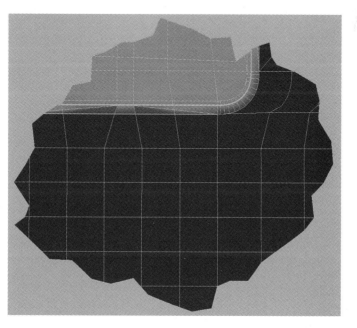

Figure 3.34
Balance the geome-
try as much as possi-
ble without altering
the surface shape or
border edge.

If you are deleting edges connected to a border, use Delete on the keyboard and not the Delete/Vertex Edge tool. Using it removes the border vertex as well, destroying the cutout shape.

Finally, the geometry is cut up by using the Split Polygon tool to create interesting and realistic shapes. You can also use the Sculpt Geometry tool to push and pull geometry around on a restricted axis, or use the Relax tool to space the edges evenly. By doing so, you do not damage the shape of the surface.

When dividing the geometry, ask yourself what type of surface you are destroying. In this case, it is pavement and concrete. Most materials fracture into smaller pieces at the epicenter. Figure 3.35 shows the finished breakaway geometry.

Figure 3.35

Use a variety of methods to split and shape the geometry in order to get it to break realistically.

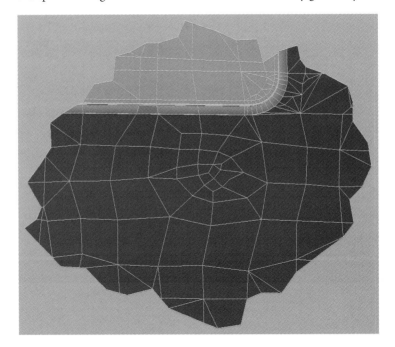

16. The nParticles are under a lot of pressure because they barely fit inside the sinkhole. The initial state established in step 13 will not keep them from popping up after the first frame of the simulation. To prevent this, the nParticles are cached for the entire simulation with a collision object sitting on top of them.

    Duplicate the breakaway model. Hide the original and make the duplicate an nCloth Passive Collider. Select the nParticles and choose nCache → Create New Cache. Figure 3.36 has the settings.

Figure 3.36

The settings for caching the nParticles

Disable the passive breakaway. It is no longer necessary but should be kept in the scene as a backup. You also may need to re-cache the nParticles to achieve different effects. Having an unaltered version of the devastated area could be useful. Figure 3.37 shows the cached nParticles slipping down the sinkhole.

17. Make the original breakaway model an nCloth object. Watch the simulation. Figure 3.38 shows the results.

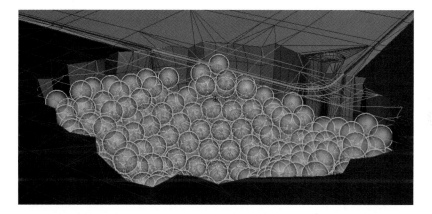

Figure 3.37

The nParticles slip down into the sinkhole.

Figure 3.38

The default nCloth breakaway object is tested before adding any constraints.

18. The nCloth surface collapses nicely. The edges fall almost immediately. Add a Component to Component constraint to keep them locked down. To do this, select the border edges for both the breakaway and sinkhole models. Choose nConstraint → Component to Component. Watch the simulation. Some of the edges pop away from the sinkhole border. Either of two attributes can be changed to fix this. You can set Exclude Collisions to On for the constraint node, effectively turning off collision for each assigned vertex. Or you could set the thickness of the sinkhole to 0. The latter was chosen for this project. Figure 3.39 shows the results.

Figure 3.39

The thickness of the sinkhole geometry is set to 0 to keep the border edges locked together.

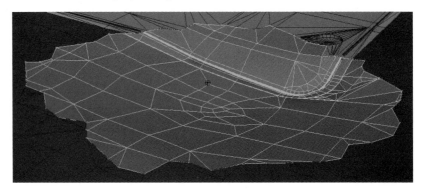

19. At the beginning of the simulation, the geometry still pops up. You can see this in Figure 3.40.

    The nParticles are not causing this. Our solution of caching the particles while covered with a passive collider is working perfectly. The problem is that the nCloth breakaway model has a greater thickness than the passive collider breakaway model used to cache the particles. Because we kept the passive collider model, copy its thickness of 0.15565 over to the nCloth's thickness. Play the simulation again to check the results.

20. It is time to do some damage! Select all of the vertices of the breakaway model, except those around the border, and choose nConstraint → Tearable Surface. Change the Glue Strength to 0.01. Test the simulation. The geometry collapses almost perfectly. Figure 3.41 shows the results at frame 20.

Figure 3.40

The breakaway geometry pops up at frame 2.

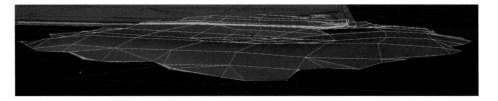

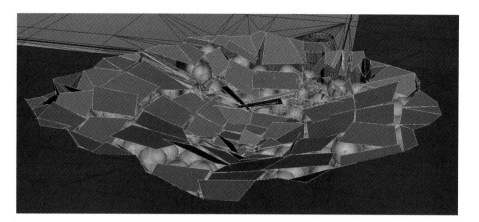

Figure 3.41
The geometry
collapses into the
sinkhole.

21. The sinkhole effect is complete, but the crumbling pieces look like shards of geometry. Give the surface the same thickness as the nCloth breakaway geometry by extruding the faces in the negative Local Translate Z. This is a good starting position, but it does not have to be maintained. You can extrude it further or add divisions. As long as the tool adds to the history stack, you can continue to make modifications without interfering with the original simulated geometry. Figure 3.42 shows frame 20 with the geometry extruded.

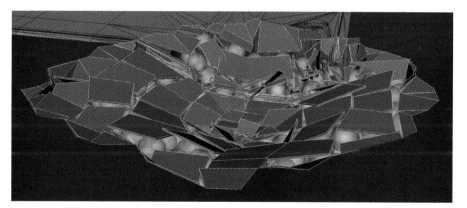

Figure 3.42
Extrusions were
added to the break-
away surface.

You can compare your final result to the saved scene file, sinkhole5.ma.

The nCloth surface and constraints mostly use default attributes. Experiment with different settings to see what you can come up with. For greater control, you could also paint values for the Glue Strength attribute on both constraints. By doing so, you can time the manner in which the pieces break up and determine their size.

CHAPTER 4

Volcanic Activity

There are numerous telltale signs of an impending eruption, but when a volcano finally erupts, nothing can prepare you for the spectacle it unleashes. From massive smoke plumes reaching miles above the planet's surface, to fiery fountains of lava, volcanoes are as captivating as they are calamitous. Their violence is legendary and always historic. Their destructive force has an ironic parallel in the computational power needed to re-create them. With a good amount of patience and a lot of megahertz, building a volcano is possible.

Volcano Formation

Many types of volcanoes cover the Earth (and other planets). Some are capable of huge catastrophic explosions, while others are merely vents that spew lava. Their formation, composition, and materialization all vary, but in the end they are nothing more than holes in the Earth's crust. As discussed in Chapter 3, "Breaking Ground," rivers of magma flow beneath the Earth's crust. Their extreme temperatures and bottled-up pressure exploit underground weak spots and find openings. Typically, volcanic activity is found where tectonic plates are pulling apart or pushing together. Their location can also be unpredictable, forming in areas where magma has melted its way through the Earth's crust.

The power of a volcano is awesome. After it starts, it cannot be stopped. Whether under water or under ice, escaping hot gas and molten rock from the Earth's mantle will vanquish anything in its path. A volcano is a great concoction for stunning visual effects and a formidable simulation.

In this chapter, our efforts focus on creating the perfect volcano. The stratovolcano is the most iconic of all varieties. With its conical shape and towering height, this type produces the most explosive eruptions. Mount St. Helens of Washington state, shown in Figure 4.1, is a perfect example of a stratovolcano.

Figure 4.1

Eruption

Volcanoes can exhibit signs prior to eruptions. Tremors, venting or steam, and small pockets of lava are all things leading up to eruption. An individual volcano can have several types of eruptions during its life span. They can even happen simultaneously. Some eruptions are merely the opening act to a much more devastating one to follow.

Your first project begins with a Plinian eruption. This type of eruption is named after Pliny the Younger of ancient Rome, who described the eruption of Mount Vesuvius in great detail. Vesuvius, Krakatoa, and Mount St. Helens all had Plinian eruptions. Columns of gases shoot straight into the air from the cone of the mountain, so powerful that the matter reaches the stratosphere. The blasts are continuous, lasting days to months. As a result, ash rains down for miles surrounding the volcano. Figure 4.2 shows the erupting smoke column of Mount Spurr in Alaska.

In this chapter, you'll create a Plinian eruption and lava. The Plinian eruption project is broken into two parts. The first creates a massive column of continuous smoke ejected from the volcano. In the second part, the smoke column is capped, which triggers exploding the top of the volcano off. Finally, you'll create lava flowing down a city street.

Project: Plinian Eruption, Part 1

Plinian eruptions are considered the most deadly of all eruptions. Several factors reinforce this. The magma is highly viscous, trapping gases and resulting in violent explosions.

This project is divided into two parts. In this first part, you'll use Maya fluids to create a column of smoke. In part 2 of the project, you'll go back just prior to the moment of eruption, capping the volcano off with an nCloth object, keeping the fluid contained until the point of eruption. The purpose of capping it is to control the time of eruption and to build pressure in the container, giving the fluid gas cloud a more explosive look. Let's get started making the smoke column.

Our eruption has been scaled down to make it more manageable. The volcano is 1,200 meters tall. The erupted smoke column will reach only 2,900 meters—which is 42,000 meters, or 420 Maya units, shy of where it realistically should be.

1. Open the scene file plinian1.ma. The scene contains a modeled volcano and a reference image of a Plinian eruption. It is roughly 11.5 units tall. Using hectometers as the scale, the volcano reaches almost 1,200 meters. Figure 4.3 shows the scene's setup.

Figure 4.3

The scene contains a modeled volcano and an image refer- ence. (USGS photo)

Create a 3D container for the column of smoke caused by the first phase of eruption. Use the settings from Figure 4.4 and translate the container to 23 in the Y axis.

The smoke column is taller than it is wide to give the smoke room to rise. The X and Z scale is large enough to accommodate the column's expected girth. The smoke column needs to be made wider as it leaves the mouth of the volcano, so you need to make the container large enough to prevent any clipping. The resolution is kept low for testing.

The column of smoke needs to rise into the stratosphere. To facilitate, set the Boundary Y to –Y Side. The fluid can now leave the container when it reaches the top. Figure 4.5 shows the container's settings so far.

2. To emit the column of smoke, use a torus surface. These work well for creating tubu- lar fluid shapes. Create a default primitive NURBS torus. Scale the torus uniformly to 0.775 and translate it to 9.95 in the Y axis. The torus is positioned about 1 unit below the top of the volcano's cone. Figure 4.6 shows the values used to position the NURBS torus.

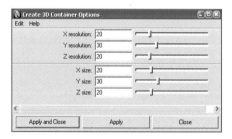

Figure 4.4

Create a 3D container by using these settings.

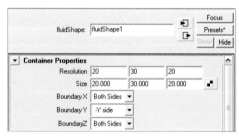

Figure 4.5

The container's current settings

Delete its history and freeze the transforms. Select the torus and the fluid container. Using the default settings, choose Fluid Effects → Add/Edit Contents → Emit from Object.

3. Make the volcano a rigid body. Select the container and the volcano and choose Fluid Effects → Make Collide. Using the volcano as a collision object helps shape the fluid. The effects cannot be seen just yet, because the voxels are too large. The fluid gets stuck in the volcano's opening. However, the following figures demonstrate the effect. Figure 4.7 shows the fluid being emitted without colliding with the inside of the volcano. In Figure 4.8, the fluid has been made to collide.

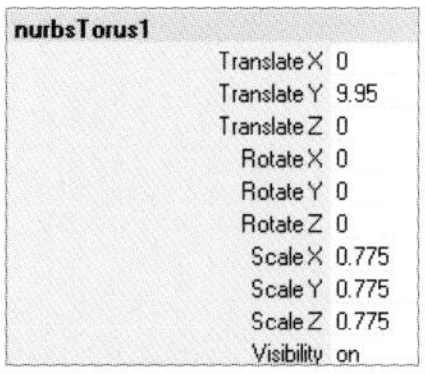

Figure 4.6
The settings used for transforming the NURBS torus

Figure 4.7
The fluid is not colliding with the volcano geometry.

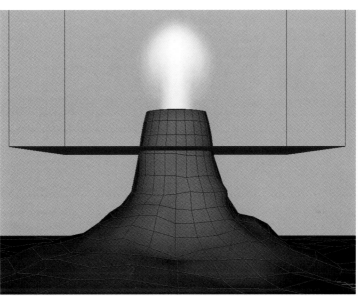

Figure 4.8
The fluid is colliding with the volcano geometry.

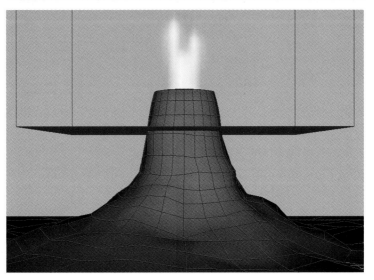

4. The smoke that pours out of a Plinian eruption is incredibly dense. Heavy with ash and sediment, it looks more like a solid mass than vapor. Change the Density/Voxel/ Sec on the emitter to 100 to give it the appropriate thickness. Set the Heat and Fuel Voxels per second to 0. You will not need to emit these.

    To view the results of your current settings, you need to disable collision on the fluid. As mentioned in step 3, the voxels are too large to pass through the cone of the volcano. After the look of the fluid has been established, the voxel resolution will be increased for greater detail and smaller size, allowing it to pass through the opening of the volcano's cone. Deselect the Use Collisions in the Dynamic Simulation option in the Attribute Editor. After the look of the smoke has been established, we will deal with the collisions. Figure 4.9 shows frame 41 of the simulation.

5. Plinian eruptions push matter out of a volcano at hundreds of meters per second. Given the scale of the scene, in an estimated 8 seconds, the fluid smoke should reach the top of the container. Because fluids do not have separate solvers, all of their calculations are done within the container. The Simulation Rate Scale is analogous to the solver scale used with a Nucleus solver node. Changing it alters the time step used for solving the simulation. Simply put, increasing the value causes the simulation to speed up, and decreasing it slows it down.

    The smoke column would actually need to be slowed down for realism. The proper value should be 0.150. Instead, for this exercise, speed up the eruption by changing the Simulation Rate Scale to 2. Keeping the value at 0.150 would add a lot of waiting time between seeing results and making changes. So we increase the value for testing purposes, but this also has some educational value. The faster the fluid is, the harder it is to maintain its stability. We will set the value back to 0.150 at the end of the project to produce the final results.

6. Smoke emitted from a Plinian eruption rolls like a ball of fire. To achieve this, change the Velocity Swirl in Content Details to 10. This alone does not make the fluid roll. You also have to turn on the High Detail Solve for All Grids option in the Dynamic Simulation window. Also increase the Solver Quality to 50. Run the simulation to see the progress. Figure 4.10 shows frame 50.

     To check your work so far, you can compare it to `plinian2.ma` on the DVD.

7. It is difficult to see how the fluid is reacting when it is a solid color. Let's jump to the shading attributes. A mixture of smoke, sediment, and hot ash, Plinian smoke tends to be a grayish green. Change the color of the smoke to match the Color Chooser in Figure 4.11. Set the Color input to Density.

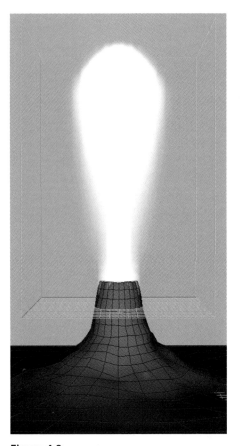

Figure 4.9
Frame 41 of the simulation

Figure 4.10
Frame 50 using the current settings

8. Incandescence plays a big role in shading the smoke as well. In the real world, smoke bounces a lot of light. To simulate this effect, use Density as the input and change the Incandescence color graph to match Figure 4.12. Black is used for the first position. Figure 4.13 shows the color used for the zero position.

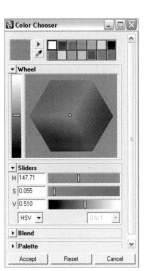

Figure 4.11
Use these values for the smoke color.

Figure 4.12
The color graph used for Incandescence

Figure 4.13

The color for position zero

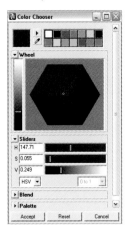

Mapping the Color and Incandescence to the Density provides a lot of needed contrast to the smoke. Figure 4.14 shows the combined results.

9. Jumping ahead briefly to the Lighting options, turn on Self Shadow. This feature helps significantly to see the details in the shape of the fluid. Figure 4.15 shows the increased contrast.

10. Going back to the Shading options, Opacity is trickier than the others. The smoke emitted from a Plinian eruption is so thick and fast that there is very little noticeable dissipation in the column. By shortening the range in the Opacity graph, you can eliminate the subtle scattering. By moving the Input Bias, you can set the desired width of the column. The base of the smoke needs to be wider. Use 0.261 to achieve a good width. Figure 4.16 shows the final settings, and Figure 4.17 shows the effect of the settings on the fluid.

Figure 4.14

The combined results of the Color and Incandescence at frame 30

Figure 4.15

Turn on Self Shadow for greater contrast.

It is important to remember that the voxel size of the fluid container is still too large. A lower size (resolution), 20 or under, makes testing faster but affects the accuracy of the final outcome. Increasing the number of voxels will decrease the proportions of the fluid shape, essentially giving it finer detail. When establishing width, through opacity, increase the number of voxels to check the actual size. The fluid will look larger than it needs to be until the final resolution is established.

A Plinian smoke column has numerous plumes, but they act as one continuous stream. To get the fine detail to replicate this effect, all three channels (Color, Incandescence, and Opacity) are textured. The Textures options in the Attribute Editor are divided into seven sections, of which we'll use four.

11. In the first section, select all three channels. Change the Texture Type to SpaceTime, a Perlin noise texture that uses time to alter its fractal pattern. Figure 4.18 shows the settings.

Figure 4.17
The effect of the Opacity settings at frame 30

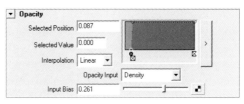

Figure 4.16
The graph used for the Opacity

Figure 4.18
Select all of the texture channels and set the Texture Type to SpaceTime.

Modifying fluid texture is time-consuming. Feedback from the viewport is sketchy at best, so software rendering is needed. If you are new to fractal textures, you can add the 2D Noise texture to the color channel of a Lambert material and assign it to a plane to view the attributes as you change them. The results do not map one-to-one to the fluid but can help you visualize what is happening.

12. Skipping over the Texture Gains section, the third set of attributes provides the biggest impact to the smoke column. Before beginning, take a look at Figure 4.19. It shows a rendered view of the smoke column with the default SpaceTime settings. Figure 4.20 shows the same settings applied to a Noise texture on a plane with a Lambert material. You can see how the attributes are affecting the fractal.

    The first value to change is the Frequency Ratio. Set it to 3. This spreads the noise patterns out further. For a denser pattern, you would decrease the value. Once again, to illustrate the value change, Figure 4.21 shows the Noise texture applied.

Figure 4.19

The smoke column in its present state

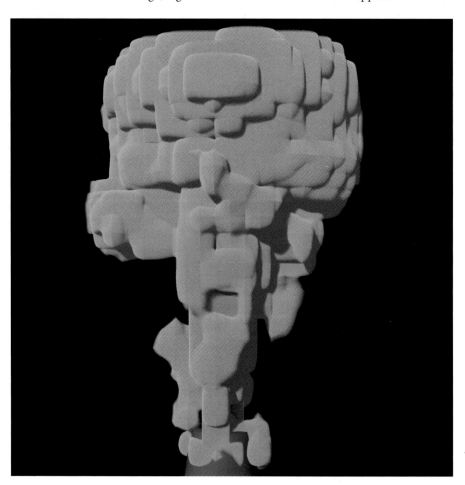

Figure 4.20
A plane has been textured with the same Noise fractal used in the fluid container.

Figure 4.21
The Frequency Ratio is set to 3 on the Noise texture.

The deeper you go into the texture settings, the harder it becomes to evaluate the results. You can use the IPR renderer for quick, accurate feedback.

Figure 4.22
The Ratio is set to 0.6 on the Noise Textured plane.

13. The next Textures section, Ratio, controls the amount of detail in the fractal. Increasing it gives you more fractal patterns. Change it to 0.6 to decrease the amount. This helps define the appropriate size of the smoke. The change is too subtle on the fluid itself; so instead, Figure 4.22 shows how the value has altered the Noise texture on the plane. The change on the texture is also quite subtle but has softened the overall look.

14. Change the Depth Max to 4. The Depth Max tells the fractal how far to calculate; increasing it has the visual effect of subdividing the detail. This adds a lot to the fluid's realism but also increases computation time by almost 60 percent. Figure 4.23 and Figure 4.24 show the fluid and the plane, respectively, with the higher Depth Max setting.

15. The last attribute to modify, in this section, is Inflection, which alters the fractal pattern. Inflection gives the texture a puffy appearance by spiking the falloff in-between the fractal pattern. Figure 4.25 and Figure 4.26 display the results on the fluid and textured plane, respectively.

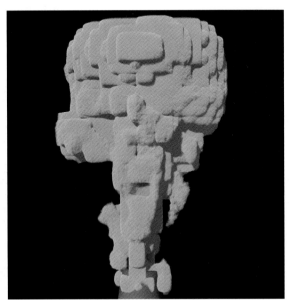

Figure 4.23
The Depth Max setting is set to 4 on the fluid.

Figure 4.24
Depth Max is set to 4 on the Noise texture.

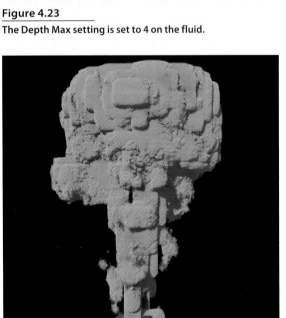

Figure 4.25
Inflection has been turned on for the fluid.

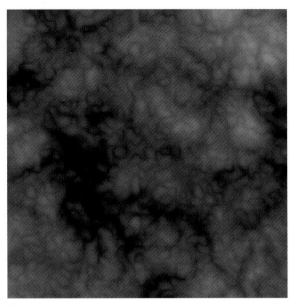

Figure 4.26
Inflection has been turned on for the Noise texture.

Figure 4.27 shows the settings for the third set of attributes.

16. The next and final section within Textures contains the Frequency. It controls the overall detail of the texture. Increasing it adds more of the fractal pattern into the texture space. Change the value to 3. Figure 4.28 shows the results on the fluid, while Figure 4.29 shows its effect on the plane.

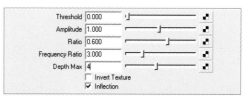

Figure 4.27

The values used to change the third section of the Texture window.

Figure 4.28

The Frequency has been set to 3 on the fluid.

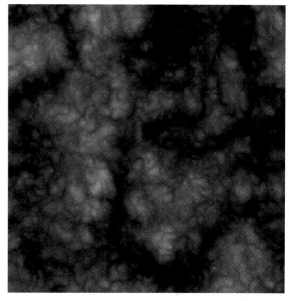

Figure 4.29

The Frequency has been set to 3 on the Noise texture.

17. Finally, you need to put the texture in motion. The SpaceTime texture is perfect because it uses time to calculate changes in the fractal itself. For the Texture Time, add the following expression:

```
fluidShape1.textureTime=time * .3
```

Multiplying the time by 0.3 slows the texture's motion by 70 percent.

Figure 4.30 shows the final settings for the last modified section. It is also a great time to save your scene.

To check your work so far, you can compare it to plinian3.ma on the DVD.

Figure 4.30

The settings for the last modified section of the texture.

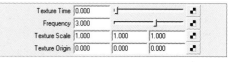

18. As you have probably noticed, the fluid looks blocky. You can almost make out each individually filled voxel. Open the Shading Quality options in the Attribute Editor. Change the Quality to 2 and the Render Interpolator to Smooth. Figure 4.31 displays the settings in the Attribute Editor, and Figure 4.32 shows the rendered results.

Figure 4.31

The Shading Quality settings

Figure 4.32

The fluid smoke rendered with the new Quality settings

19. The Plinian column of smoke is almost finished. In Container Properties, set the Resolution to 40, 60, and 40 in the XYZ axes. In addition, change all of the Boundary options to None. This changes the pressure inside the container, allowing the smoke to rise more freely. Also, with the smaller voxel size, you can re-enable collisions. Figure 4.33 shows the new Container Properties in the Attribute Editor.

Figure 4.33

The Container Properties settings

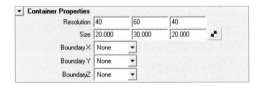

20. When played back, some of the smoke trails off and does not maintain the speed of the column. To keep the smoke rising, increase Buoyancy in the Density options to 2. Figure 4.34 shows the final settings.

21. In step 5, we decided to use a faster-than-normal Simulation Rate Scale to quickly push the smoke out of the volcano. This reduced the playblack time needed to see how the smoke was progressing, but it also causes the simulation to fall apart at later frames. To solve this problem, add 0.1 to the Damp attribute in the Dynamic Simulation options. Furthermore, change the Viscosity to 0.2 and the Friction to 0.1. Figure 4.35 shows the Dynamic Simulation options.

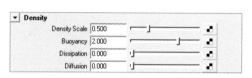

Figure 4.34
The final Density attributes

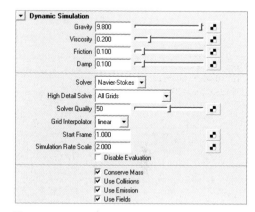

Figure 4.35
The Dynamic Simulation options

Viscosity makes the fluid move and act as a thicker substance. Inadvertently, it does help stabilize the fluid by increasing its resistance to flowing. The Friction increases the fluid's internal resistance. This helps simulate the roughness of the sediment blown up in a real Plinian eruption.

The first part of the Plinian eruption is finished. Make sure to save your scene file before moving on. Figure 4.36 shows a render of the eruption at frame 50.

To check your work so far, you can compare it to `plinian4.ma` on the DVD.

Figure 4.36
Frame 50 of the finished smoke column

Project: Plinian Eruption, Part 2

In this second part of the Plinian eruption, the cap of the volcano is activated, allowing you to contain the fluid until you are ready to make it blow. The cap also builds pressure, giving the fluid a better explosive look at the time of eruption. The cap geometry is made into nCloth and then into a tearable surface. Fluids cannot directly influence nCloth, so an air field is used to invoke the eruption.

As described earlier in the chapter, a Plinian eruption is a pressure cooker that finally explodes. By keeping the fluid bottled up, we allow the pressure to build. Check out the differences. Figure 4.37 shows the normal distribution of the smoke column. It is uninhibited by any blockage. Figure 4.38 shows the column after 120 frames of bottled-up pressure. Notice that when the volcano is plugged, the fluid blooms into a multi-tiered mushroom cloud after being released.

1. Open the scene file `plinian4.ma`. It picks up where Plinian Eruption, Part 1 left off. To fine-tune the cap exploding off the volcano, disable the fluid. Next, turn the visibility on for the CAP layer. Select the cap geometry and make it an nCloth object. Reselect the geometry and add a Tearable Surface constraint. Animate the Glue Strength, using Figure 4.39 as a guide.

2. The nCloth geometry does not stay put by itself. Select all of the border vertices and add a Transform constraint. Animate its Glue Strength with the same values used on the Tearable Surface constraint.

Figure 4.37
The smoke without being capped

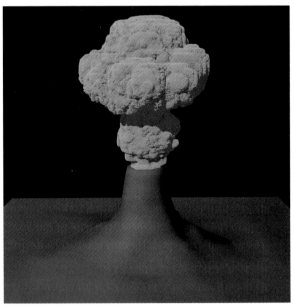

Figure 4.38
The smoke after it has been bottled up and then suddenly released

3. Add an Airfield to the nCloth cap, using the default settings. Translate it to 9 in the Y axis. Animate its Magnitude, using Figure 4.40 as reference.

Keys	Time	Value	InTan Type	OutTan Type
0	100	1	Clamped	Clamped
1	101	0	Clamped	Clamped

Figure 4.39

The values and keys for animating the Glue Strength

Keys	Time	Value	InTan Type	OutTan Type
0	100	0	Clamped	Clamped
1	101	500	Clamped	Clamped
2	103	0	Clamped	Clamped

Figure 4.40

The values and keys for animating the Airfields Magnitude

Next, turn on Enable Spread and use 0.4 for the Spread. Last, set the Speed to 500. Play the simulation. The nCloth explodes out with tremendous uniform force. Figure 4.41 shows the results.

4. During the first part of the Plinian eruption project, the scale was established in hectometers, with 1 unit being equal to 1 hectometer, or 100 meters. The Nucleus's Solver Scale should be set to 100. However, we cheated the scale in order to expedite fine-tuning. To match these settings, change the Solver Scale to 7.5. In addition, change the Time Scale to 3, forcing the simulation to run eight times faster than normal. This will keep it in sync with the fluid's speed. Because the nCloth is not affected by the fluid, but the fluid is affected by the nCloth, it is important to keep the nCloth ahead of the fluid until it breaks up. Otherwise, the fluid will be blocked by the cap geometry as it rises. Also, the nCloth's point mass is at its default value of 1, far too light for volcanic rock. Change the Mass to 3.

Figure 4.41

The cap explodes uniformly.

5. The nCloth explodes with uniform precision. To break this up, add a Turbulence field to the nCloth cap, using the default settings. Set the Frequency to 10. Animate its Magnitude from 0 to 100, using frames 100 and 101, respectively. Figure 4.42 shows the improved results at frame 180.

Figure 4.42

The cap explodes in a turbulent fashion.

6. The nCloth passes through the volcano when the pieces come back down. Make the volcano an nCloth Passive Collider. Figure 4.43 shows the nCloth colliding with the volcano.

Figure 4.43

The nCloth collides naturally with the volcano geometry.

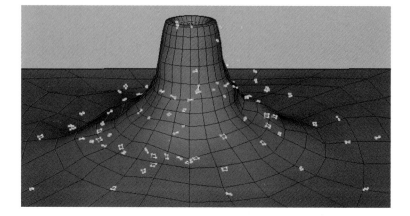

7. The pieces of nCloth slide along the volcano geometry. Change the Friction to 0.5 and the Stickiness to 0.2 for a more natural collision.

8. The cap is ready. The only thing left is to enable the fluid and make it interact with the nCloth. Select the cap geometry and the fluid. From the Dynamics module, choose Fluid Effects → Make Collide. The eruption is ready. Figure 4.44 shows the result at frame 140.

Figure 4.44

The nCloth and fluid
seemingly interact
with each other.

The Plinian eruption is finished. Make sure to save your scene before moving on. The
final scene file is on the DVD as plinian5.ma.

ADDING REALISM

As discussed during both parts of the project, time was altered to speed up production. To
achieve a more realistic simulation, you can use the following parameters:

Fluid Smoke Column (fluid1)

Simulation Rate Scale: 0.150

Nucleus nCloth cap (nucleus1)

Time Scale: 10

Lava

Spewing, spattering, and rolling, lava is an amazing act of nature. Its evolving forms provide spectacles to be admired and respected. *Lava* is the term used to describe magma that has reached the earth's surface.

Lava's composition varies, and its makeup is what defines its behavior. Flowing lava, such as Basaltic lava, is made primarily of iron and magnesium. It is a thick material that can form walls of slow-moving rock as high as 10 feet. Flowing lava typically has an internal core temperature of more than 1,000 degrees. Its exterior cools rapidly, creating an underground river of molten lava.

Project: Lava in the Streets

In this project, you will create a wall of lava that crawls down the street. For dramatic effect, we'll make the lava move faster than it usually would along a flat city street. We will use the temperature to provide the hot molten look of the lava, while the density is used for its cooler rock-like state. Texturing the fluid's opacity will provide the final look.

1. Open the scene file `lava1.ma`. The scene contains a small city section. All of the geometry has been assigned to a layer. The scale is in feet. Figure 4.45 shows the environment.

Figure 4.45

An overview of the city environment

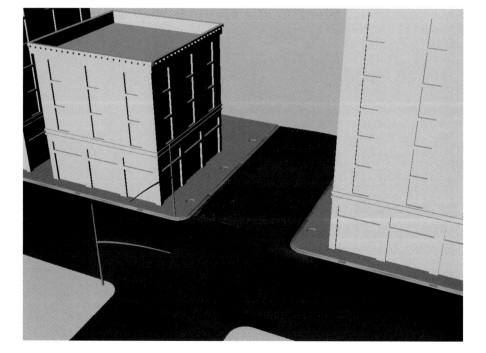

Choose Fluid Effects → Create 3D Container with Emitter. Use 40, 20, and 60 for the size in the X, Y, and Z axes. Set the resolution to half of the container's size. Make the emitter a volume cube with the default density/voxel/sec of 1. Figure 4.46 shows all of the settings.

Position the container in the street by using the coordinates shown in Figure 4.47.

2. The container fills the entire street. The lava will slowly make its way toward the intersection. In order to create a wall of lava, the emitter needs to be large. Use the coordinates from Figure 4.48 to translate and scale the emitter.

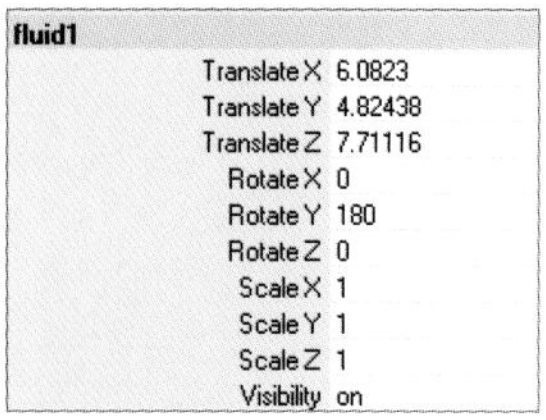

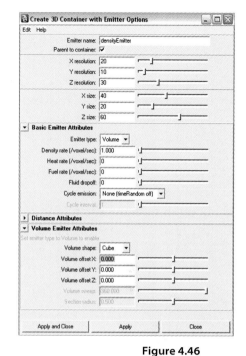

Figure 4.46

Use these settings to create a fluid container.

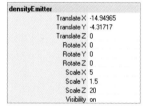

Figure 4.47

Use these coordinates to position the container.

Figure 4.48

Use these coordinates to position the densityEmitter.

3. The fluid density emits up into the container, dispersing as the fluid hits the top. Figure 4.49 shows an example.

Figure 4.49

The fluid rises to the top of the container.

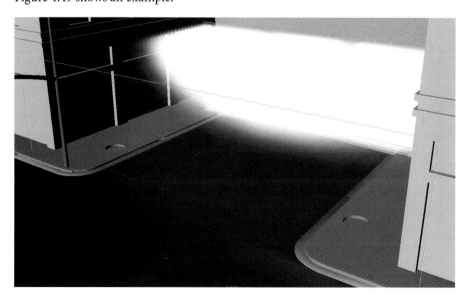

4. Lava is a hard surface, unlike the gaseous appearance of the fluid's current settings. In the Attribute Editor, choose Surface Render and Hard Surface from the Surface options. The fluid is now represented by an implicit surface. Its shape is defined as the fluid is emitted. Hard Surface makes the transparency of the fluid a constant. Because lava has no transparency, we will set it to zero in a later step. Next, drop the Surface Threshold to 0.001. This threshold controls how the fluid is translated into a surface. Last, set the Specular Color to white. Figure 4.50 shows the Surface settings.

Figure 4.50

The altered Surface settings

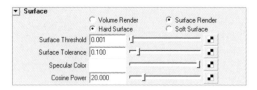

The fluid now looks solid. It no longer has soft edges or a gaseous appearance. Figure 4.51 shows the result.

Figure 4.51

An implicit surface represents the fluid shape.

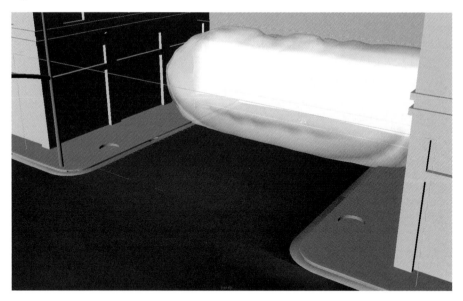

5. Before making any adjustments to the lava's behavior, let's change its shading. Go to the Shading section of the Attribute Editor. As mentioned in step 4, lava has no transparency. Change the setting to zero or black. Also use black for the Constant Input for the Color channel. Figure 4.52 shows the settings in the Attribute Editor.

The black shade represents the color of the lava after it has cooled. You could think of this as the lava's rest color. It remains as black rock until the temperature gets hot enough to melt it.

This is a good time to save your scene file; my version is on the DVD as lava2.ma.

6. At this point, the lava is a solid mass. To give it life, we'll use a second emitter to emit heat into the container. The heat or temperature is then used to drive the Incandescence. Change the Temperature Contents Method to Dynamic Grid.

7. Create an emitter by using the settings from Figure 4.53. The Heat Rate is high, just as it is in real life.

The temperature is the driving force of the lava. Transform the emitter by using the values in Figure 4.54.

To see the effects of the new emitter, open the Attribute Editor. Under Display, set the Shaded Display to Temperature. The density is hidden, and only Temperature can be seen now. For a more solid appearance, change the Opacity Preview Gain to 1. Figure 4.55 shows the settings.

Play the simulation. The temperature quickly floods the street, with an effect similar to Density. Figure 4.56 shows the result at frame 50.

Figure 4.52
The transparency and color are set to black.

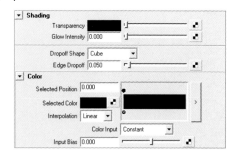

Figure 4.53
Create an emitter with these settings.

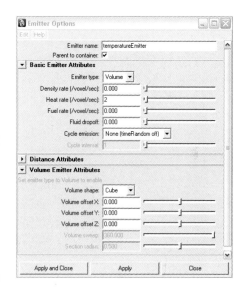

Figure 4.54
Translate and scale the emitter.

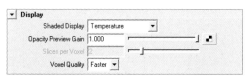

Figure 4.55
The settings used for displaying only the Temperature

Figure 4.56

Frame 50 of the
simulation

8. Change the Incandescence to be the color of molten lava. The Incandescence is already set up to be driven by the Temperature; only the colors need to be established. Use Figure 4.57 for reference.

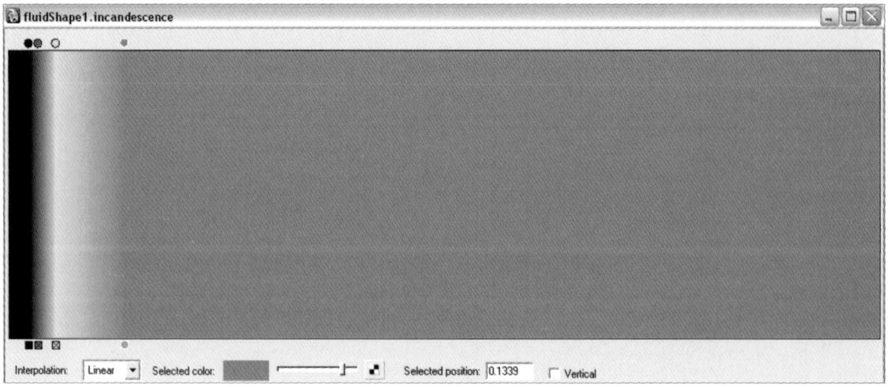

Figure 4.57

Change the
Incandescence
graph to match.

9. The lava needs to expand in the X and Z coordinates as it oozes forward. Any Y motion needs to be kept to a minimum. You don't want to eliminate it, just reduce it to prevent the lava from rising. Change the Y Velocity Scale to 0.1. Figure 4.58 shows the settings.

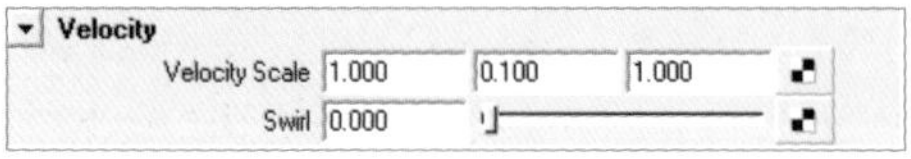

Figure 4.58

The settings for the
fluid's velocity

10. The extreme temperature of the lava needs to be out front, leaving a cooling, dense mass behind. By making the temperature's Buoyancy negative and the density's positive, you can accomplish these effects. Change the Density parameters first. Set the Buoyancy to 2 and the Diffusion to 0.1, allowing the fluid to spread into adjacent voxels. Figure 4.59 shows the settings in the Attribute Editor.

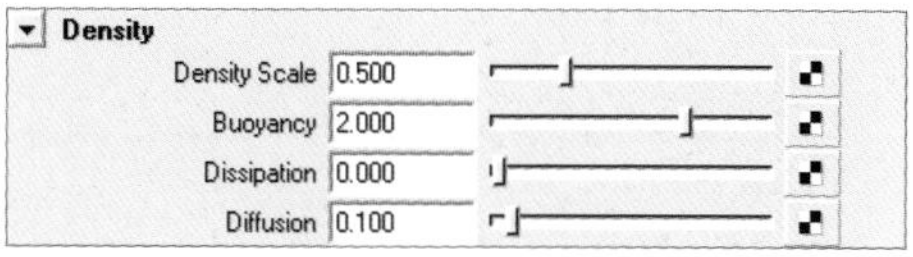

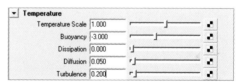

Figure 4.59

The settings for the fluid's density

11. When it comes to temperature, the heat from the lava needs to be continuous; it should not dissipate. Set the Dissipation attribute to 0. You also do not want the temperature to have any diffusion. There is a fine line between the molten lava and cooled rock. Adding too much diffusion will cause the temperature to overpower the density. Set the Diffusion option to 0.05. Next, set the Turbulence to 0.2. This provides motion to the fluid's temperature. Adding too much turbulence, a value of 1 or more, causes the bulbous extrusions in the Y, an interesting effect but not suitable for our purposes. Finally, set the Buoyancy to –3, slightly greater than the density's. Figure 4.60 shows the Temperature values.

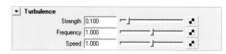

Figure 4.60

The Temperature values

12. To give the lava a little extra motion, add some turbulence. It needs only a little because the Temperature also has turbulence. Change the Strength to 0.1 and the Frequency and Speed to 1. Figure 4.61 has the settings.

    This is also a good time to save your scene; mine is on the DVD as lava3.ma.

Figure 4.61

The settings for the fluid's Turbulence

13. The temperature is still hidden behind the density, as seen in Figure 4.62. Two things need to be set in order to alter this.

    First, change the Density/Voxel/Sec on the densityEmitter to 0.1. Decreasing the density gives way to the increasing heat, but still not enough to make the molten lava visible.

Figure 4.62
Frame 100 of the simulation shows that the temperature is not making it through the density.

14. The next thing to bring the temperature out is the addition of a texture. Adding texture is a major factor in making the lava's appearance convincing. It will make the cool lava look rocky and the molten lava, gooey. Texturing the Opacity cuts away portions of the rock to reveal the molten lava underneath. Because the texture offers the most dramatic changes, we will examine how each attribute affects the look of the lava over the next five steps. To begin, take a look at Figure 4.63. It shows the fluid in its current state, before the texture is added.

The following images are all rendered by using Mental Ray. They were done with the Draft preset and default Final Gather settings.

Figure 4.63
The lava prior to texturing

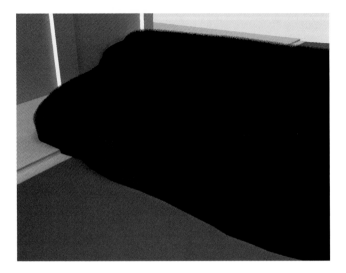

For the overall appearance, use Perlin as the Texture Type. It immediate cuts away density, revealing the hot temperature underneath. Figure 4.64 has the results.

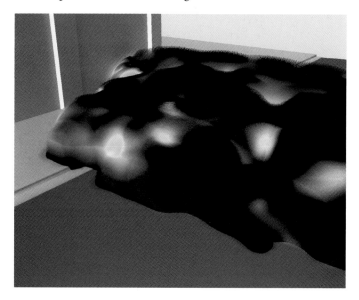

Figure 4.64
Texture the Opacity with a Perlin fractal.

15. The Perlin texture type isn't very suitable for a rocky surface until Inflection is turned on. The large spike in the fractal's falloff reveals most of the temperature. Figure 4.65 shows the dramatic change.

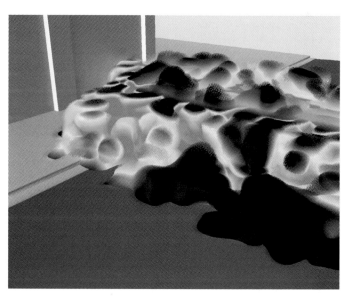

Figure 4.65
Selecting Inflection removes almost all of the black rock.

16. Depth Max is next. Set it to 4 to increase the varied layers within the fractal texture. The higher value brings back some cooler rock to the lava. Figure 4.66 shows the results.

Figure 4.66

Increasing the Depth Max option to 4 adds levels of complexity.

17. Change the Frequency to 3 to add more of everything. The frequency increases the number of patterns within the fractal. For the lava, this setting makes the details smaller, ultimately making the lava look bigger. Figure 4.67 has the results.

Figure 4.67

The Frequency increases the number of patterns within the fractal.

18. Some of the texture's definition is being lost from low quality. Before finishing the texture attributes, change the Shading Quality. Increase the Quality to 20 and set the Render Interpolator to Smooth. Figure 4.68 shows the results.

Figure 4.68
The Frequency increases the number of patterns within the fractal.

19. To give the cooled rock more of a crumbled appearance, set the Ratio to 0.8. This adds finer detail to the fractal, breaking up the black masses into crumbled rock, as shown in Figure 4.69.

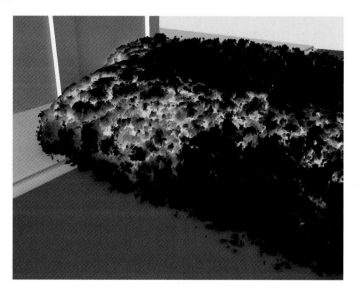

Figure 4.69
Increasing the Ratio adds finer detail.

20. Changing the Coordinate Method to Grid makes the texture move with the fluid. The Coordinate Speed scales how fast the texture moves in accordance with the Velocity. Increase it to 1. A value this high has a side effect of stretching the texture. In this case, it actually adds to the look of the molten rock, providing a thick, gooey appearance. The lava must be resimulated in order for the effect to be noticeable. In Figure 4.70, you can see the change in the fluid after the lava was simulated again to frame 100. Figure 4.71 has the final texture settings.

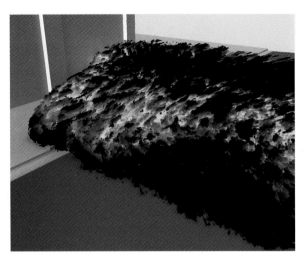

Figure 4.70
The lava with Grid for the Coordinate Method

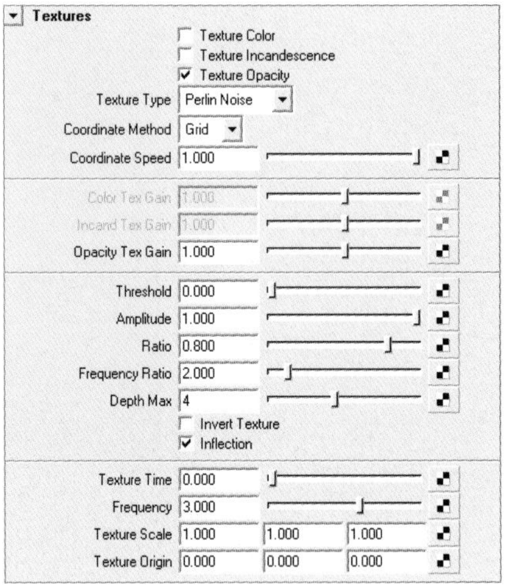

Figure 4.71
The texture settings

21. The lava is so hot, it should glow. The Incandescence setting only makes the surface brighter; it doesn't make it appear to give off light. Changing the glow can produce the desired results. Set the value to 0.2. Glow is a postrender effect, added only after the render is complete. Figure 4.72 shows the results of rendering frame 100 with Maya Software.

Glow works off the rendered color of the fluid. If the fluid is red, it will glow red. The lava is a mixture of colors, the most important one being black. If the lava rock was anything other than black, even a hint of another shade, the glow would take on that color, because it would be the most prominent color in the lava. Keeping the lava black prevents a glow from being added to the rock, illuminating only the molten parts.

22. For the finishing touches, set the Viscosity to 0.8 and the Friction to 0.3 to give the lava a nice gooey, and sometimes stubborn, motion. Overall, the simulation moves too fast. Change the Simulation Rate Scale to 0.6. It's still not slow enough to be physically accurate, but enough to be convincing and build cinematic tension. To reduce its momentum further, set Damp to 0.1. Figure 4.73 has the settings.

To check your final scene file, you can compare it to lava4.ma on the DVD. Figure 4.74 shows the final look of the lava at frame 200.

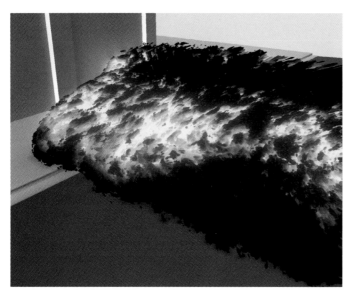

Figure 4.72
The lava rendered with glow

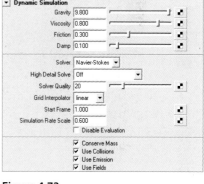

Figure 4.73
The Dynamic Simulation settings

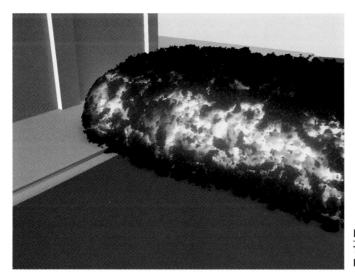

Figure 4.74
The final look of the lava at frame 200

CHAPTER 5

Tornadoes

It sounds like a freight train heading in your direction, a vortex of wind spinning toward your home, rumbling and shaking it before ultimately ripping away everything but the foundation. The tornado is a ferocious act of nature, elusive and dangerous. Tornadoes have caused miles of destruction in minutes. In this chapter, you'll create an F5 tornado, the fastest, largest, and most destructive grade of all.

Spinning Air

A tornado stretches, most commonly, from cumulonimbus thunderstorm clouds to the surface of the earth. Like all acts of nature, a tornado takes many shapes and sizes, but nothing is more iconic than the funnel cloud. Figure 5.1 shows an F5 tornado that touched down in Canada in 2007.

Tornadoes begin with winds spinning horizontally in the lower atmosphere of a thunderstorm. Rising warm air—an updraft—tilts the spinning air vertically. This creates an area several miles wide called a *rotating wall cloud*. It is within this wall cloud that a tornado will touch down.

A tornado is just spinning air. It rotates counterclockwise in the northern hemisphere and clockwise in the southern hemisphere. If it wasn't for water vapor and debris, you would never see one. Tornadoes can spin at speeds in excess of 200 miles per hour. They are most recognizably measured by the recently enhanced Fujita scale, where EF0 tornadoes are the weakest and EF5 the strongest. A major component in a tornado is its *helicity*, the amount of corkscrew-type motion it has. The winds spin, but they also travel upward, creating this spiraling effect.

Replicating the look of a tornado in Maya is all about speed. It is a delicate balance between upward motion and spinning motion. When the two are out of sync, the funnel cloud falls apart. When you don't have enough upward momentum, the tornado spins itself out of control. Too much upward motion, and the fluid is expelled from the container.

There are three main elements you will focus on creating in this chapter: the debris fountain, the dust shroud, and the condensation funnel. The *debris fountain* is the area surrounding the bottom of the tornado. It is where material from the ground is being sucked up into the tornado. You can see it in Figure 5.1. The *dust shroud* envelops the funnel. It may not always be noticeable, but it circles the funnel nevertheless. Last is the condensation funnel, or for all intents and purposes, the tornado itself.

Project: Funnel Cloud

The first project is to create a basic funnel cloud. You will build the effect from scratch by using Maya fluids and a Volume Axis field. The purpose of this exercise is to learn how to spin a fluid. The look of the cloud is addressed, but refining it is for another project. Our focus is to establish the motion and not the look. There is no scene to start from; you will create the fluid from scratch.

1. Create a 3D container by using the settings shown in Figure 5.2.

2. Create a primitive NURBS torus by using the defaults. Use Figure 5.3 to transform it to the bottom of the fluid.

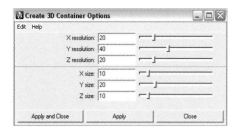

Figure 5.2

The settings for creating the container

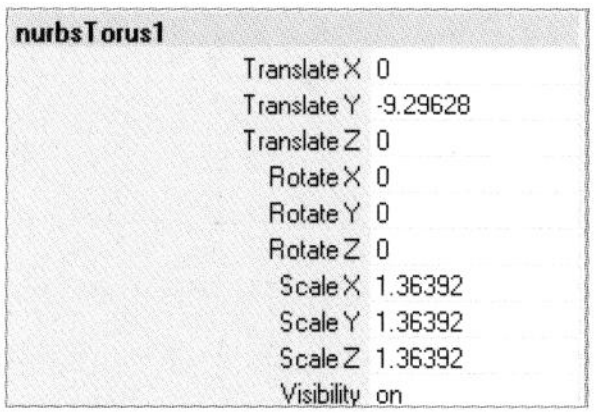

Figure 5.3

Translate and scale the torus.

Add the torus as an emitter to the fluid. You can use the defaults or optimize it by emitting only density. Run the simulation to see the progress so far. Figure 5.4 illustrates frame 150.

3. To get the rising fluid to twist and spin, use a Volume Axis field. A cone is used for the field's shape. The conical shape is used over a cylinder to allow the fluid to have more freedom of movement and to produce a stronger vacuum force within the fluid container. Figure 5.5 shows the settings for its creation.

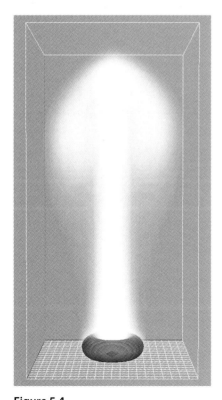

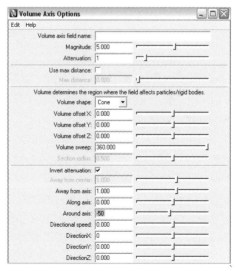

Figure 5.4

The torus is made into an emitter and tested.

Figure 5.5

The settings for creating a Volume Axis field

```
volumeAxisField1
        Translate X  0
        Translate Y  10
        Translate Z  0
        Rotate X  180
        Rotate Y  0
        Rotate Z  0
        Scale X  5
        Scale Y  20
        Scale Z  5
        Visibility  on
```

There is one main attribute contributing to the success of the funnel cloud: Around Axis. It is the speed the fluid travels around the central axis of the field. Positive values spin counterclockwise, and negative values clockwise.

The Attenuation is also adjusted. It controls the tapering of the field's strength. A value of 1 is used, making the field's power strongest at the central axis and diminishing in a linear manner to the outermost edge of the volume axis field. In terms of creating a tornado, the force should not radiate from the center. Instead, the force needs to be around the edge of the field and pushing in. Selecting the Invert Attenuation option flips the force so it does exactly that.

Transform the field by using the settings from Figure 5.6. It is important to recognize the orientation of the field. As you learned, real tornadoes form from an updraft. Placing the field above the presumed ground and setting it to suck the fluid up reenacts the rapid upward motion of warm air.

4. To get the fluid to twist properly, you must turn on High Detail Solve. In the Dynamic Simulation window, turn it on for All Grids. Figure 5.7 shows the results at frame 100. When you run the simulation, the effect is most noticeable down by the torus emitter.

5. The fluid starts to rise but never achieves a funnel shape. The Volume Axis field is not creating suction. Having the cone of the field at the bottom of the fluid container causes the fluid to twist upon emission. But because the field is so close, there isn't an opportunity for upward pressure to build. You can visualize this by turning on Velocity Draw under Display in the Attribute Editor. Figure 5.8 shows the velocity vectors circling the interior of the cone and pushing the fluid outward. The vectors along the container walls push the fluid up.

The longer the display vector, the greater the magnitude of the velocity. The arrows can get numerous and long. Control them with Draw Length and Draw Skip.

To get the desired results, raise the Volume Axis field to 20 in the Y axis. Watch as the field immediately rotates velocities within the cone. Within a few frames, the spinning force causes upward momentum. Figure 5.9 illustrates this momentum.

Run the simulation. By frame 50, a funnel cloud forms. As the fluid continues to emit, the container begins to fill up. If you keep watching, you can still catch a glimpse of a solid funnel from time to time. Figure 5.10(a) shows frame 50, and Figure 5.10(b) shows frame 96. Go ahead and save your scene before moving on.

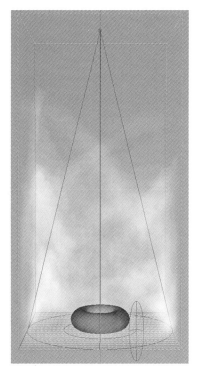

Figure 5.7

Turning on the High Detail Solve option allows the fluid to rotate or twist.

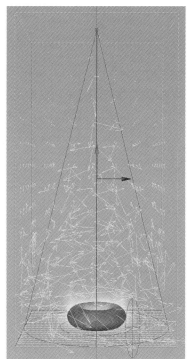

Figure 5.8

Display the velocity vectors to understand the motion path of the fluid.

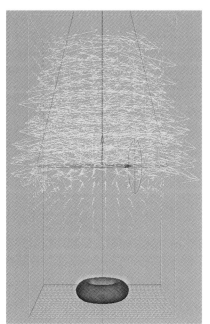

Figure 5.9

The velocity vectors are pushing the tornado upward.

Figure 5.10

(a) A funnel cloud
forms by frame 50;
(b) the funnel cloud
at frame 96.

To check your work so far, you can compare it to `funnel1.ma` on the DVD.

6. To keep the container from filling up, change all of the Boundaries under the Container Properties window to None, except for the Y Boundary. Change it to –Y.

7. The Volume Axis field is too far from the emitter. Moving the field high in the container was good for demonstrating velocity direction, but it creates too much upward motion on the fluid. It needs to be moved closer to the emitter; however, doing so also reduces the height of the funnel. The solution is to make the field larger and then reposition it. Use Figure 5.11 to set the field's new transforms.

Figure 5.11

Translate and scale the volume axis field.

Run the simulation. The results are shown in Figure 5.12.

8. The funnel cloud is not stable. It begins to lose stability at the top of the container, around frame 80. By frame 110, the funnel cloud is in total collapse. Figure 5.13 shows its demise.

   The funnel falls apart primarily because we opened the container. This causes a gradual buildup of forces or wind inside the container. To temper its volatility, add 0.05 to the Damp value under the Dynamic Simulation settings. The Damp value takes away velocity at each time step, thus reducing the wind in the container. Run the simulation again and notice the difference.

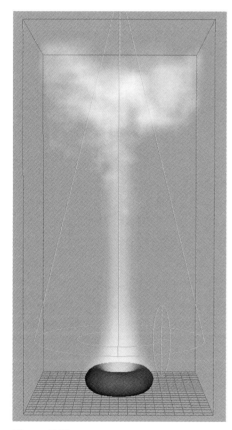

Figure 5.12
The funnel cloud is the full height of the container.

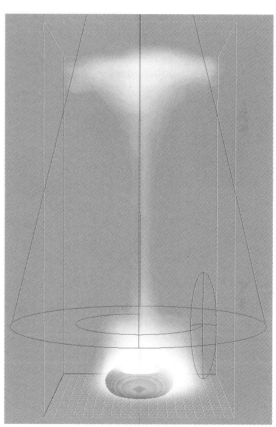

Figure 5.13
The funnel cloud falls down at frame 110 and never regains its shape.

9. As with the other projects, adding color helps us understand the motion of the fluid. Use Figure 5.14 to set the color graph. In addition, set the Color Input to Density and the Input Bias to 0.4. Remember, this is an exercise in function rather than aesthetics; the coloring is not critical. Its purpose is to provide contrast. After establishing the funnel's color, save your scene.

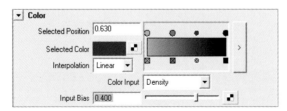

10. The funnel cloud is too transparent. Change the Transparency Color Value to 0.025.
11. The fluid forms a good-looking funnel cloud. Its motion, however, is too stiff. On the Volume Axis Field, set the Turbulence to 1. Watch the simulation again. Figure 5.15 shows frame 120.

    To check your work, you can compare it to funnel2.ma on the DVD.

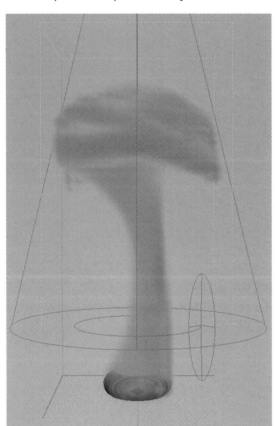

Twister

The previous project created a funnel cloud by using a Volume Axis field. The problem with using this type of field is the lack of control. It does the job, but you are left with little ability to influence its shape and size. It is possible to gain this control and more, without sacrificing the natural look of the simulation, by using a Volume Curve field. The next project focuses on providing control and making the tornado look real.

Project: Twister

In this project, a Volume Curve field is used to control a Maya fluid. The Volume Curve field is unique in that it allows you to customize the area of influence. The field is used to scale the beginning and the end of the twister, giving it its unique funnel appearance. The curve is used to alter the tornado's shape. Once again, you will start this project from scratch.

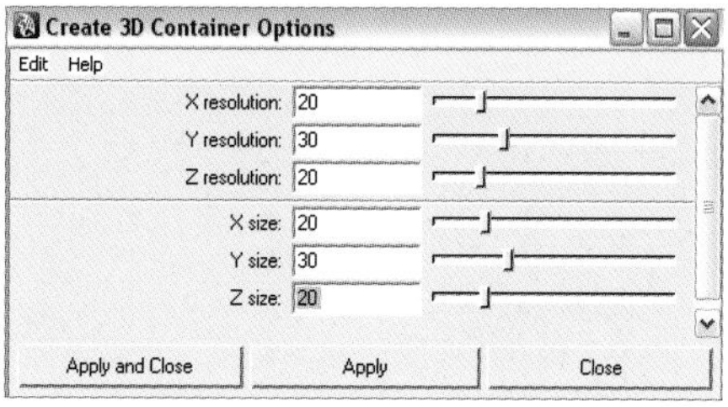

1. Create a 3D container by using the settings from Figure 5.16.

Figure 5.16

The settings for creating the container

2. A tornado's force is not specific to a point on the ground; it affects a circular area. To replicate this, you'll need a surface emitter. Create a default primitive NURBS circle. Duplicate it and scale the duplicate uniformly to 2. Select the inner curve and then the outer curve. From the Surfaces module, choose Surfaces → Loft. The defaults create the surface shown in Figure 5.17.

3. Delete the lofted surface's history. Rename the surface to **twisterSurface**. Add a default fluid surface emitter and place it 1 unit above the bottom of the container. Increase the surface's scale to 1.5. Figure 5.18 shows the progress so far.

Figure 5.17

Create a lofted surface by using the default options.

4. Draw a linear curve, with a single span from the emitter to the height of the container. The curve represents the tornado. Rename the curve to **twisterCurve**. Select it and the fluid. Choose Fields → Volume Curve. Volume Curve fields have no creation options. The field is added, with a series of circles running the length of the curve. They are the field's radius. Figure 5.19 shows the setup.

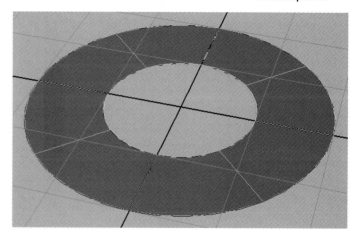

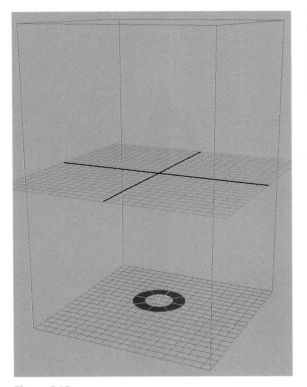

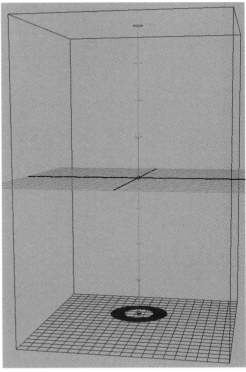

Figure 5.18

Place an emitter at the bottom of the container.

Figure 5.19

Add a Volume Curve field.

5. Select the Volume Curve field and open the Attribute Editor. Change the Section Radius to 8. The radius circle icons expand. Next, modify the Curve Radius graph to shape the funnel cloud. Use Figure 5.20 for reference.

Figure 5.20

Shape the funnel cloud with the Curve Radius graph.

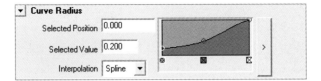

6. Go down to the Volume Speed Attributes. To move the fluid along, change the Along Axis value to 2. Furthermore, set the Directional Speed to 3 for the Y axis. These settings are strong, but they are necessary for the proper upward motion. For the spinning wind, change Around Axis to 8. To determine the direction of spin, you must decide whether your tornado is in the northern or southern hemisphere as described earlier. Positive values for Around Axis spin the fluid clockwise. Figure 5.21 shows the settings. Save your scene before moving on to step 7.

To check your work so far, you can compare it to `twister1.ma` on the DVD.

7. The spinning effect can't be seen until you turn on High Detail Solve. Select the fluid and set it to All Grids. In addition, set the Boundary in the X and Z to None and the Y to –Y Side, just as you did in the previous project. Confirm your settings with Figure 5.22.

8. At this point, it is difficult to see the fluid's reactions to the previous settings. Let's work on the shading and return later to the fluid's behavior. Set the Transparency value to 0.04. Go to the Color graph and use Figure 5.23 to set the color values. Also, set the Color Input to Y Gradient.

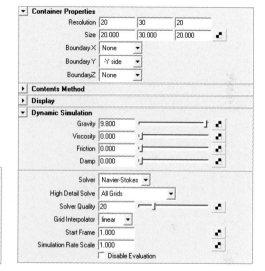

Figure 5.21
Use Along Axis and Around Axis to put the tornado in motion.

Figure 5.22
Change the boundaries and turn on High Detail Solve for All Grids.

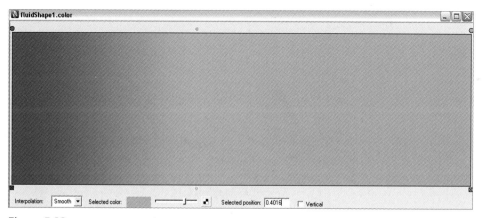

Figure 5.23
The color settings for the color graph

9. The fluid is still difficult to see. The power of the Volume Curve field is clearing the voxels faster than the emitter is filling them. Select the emitter. Change the Density/Voxel/Sec to 20. Run the simulation to check your progress. Figure 5.24 shows frame 39.

10. You can now return to working on the tornado's behavior. The fluid is reacting too much to the Volume Curve field. You do not want to reduce the settings of the field. You need to gain control over the fluid by damping its motion. Change the Damp parameter on the fluid to 0.2. Test the simulation. It runs much slower and begins to fill out the radius of the Volume field. Figure 5.25 has the results.

11. When you watch the simulation, it appears that the fluid is not moving in the X and Z directions. It looks as if it is not twisting. The problem, however, is that the fluid's motion is not varying from frame to frame. It has the same velocity, shape, and speed. Therefore, it looks stationary. You can witness this by turning on Velocity Draw. To fix this, you need to disrupt the fluid's monotonous behavior. Add 5 to the Velocity Swirl. Furthermore, in Turbulence set the Strength and Frequency to 10 and the Speed to 1. Figure 5.26 shows the Attribute window.

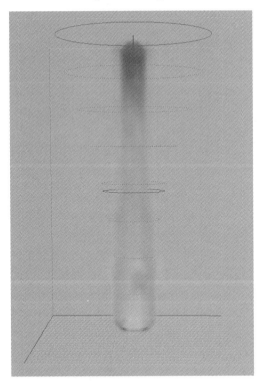

Figure 5.24
The progress of the tornado so far

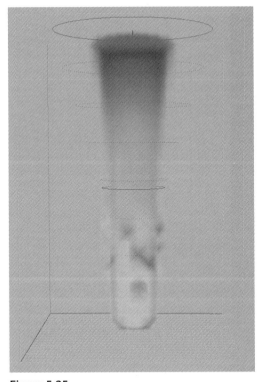

Figure 5.25
The simulation at frame 100

Run the simulation again with Velocity Draw on. The arrows now shift in the X and Z. Figure 5.27 shows frame 100 for comparison. Save your scene file after analyzing the changes.

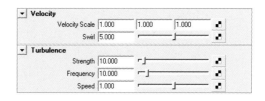

Figure 5.26

The values for the Swirl and Turbulence

To check your work so far, you can compare it to twister2.ma on the DVD.

Controlling the Fluid Spread

The fluid is flowing and twisting up the Volume Curve, but the fluid's rotational speed also throws it out of the field. This is the largest problem with using fluids for tornadoes. Several attributes need to be modified in order to get control over this, including increasing the resolution. The next three steps address the issue:

1. Under the Dynamic Simulation menu of the fluid, change the Simulation Rate Scale to 3. The Damp is slowing the fluid; because of this, the Rate Scale is increased.

2. Next, you want the density to disappear quickly when the fluid is thin, showing only when it is accumulated together. Change the Dissipation and the Diffusion to 0.2. The diffusion helps soften the look by dispersing the fluid into adjacent voxels. Next, set the Buoyancy to 10. Increasing the Buoyancy causes the fluid to rise, helping to prevent the fluid from accumulating inside the container. Figure 5.28 shows the new settings.

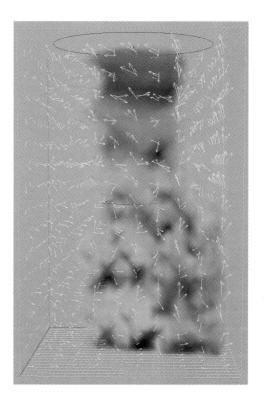

Figure 5.27

The simulation at frame 100 with swirl and turbulence added

Figure 5.28

The new Density parameters

3. The final setting to modify is the fluid resolution. The look of the tornado changes depending on the resolution you choose. Take a look at Figure 5.29(a). It shows the

tornado at frame 100 with the XYZ resolution at 40, 60, and 40. Figure 5.29(b) shows the fluid at the same frame but with an XYZ resolution of 60, 90, and 60. You can see a change in the silhouette of the fluid as well as an increase in internal detail.

Both resolutions are good, but they provide different looks. For this project, stick with the higher resolution of 60, 90, and 60. Make sure to save your scene before moving on.

To check your work so far, you can compare it to `twister3.ma` on the DVD.

Adding a Dust Cloud

The next part of the project adds a separate dust cloud, or debris fountain, that circles the ground. Adding dust to the bottom of the tornado is a great finishing touch. It provides extra realism and way to conceal the sometimes awkward look of the fluids as they are emitted at the base of the tornado. A cylindrical volume field is used to keep the dust fountain under control and provide the spinning motion.

1. Hide all parts of the tornado on a layer. The fluid tornado does not calculate when hidden, freeing up your processor to work on the fluid dust cloud. Create a new 3D container by using the settings from Figure 5.30. Name the container **debrisFountain**.

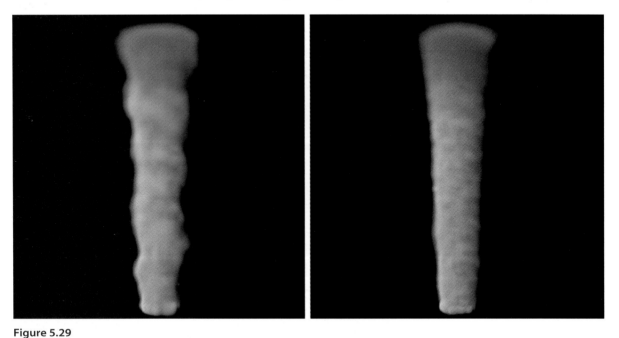

Figure 5.29

The tornado with (a) an XYZ resolution of 40, 60, and 40; (b) an XYZ resolution of 60, 90, and 60

2. Duplicate the twisterSurface node. Delete the child emitter node that was duplicated along with the surface. Rename the surface to **dustSurface**. Figure 5.31 shows the progress so far.

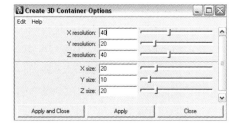

Figure 5.30

Create a 3D container.

3. Make dustSurface an emitter for the debrisFountain fluid node. Set the Density/Voxel/Sec to 3.

You could have used the tornado's surface emitter for the debris fountain emitter as well. It is still a good idea to have separate emitters in the event you need to scale or alter one component and not the other in future developments.

4. The dust cloud spins around the tornado. To accomplish this, use a cylinder Volume Axis field. Figure 5.32 shows the necessary settings for creating the field. A cylindrical volume is ideal for getting fluids to rotate. It functions just like the Volume Curve field but lacks the ability to change shape.

Figure 5.31

Duplicate the twisterSurface node.

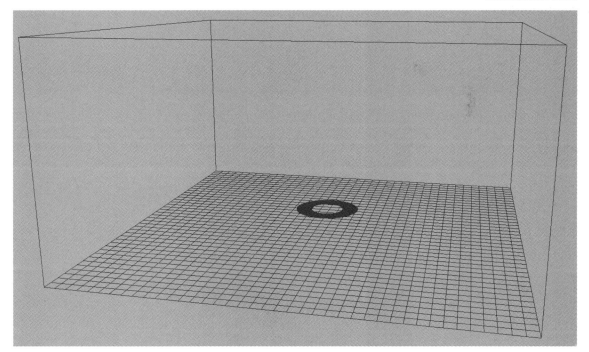

Figure 5.32

Create a Cylinder Volume Axis field.

To get the fluids to respond accordingly, the Attenuation is turned completely off with a zero value, effectively applying the same amount of strength across the fluid. Force is being applied around the axis as well as along the axis to get the fluids to spin and move up. Further assisting the upward motion is the Directional Speed, set to 1.0 in the Y.

5. The position of the cylinder is important and can change the field's influence dramatically. Transform the cylinder by using the settings from Figure 5.33.

Run the simulation to see its effects. Figure 5.34 shows frame 105.

Figure 5.33

Transform the Cylinder Volume Axis field.

Figure 5.34

The dust cloud at frame 105 with the Volume Axis Field.

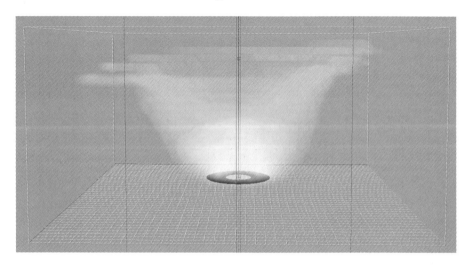

6. The debrisFountain fluid is similar to the tornado fluid, but with less organized fury. Using the twister settings as a comparison, we can establish the debris fluid. The Velocity Swirl and turbulence values are lower than those used for the twister. The turbulence is subtle, comparatively speaking, to keep the fluid from going out of control. You are also not trying to suck the fluid to the top of the container, so the Buoyancy is cut in half. The Dissipation is increased to prevent the fluid from becoming too dense and lingering in the container, and the Diffusion is dropped to 0, creating a dirtier, rougher look. Use Figure 5.35 to set debris fountain values.

 To check your work so far, you can compare it to twister4.ma on the DVD.

Shading the Dust Cloud

The motion of the dust fountain is complete. You can now move on to shading it. A texture is also used to give the fluid greater detail. Let's get started.

1. Modify the color of the fluid by using Figure 5.36. Make sure the Color Input is set to Density.

2. Set the Transparency Value to 0.02. You also need to make sure the fluid dissipates before it reaches the top of the container. Instead of relying on the Density Dissipation, change the Dropoff Shape to Y Gradient and set the Edge Dropoff to 0.5. Figure 5.37 has the settings.

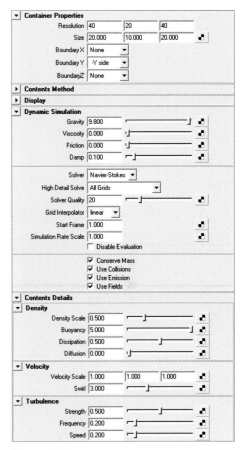

Figure 5.35
Set the values for the debrisFountain fluid.

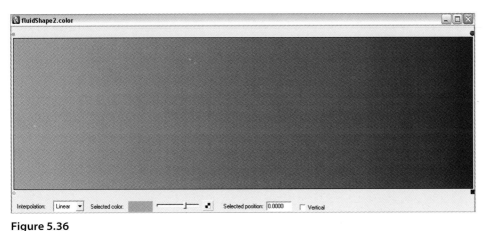

Figure 5.36
The colors for the dust cloud

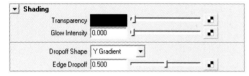

Figure 5.37

The settings for the Transparency Dropoff

3. As in the funnel cloud project, you need to be able to see as much detail and contrast as possible in the viewport. Select the Self Shadow option under the Lighting menu. Figure 5.38 shows the progress so far.

4. The dust cloud is almost there. To give it more detail, add Texture to the Opacity. Change the Texture Type to Space Time, the same texture you used for the plinian eruption in Chapter 4, "Volcanic Activity." Figure 5.39 shows the rest of the Texture settings.

Run the simulation to see the results, shown in Figure 5.40.

Figure 5.38

The dust cloud at frame 100 with self-shadowing turned on

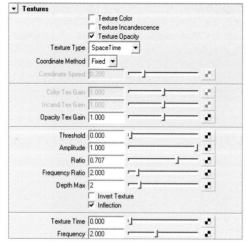

Figure 5.39

Texture the Opacity to give the dust cloud detail.

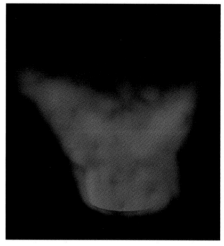

Figure 5.40

The textured fluid at frame 100

5. The texture looks good when the dust cloud is still, shown in Figure 5.40, but it lacks motion. The dust detail should spiral around just like the funnel cloud. Although the fluid is moving appropriately, the texture is not. The fix is to add an expression to the texture's origin to move it with the flow of the twister. Enter the following expression for the fluid shape:

```
debrisFountainFluidShape.textureOriginX=time*.2;
debrisFountainFluidShape.textureOriginY=time*-.12;
debrisFountainFluidShape.textureOriginZ=time*.2;
```

To finish the look of the texture, add the next line to the expression to animate the texture's pattern over time:

```
debrisFountainFluidShape.textureTime=time*.5;
```

To check your work so far, you can compare it to `twister5.ma` on the DVD.

Combining the Parts of the Tornado

The parts of the tornado are complete. You can now incorporate the dust cloud and the tornado into one effect. We will also give the twister more life, by using a dynamic hair curve to manipulate its volume curve field. After the parts are complete, a simply hierarchy brings all of them together.

1. Unhide all of the tornado parts. The first thing to do is alter the original curve used to generate the Volume Curve field. Currently, it is a linear curve. By rebuilding the curve to cubic, you can control its curvature, allowing tendril-like tornadoes to be created. Select twisterCurve and rebuild it by using the options shown in Figure 5.41.

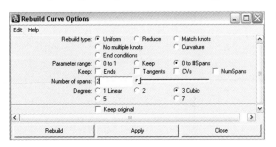

Figure 5.41
Rebuild twisterCurve.

2. Controlling the curve is a bit more challenging. After rebuilding, it now has five control vertices. Maya has numerous options for manipulating curve points, all of which are acceptable and provide adequate results, but some require more work to be animated than others. To keep within the context of this book, the curve will be set up with its own dynamic simulation using a hair curve.

Select twisterCurve. Choose Hair → Assign Hair System → New Hair System. The twister curve becomes a child of the hair system follicle and duplicated. Its duplicate becomes the dynamic curve. Figure 5.42 shows the setup in the Hypergraph.

Figure 5.42

Assigning a new
hair system to the
twister curve results
in these nodes.

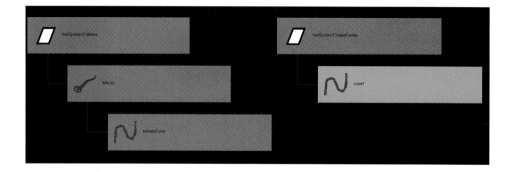

3. The Volume Curve field is still attached to the original twister curve. There isn't an automatic way to move the field to another curve, but it can be done manually through the Connection Editor. Select curveShape1 from under the HairSystem1-OutputCurves node. Make sure you are selecting the shape node and not the transform node. Next, select the Volume Curve Field. Choose Window → General Editors → Component Editor. Choose World Space from the left column, and inputCurve from the right column. Use Figure 5.43 for reference.

Figure 5.43

Use the Connection
Editor to change the
field's input curve.

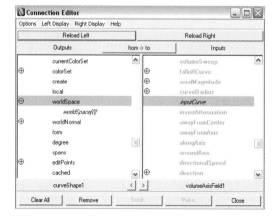

4. The curve has little response at this point to the hair simulation. This is actually what you want. The point of the hair system is to create a structure to control the direction and shape of the funnel. Go to the start frame, to make sure the hair curve is in its original state. Select curve1 and then choose Hair → Create Constraint → Transform. Snap the newly created locator to the bottom of the curve. Rename it to **twisterBottom**. Create another Hair Transform constraint and snap it to the top of the curve. Rename it to **twisterTop**. Figure 5.44 shows the setup.

5. Hair curves are automatically attached to a fixed point, depending on the direction of the curve. Because you are using a Transform constraint to control the hair curve, all of the default attachments need to be turned off. Select the follicle1 node. In the Channel Box, change Point Lock to No Attach. You can now move the locators to shape and move the tornado. Keep in mind, however, that the hair curve updates only during simulation. Figure 5.45 shows the Volume Curve field responding to the new setup.

6. When the locators are moved, certain nodes should move with them to keep the effect intact. Parent the debrisFountainSurface, debrisFountainFluid, debrisFountain-VolumeAxisField, and twisterSurface to twisterBottom. Next, parent twisterFluid to twisterTop. Figure 5.46 shows the setup in the Hypergraph.

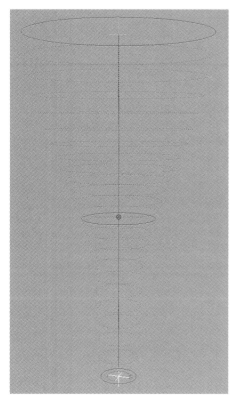

Figure 5.44

Create two Hair Transform constraints. Snap one to the top of the curve and the other to the bottom.

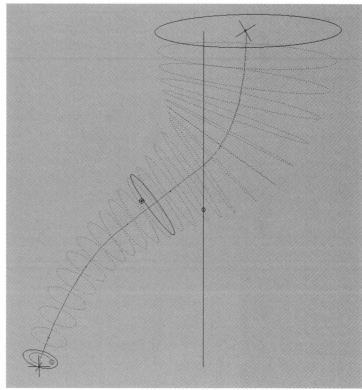

Figure 5.45

The twister's Volume Curve field is manipulated by the Hair Transform constraints.

Figure 5.46

The hierarchies
used to control the
twister

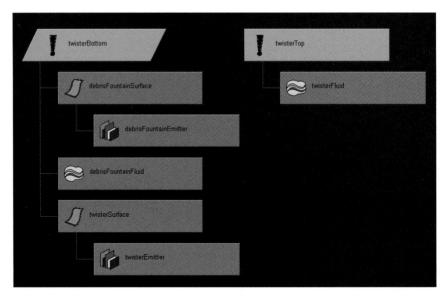

7. Select curve1 under the hairSystem1OutputCurves node and debrisFountainVolume-AxisField, in that order, and open the Options box for Constrain → Tangent. Use the settings from Figure 5.47 to add a Tangent constraint.

Figure 5.47

Add a Tangent
constraint to debris-
FountainVolume–
AxisField.

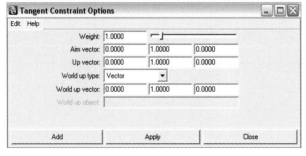

By adding a Tangent constraint, we make the field automatically rotate to stay aligned, in the Y, with the curve. Along with parenting the field, the Tangent constraint gives the dust cloud the appearance of being created by the tornado by matching its movements.

8. The twister is done. The only thing remaining is to change the Shading Quality for both fluids. Set the Render Interpolator to Smooth. Figure 5.48 shows all of the Shading Quality settings.

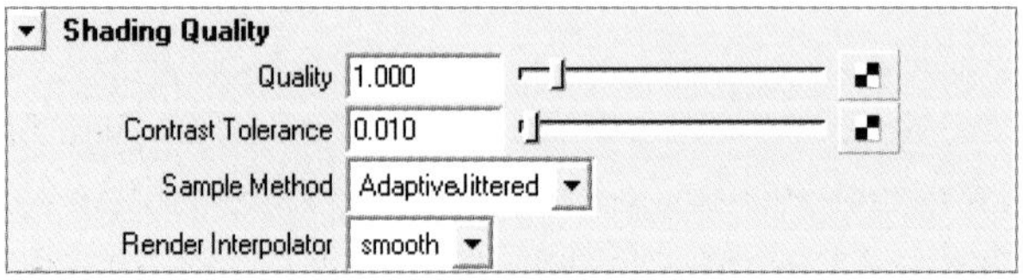

Figure 5.48

The Shading Quality
settings for both
fluids

Figure 5.49(a) shows a snapshot of the viewport at frame 115, and Figure 5.49(b) shows a rendered image of the simulation using the Draft preset of Mental Ray. A ray-tracing directional light was also added to match the shadows shown in the viewport.

To check your work, you can compare it to `tornado6.ma` on the DVD.

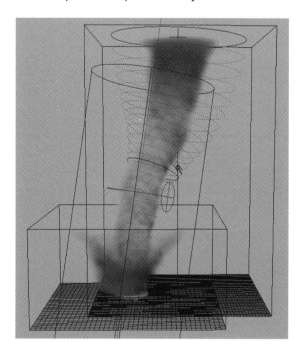 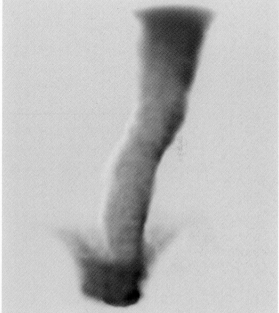

Figure 5.49

The simulation (a) as seen in the viewport and (b) rendered with Mental Ray

Tornado Winds

The rating F5 on the Fujita scale means that winds exceed 261 miles per hour, delivering total devastation. When a tornado has such magnitude, the tornado itself is only half of the problem. Some of the worst destruction comes from the objects the tornado hurls from its path. The powerful winds are capable of leveling structures and throwing the parts for miles in all directions.

It's time to put all of your knowledge to use. The next project entails creating an F5 tornado. But creating the tornado is not your only task; you must also use the destructive force of an F5 tornado to destroy a small cabin.

Project: Creating an F5

In this project, you will take an existing tornado and use its winds to level a cabin. The tornado is built from a fluid similar to the tornadoes built in the previous projects. The cabin will be made into an active nCloth object so it can be destroyed. Fluids cannot influence nCloth vertices; therefore, nParticles are combined with the fluid to create a destructive force. Although the tornado's path of destruction is a glancing blow to the cabin, the wind generated by the nParticles will cause its devastation.

1. Open the scene file F5_1.ma. The scene contains a cabin and ground terrain. The cabin is missing its back wall in order to reduce the amount of geometry in the simulation. The terrain has been made into a Passive Collider. A fluid tornado is also in the scene. It was created using a Cylinder Volume Axis Field. The fluid and field use similar settings to those in the twister project. Figure 5.50 shows the scene.

   The fluid is currently disabled. Click Play to see the animation applied to the tornado setup. The tornado's path takes it across the back-right corner of the cabin; because of its size, the tornado makes a direct hit.

   The first thing to address is the surface emitter. You can see in Figure 5.50 that it is partially below the terrain. The terrain is a collision object, potentially preventing emissions. Furthermore, having the tip of the tornado follow the terrain would add to the effect. A quick way to achieve this is to use the terrain as a sculpt deformer to the surface emitter.

Figure 5.50

F5_1.ma **is set up with an environment and tornado.**

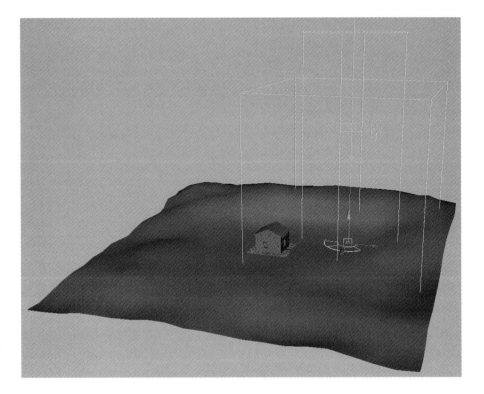

Select tornadoSurface and then the terrain. Open the options for Create Deformers → Sculpt Deformer. Set the mode to Flip and select Use Secondary NURBS or Polygon Object. Figure 5.51 has the rest of the settings.

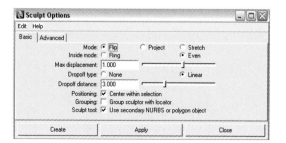

Figure 5.51

The Sculpt Deformer settings

2. The surface emitter deforms along the terrain but does not stick to the surface. Select the terrain and then tornadoSurface. Choose Constrain → Geometry. The surface emitter now deforms as you move it across the terrain.

> Project is a better choice than Flip for the sculpt deformer Mode option. However, Flip works so well that the sculpt deformer and deformed occupy the same space, also causing particle emissions to become trapped below the terrain. In areas of extreme elevation, the surface emitter will fall through the terrain. You can compensate by manually rotating the surface. This will not entirely fix the problem. Ultimately, the surface emitter does not have enough geometry to deform properly.

3. In order for the tornado to destroy the cabin, you need to incorporate nParticles. You can use the fluid surface emitter to emit the nParticles. Select tornadoSurface. Choose Create nParticles → Balls. Open the options for nParticles → Create nParticles → Emit from Object. Only a few adjustments need to be made. Use Figure 5.52 to change the settings.

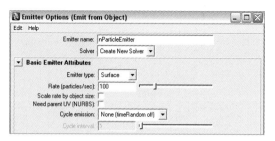

Figure 5.52

The settings for creating nParticles

The number of nParticles emitted has a big impact on influencing other nCloth objects. The more nParticles you have, the greater wind force the nParticles create.

4. When emitted, the nParticles fall to the terrain. You want them to mimic the motion of the fluid tornado. The best way to accomplish this is to add another Volume Axis field. The fluid, and the Volume Axis field affecting the fluid, do not have the settings to move the nParticles correctly. Because fluids and nParticles use different solvers, their reactions to fields are not the same. Select nParticle1 and open the options for Fields → Volume Axis. Use Figure 5.53 to set the values.

Figure 5.53

The settings for creating a Volume Axis field

Volume Axis Options		
Edit Help		

Volume axis field name: nParticleVolumeAxisField
Magnitude: 15
Attenuation: 0.000
Use max distance: ☐
Max distance: 0.000

Volume determines the region where the field affects particles/rigid bodies.
Volume shape: Cylinder ▾
Volume offset X: 0.000
Volume offset Y: 0.000
Volume offset Z: 0.000
Volume sweep: 360.000
Section radius: 0.500

Invert attenuation: ☐
Away from center: 1.000
Away from axis: 0
Along axis: 1
Around axis: 200
Directional speed: 50
DirectionX: 0
DirectionY: 1
DirectionZ: 0.000

5. Translate and scale the volume field by using the settings from Figure 5.54. Make sure to save your scene as well.

To check your work so far, you can compare it to F5_2.ma on the DVD.

6. Make nParticleVolumeAxisField a child of tornadoGrp. Run the simulation. The nParticles shoot out from their emitter in an uncontrollable fashion. In a sense, they are receiving double transforms. They are getting information from the nucleus solver and the field. They need to be affected by only the field. Select the nParticle and change Conserve to 0. Also, change their Radius to 1 to make them easier to see. Run the simulation again. Figure 5.55 shows the results.

Figure 5.54

Translate and scale the Volume Axis field.

```
nParticleVolumeAxisField1
   Translate X  39.19468
   Translate Y  53.38937
   Translate Z  -26.6705
   Rotate X  0
   Rotate Y  0
   Rotate Z  0
   Scale X  30
   Scale Y  70
   Scale Z  30
   Visibility  on
```

7. The nParticles mimic the motion of the tornado. You can now shift your attention to the cabin. The cabin was built in pieces and then combined into one object. None of the vertices have been merged. Keeping the original pieces separate will allow them to blow apart. Select the cabin and choose nMesh → Create nCloth. Use the default options.

8. The cabin needs to stay intact until the force of the tornado becomes too overpowering. A Transform constraint does the job perfectly. Select the cabin and choose nConstraint → Transform. The constraint covers the cabin as shown in Figure 5.56.

Figure 5.55

The nParticles at frame 46

Figure 5.56

Add a Transform constraint to the cabin.

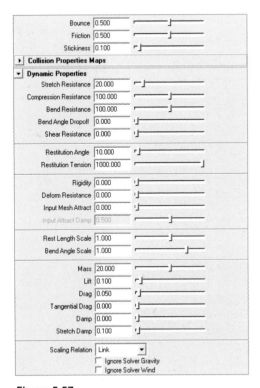

Figure 5.57

The values for the nCloth cabin

9. To keep the cabin together until the right time, lower the Glue Strength. Select the Transform constraint and change the Glue Strength to 0.05.

10. The nCloth properties on the cabin, with the exception of the mass, do not contribute to the simulation until the cabin breaks apart. Use Figure 5.57 for the settings.

   The Bounce, Friction, and Stickiness options influence how the cabin parts interact with the terrain. You do not want your parts to go sliding across the surface. The combination of values provides a realistic stop to their turbulent flight.

   The next set of attributes—Stretch, Compression, and Bend Resistance—attempts to keep the shape of the parts being flung around. Coupled with a low Restitution Angle, the parts will tumble but still receive damage when they impact other objects.

   Last, the Mass gives the previously set values power. Even though an F5 tornado would blow through the cabin as if it were a stack of papers, the increased mass keeps the cabin from looking like a toy. The Lift was also raised to give the pieces more flying time. Now is also a good time to save your scene.

To check your work so far, you can compare it to `F5_3.ma` on the DVD.

11. Select the nucleus1 node and change the Space Scale to 0.304 to match the scale of the scene. Figure 5.58 shows the settings.

Figure 5.58

The settings for nucleus Scale Attributes

12. The cabin is ready to be destroyed. The only thing missing is the 261 mph wind. Select the nParticles. Find the Wind Field Generation attributes. The first setting, Air Push Distance, controls how far out the wind field influences. Change it to 100. The next, Air Push Vorticity, is the amount of circular motion and curl within the wind being generated. Set it to 4. Figure 5.59 shows the settings.

Figure 5.59

The settings for Wind Field Generation

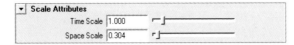

The force of the wind rips boards off the cabin before the fluid tornado touches it. Because the cabin doesn't have a back wall, the boards break away easily. Take a look at the inevitable devastation in Figure 5.60.

Figure 5.60
The nParticle wind begins to rip the cabin apart.

13. At almost 10,000 triangles, the cabin is expensive to simulate. A playblast using video resolution can take hours. Make sure to save your scene before running the simulation. If your computer is having a hard time with a playblast, render it by using low-quality settings with either Maya Software or Mental Ray. If you are satisfied with the simulation, you can cache the cabin. There is no need to cache the nParticles, because they will never be seen and eventually will be deleted.

To cache the cabin, choose nCache → Create New Cache. Make sure the cache directory is valid and set the cache name to **cabin**. Use Figure 5.61 for the rest of the settings. After the cabin is cached and you are satisfied with the results, you can delete the nParticles.

Figure 5.61
The settings for caching the nCloth cabin

Caching the fluid is addressed in the next project. You will also tackle rendering a high-quality version of the finished scene. To check your work, you can compare it to F5_4.ma on the DVD.

Project: Rendering the F5

The previous project had an F5 tornado destroy a cabin. The next step is rendering. The cabin has already been cached and is included in the project's scene file. Several things still need to be addressed before we can render. In this project, you will cache the fluid and then set up Mental Ray to render the scene.

1. Open the scene file renderingF5_1.ma. The scene file picks up where the previous project left off. The nCloth cabin has been cached. The nParticles, emitter, and volume field have been deleted. Only the fluid remains.

   Before caching the fluid, you want to establish an initial state. This way, the F5 tornado will be at full force at the start of the simulation, eliminating its creation period. Run the simulation to frame 90. Select the fluid and choose Fluid Effects → Set Initial State. Return to frame 1.

2. With the Initial State set, you can now cache the fluid. Choose Fluid nCache → Create New Cache. Figure 5.62 shows the settings. Fluid cache files can be large. After the tornado is cached, the file is almost a full gigabyte.

> Some file systems cannot manage files larger than 2GB. If your cache files get this large, an alternative is to use the One File per Frame settings in the Create Fluid Cache options. This creates a small file for every frame instead of combining them into one large file.

3. You can now delete the tornadoSurface and its emitter. The fluid runs on its own through the cache file.

Figure 5.62

The settings for caching the fluid tornado

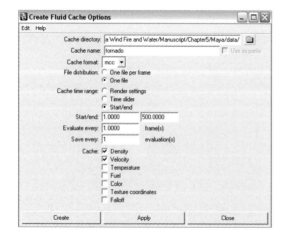

4. Open the render settings. Choose Mental Ray for the renderer. Under the Common tab, disable the default light.

5. Go to the Indirect Lighting tab and Create a Physical Sun and Sky from the Environment section. Choosing this does several things. First, it automatically checks Final Gather. Then, it adds a directional light for the sun. It also creates a simple Exposure node and Physical Sky node connected to the perspective camera. Figure 5.63 shows the connections in the Attribute Editor.

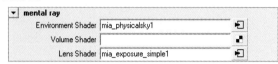

Figure 5.63

An exposure and Physical Sky node are connected to the perspective camera.

Rendering a frame, shown in Figure 5.64, reveals a bright, washed-out look, not very suitable for tornado weather.

Figure 5.64

The scene rendered with the default Physical Sky settings

6. To get rid of the washed-out look, open the mia_exposure_simple1 node attached to the perspective camera. Change the Gamma to 1. Figure 5.65 shows the settings. Figure 5.66 shows the rendered results.

Figure 5.65

The settings for the mia_exposure_simple1 node

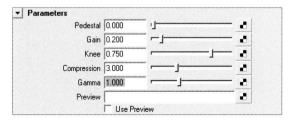

Figure 5.66

The scene rendered
with the gamma
turned down

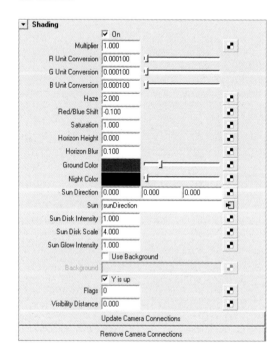

7. Open the Physical Sky node. To create an atmosphere more suited to an F5 tornado, use the settings from Figure 5.67.

The Haze and Red/Blue Shift give the scene a dirty, bluish look. Figure 5.68 shows the render.

Figure 5.67

The settings for the
Physical Sky node

8. The angle of the sun or directional light dictates the time of day. For the final adjustment, select the sun and rotate it to –25, setting the time to dusk. Figure 5.69 shows the render.

To check your final work, you can compare it to rendering F5_2.ma on the DVD. The fluid cache file is not included, because of its size of almost 1GB.

Figure 5.68

The scene rendered with haze and a bluish tint

Figure 5.69

The scene rendered with a sun angle for dusk

CHAPTER 6

Playing with Fire

From a single match to a blazing inferno, fire is nature's mischievous child. Its presence is hypnotic. Its dancing flames, welcoming heat, and warm color fill you with a false sense of security. In an instant, fire can go from a life-saving instrument to a tool of destruction. Left to its own devices, fire would consume anything it came into contact with. This chapter uses fluids to build realistic fire, from a single flame to a house engulfed in flames.

Fuel

Fuel is arguably the most complex and interesting parameter of fluids. What makes it so unique is its ability to be reactive in a chemical sense. Other content methods fill containers and are modified by altering their own attributes. Fuel, however, can do nothing without another method, such as density or temperature, influencing it. Fuel relies on these to exist or be destroyed. On its own, it is a stagnant volume of untapped energy.

The premise behind fluid fuel is relatively simple. It is a catalyst, just like its real-world counterpart. When emitted, it flows as part of the density. If it comes in contact with temperature, it releases heat. The heat it releases is added to the current temperature values. The first project in this chapter introduces you to the concept of fuel.

Project: Igniting Fuel

To understand fuel's role in creating fluid effects, you will paint fuel into a container. From there you will add an emitter to cause a reaction through heat or temperature.

1. Create a default 3D container. Translate the container to 5 in the Y, setting it on top of the grid.

2. To paint fuel, choose Fluid Effects → Add/Edit Contents and open the Paint Fluid Tools options. A painting slice appears in the container. The goal is to fill the bottom of the container with fuel and density. Adding density makes the fuel visible. Tumble your camera view until the painting slice switches to the Y axis. Use Figure 6.1 for reference.

3. Click the lock icon to keep the manipulator set to the Y. You can now move the camera freely. Translate the manipulator to the bottom of the container. It won't go to the border of the container; it always sits in the middle of a voxel.

4. Click the target icon, enabling you to scale the manipulator. Scale it down to the size of a single voxel. Use Figure 6.2 for reference.

5. Scaling the manipulator establishes a subvolume. You can now flood the entire subvolume. In the Paint Tool settings, choose Density and Fuel for the Paintable Attributes. A window pops up, asking whether you want to change the attribute to Dynamic. Choose Set to Dynamic to continue. Click the Flood button to fill the subvolume. Figure 6.3 shows the results of the completed step.

6. If you play the simulation, the fluid rises and fills the entire container. You want the fuel to sit motionless on the bottom until it reacts with another component. Open the Fluid's attributes. Change the Density's Buoyancy to 0.

To check your work so far, you can compare it to `ignitingFuel1.ma` on the DVD.

7. Let's add our catalyst. Add an emitter by using the settings from Figure 6.4 to the container. The emitter will emit Density and Temperature.

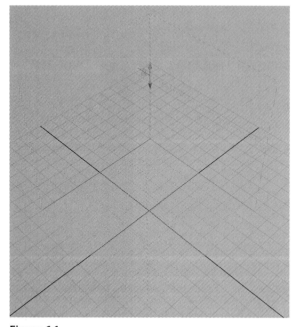

Figure 6.1

Position the camera to switch the manipulator to work in the Y axis.

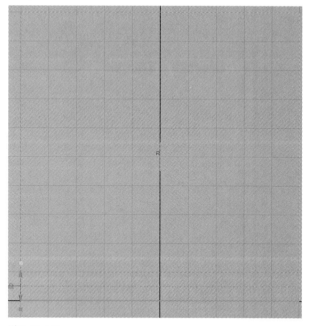

Figure 6.2

Scale the manipulator down to the size of a single voxel.

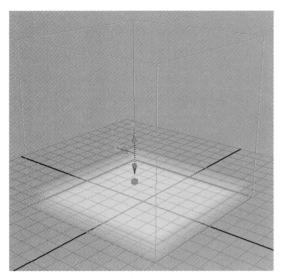

Figure 6.3
Flood the subvolume with Density and Fuel.

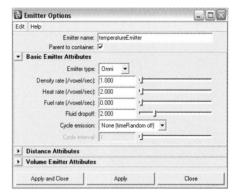

Figure 6.4
The settings for adding a temperature emitter

As mentioned in step 2, adding density to the emitter is done only to make the temperature visible, just like the fuel. The density is not necessary to create a reaction. It does, however, play an integral part in our ability to see it. Either temperature, fuel, or both can have density. If neither has density, the reaction still occurs; it just won't be visible through rendering.

Figure 6.5
The temperature and fuel mix together.

8. Select the fluid. Change the Temperature Content Method to Dynamic. The temperature can now flow into the container. Playing the simulation yields little effect. The two different emissions eventually mix together, as shown in Figure 6.5.

9. To simplify the effect, change the Surface parameters to Surface Render and Hard Surface. Figure 6.6 shows the settings.

Figure 6.6

The settings for the
surface attributes

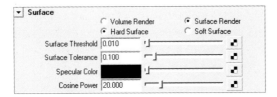

10. Move the temperature emitter into the fuel. Translate it to −4. Putting the emitter in the middle of the fuel expedites the reaction.

11. Playing the simulation causes a large mushroomlike formation to fill the container, as shown in Figure 6.7.

Figure 6.7

A mushroom cloud
forms during the
simulation.

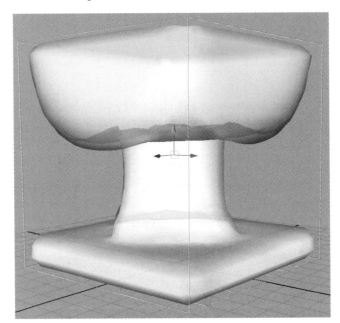

A reaction is taking place, but it is hidden by the temperature's density. We can use the fluid's opacity to focus on the effects of the fuel and temperature coming into contact with one another. Change the Opacity Input to Density and Fuel. Figure 6.8 shows the settings.

Figure 6.8

The fluid's Opacity
settings

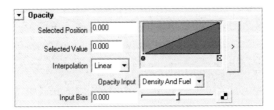

12. Playing the simulation again reveals a very different simulation. The temperature seems to disintegrate the dense fuel mass at the bottom of the container. The affected area gives off a reddish hue. The coloring is from the Incandescence, which by default is mapped to the Temperature. Figure 6.9 shows frame 175.

Figure 6.9

The temperature eats away at the fuel.

Improve the look of the effect by setting the Transparency to 0 and the color to black. Figure 6.10 shows the finished effect at frame 135.

To check your work so far, you can compare it to `ignitingFuel2.ma` on the DVD.

Figure 6.10

The finished effect at frame 135

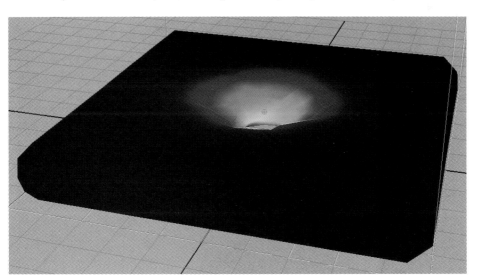

Temperature and Fuel

Let's take a closer look at the relationship between the content methods Fuel and Temperature. They both emit details into a container, but under the right conditions fuel will ignite, causing heat to be added to the Temperature. When this happens, there is an increase in Temperature density and a decrease in Fuel density as the fuel burns away.

Figure 6.11
The Fuel attributes

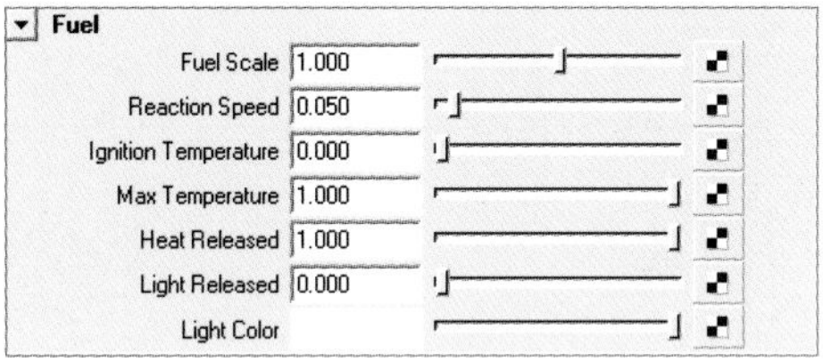

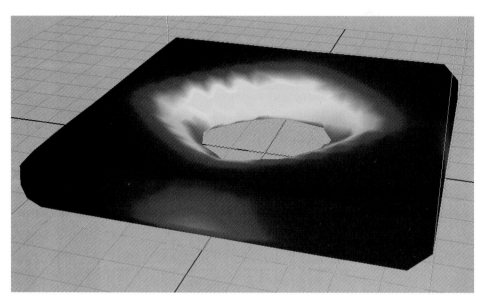

To get fuel to ignite, you must have temperature or emit Heat/Vox/Sec into the container where the fuel is also present. When the ignition temperature of the fuel is reached by the temperature contents in the container, a reaction takes place. We will use the Igniting Fuel project to help explain the Fuel parameters and how they influence temperature contents. Figure 6.11 shows all of the Fuel settings.

Heat Released

The Heat Released value is added directly to the temperature content methods. Raising this value adds more incandescence. It also plays a part in the fuel's own demise by increasing the temperature, because the higher the temperature, the greater the opportunity for a reaction. This does not have the same effect as adding temperature; it only adds to the heat of the temperature at the reaction point. This causes a chain of reactions, burning up the rest of the fuel. The Heat Released attribute is grayed out until Ignition Temperature is activated. Figure 6.12 shows what happens when the Heat Released attribute is set to 5.

Figure 6.12
The Heat Released is set to 5.

Ignition Temperature and Max Temperature

Fuel has an ignition temperature. In terms of Maya fluid mechanics, this is the amount of heat required to cause a reaction in the fuel. By default, this attribute is set to 0, which means the slightest bit of temperature deviation causes the fuel to react. At this setting, fuel will keep its state only if temperature is not being emitted into the container. The rest of the parameters are waiting to see whether a reaction will occur. If temperature is present, the Reaction Speed has an effect. The Reaction Speed controls how fast the reaction happens. In the real world, it's the difference between a slow-burning material and a fast-burning material. A value of 1.0 speeds up the reaction, dissolving the fuel faster.

The Max Temperature is the range of allowable temperatures a fuel can have. In a real-world comparison, this indicates how volatile the fuel is. Does it combust quickly, or does it take a lot to get it going? Wood, for instance, is stable; it takes a sustained high temperature to ignite. Gasoline, on the other hand, is extremely combustible and burns instantly.

Raising the Ignition Temperature to 1 makes the fuel rise with the temperature, and the reaction does not occur. It won't occur until the Ignition Temperature is lowered. Lowering the Ignition Temperature to 0.75 causes the fluid to rise. The heat builds and eventually reacts with the fuel. Figure 6.13 shows the reaction taking place in the bright yellow areas.

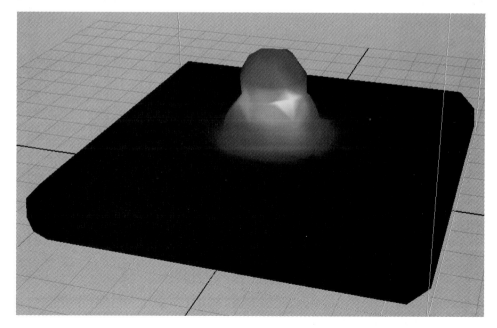

Figure 6.13

The Ignition Temperature is set to 0.75.

Light Released

Another capability of fuel is to release light. The Light Released attribute does not actually produce light in the 3D illumination sense but adds the Light Color to the fluid's incandescence. Figure 6.14 shows an example. The Light Released was set to 100 and the color to green.

Figure 6.14

The fuel has a green halo at the point of reaction.

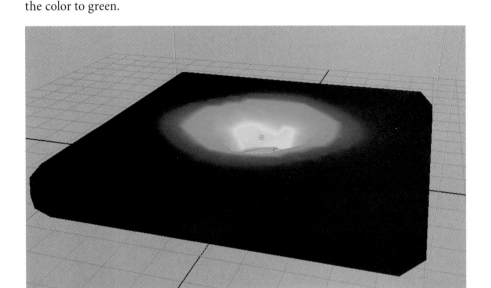

Making Fire

A fire starts when a combustible material is exposed to enough heat in the presence of oxygen. In reality, fire follows a complex chain of events. Creating fluid fire in Maya doesn't require the same elements as its real-world counterpart does. However, creating fire is still one of the more complex tasks in fluid effects. It is difficult to get the right look as well as the right motion.

One thing to keep in mind when creating fire is the old saying "Where there's smoke, there's fire." Unless you add smoke to your fire, the results look artificial. As real fire burns, the combusting particles, or soot, cause the familiar orange glow of a flame. The temperature of the soot changes the flame color. It will go from white hot to a dark orange. When the soot cools, it turns black, creating smoke.

Project: Making Fire

Creating a reaction with fuel isn't too difficult. Creating fire, however, is a bit more involved. You must maintain a balance of heat and fuel, just as in the real world, to keep the fire burning. Starting from scratch, this project builds a small flame and then turns it into a roaring fire. The focus is on understanding the properties contributing to the fire's look and learning how to control those properties.

1. Create a default 3D container with an emitter. Increase the resolution and size of the container to 15 in the Y. Change the Y Boundary to –Y.

2. Move the emitter –6.0 units in the Y, placing it close to the bottom of the container. Figure 6.15 shows the setup.

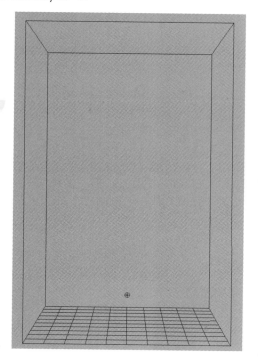

Figure 6.15

Create a container and emitter.

3. Select the fluid container. Set the Content Methods for the temperature and fuel to Dynamic Grid.

4. We'll establish the Density parameters first. Fire requires a high buoyancy to keep it from collapsing under the stress of its own flickering motion. It also provides its constant upward momentum. Dissipation makes the flame effect die out before too much of the fluid reaches the top of the container. A little fluid at the top is okay. Eventually, we will use transparency to fade out any extra fluid. Use Figure 6.16 to set the parameters for the Density.

5. The Velocity Swirl provides the look of fire, making the fluid waver as it rises. In the Velocity window under Contents Details set the Swirl to 5.

6. The Turbulence gives the flame its flicker, twisting and bending the fluid. Without the previously added strong buoyancy, the turbulence would take over, making the flame look as if it is being blown out. Use Figure 6.17 for the settings.

To check your work so far, you can compare it to flame1.ma on the DVD.

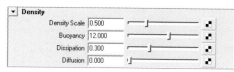

Figure 6.16

The Density parameters

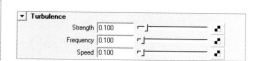

Figure 6.17

The Turbulence settings

7. The low resolution of the container was fine for establishing the fluid's motion, but as we add more detail, we need to increase it. Use Figure 6.18 to change the container's resolution.

Figure 6.18

Change the container's resolution.

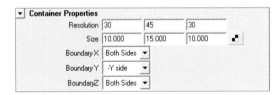

8. Now let's add the shading. Change the camera environment color to dark gray. Use a preset from the Color Chooser. It is important not to render on black. Part of our fire effect is the soot and smoke, which will not be visible on a black background. In addition, a black background makes it impossible to set the proper transparency values.

9. As noted earlier, a flame is actually glowing soot. When all the energy escapes the particles, the only thing left is black dust. Using this information, make the color of the fire black, representing the extinguished soot. This serves another purpose as well. Although a simple change, it is an important one. The black provides the color of soot, which is also the smoke. The effects of this will become clearer after the next step. Figure 6.19 shows the progress so far. It is a render of frame 150.

Figure 6.19

Frame 150 of the fire

10. At this point, the flame isn't much to look at. The incandescence provides the illuminated look of the flame. It starts as black, goes to an extreme orange, and then to black again. The orange values are very important. If they are not set right, the color will be off. Use Figure 6.20 to set the orange.

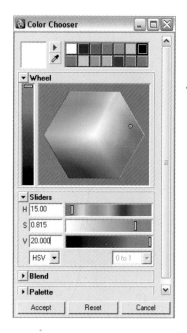

Figure 6.20

The intense orange color values

11. Remember that the incandescence isn't producing color; it is adding shading to the color. By starting and ending with black, we are removing the glowing look. At the beginning of the graph, black adds dimension to the flame by providing soot to mix with the flame. At the end, the flame turns to smoke. The high value of the orange blends to the black, giving us a full spectrum of flame intensities. Use Figure 6.21 to set the Incandescence graph.

12. By default the Incandescence input is set to Temperature. This is exactly where we want it. However, the input bias needs to be altered. Change it to −0.5. Figure 6.22 shows the flame's progress at frame 150.

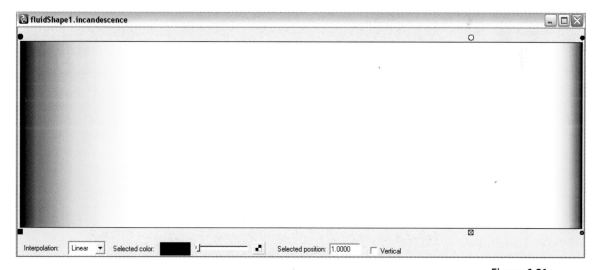

Figure 6.21

The Incandescence graph

Figure 6.22

**The flame at
frame 150**

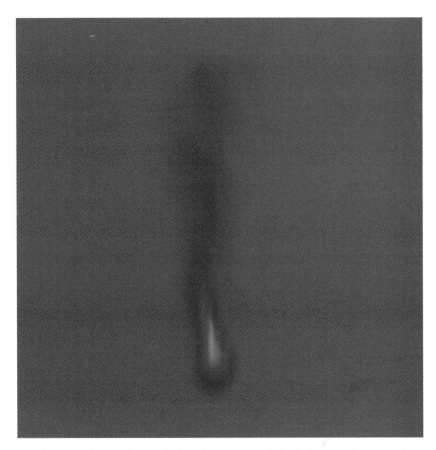

13. The flame looks too thin. It lacks substance. By default the opacity is consistent throughout the fluid. Use Figure 6.23 to change the Opacity and give the fire some body.

Figure 6.23

The Opacity graph

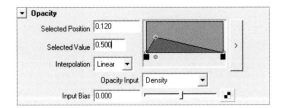

Rendering the fire again at frame 150 reveals a much improved flame. Take a look at Figure 6.24 for the results.

To check your work so far, you can compare it to flame2.ma on the DVD.

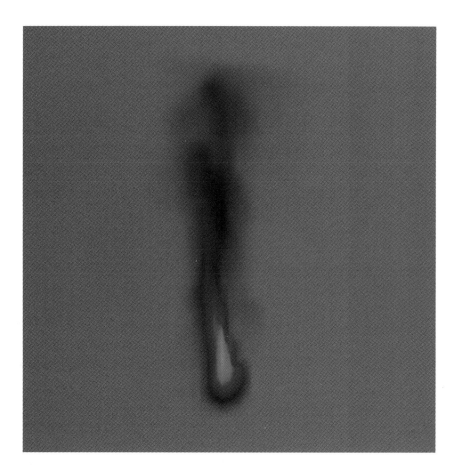

Figure 6.24
The flame with its new Opacity settings at frame 150

14. Now you can refine the reaction between temperature and fuel. The first step is to make sure enough fuel and temperature are being emitted into the container. Select the emitter. Increase the heat and fuel emissions to 2 and 4, respectively. Maintaining the delicate balance between fuel and heat is usually done best with a 2:1 mixture, two parts fuel to one part temperature. Use Figure 6.25 for reference.

Play the simulation. Figure 6.26 shows frame 150.

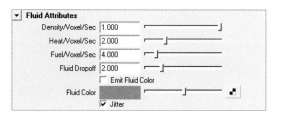

Figure 6.25
Increase the heat and fuel emissions.

Figure 6.26

The flame with
increased heat and
fuel emissions

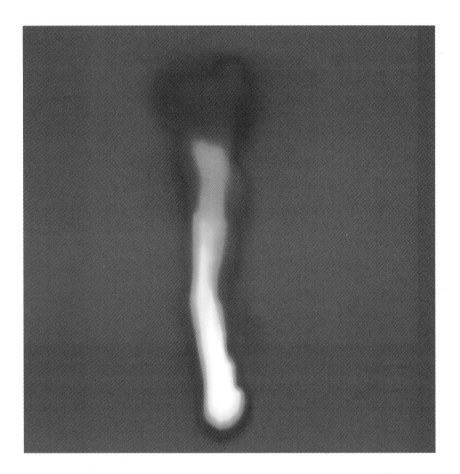

15. The flame is close to what we want, but it lacks that internal turbulence. This isn't a result of the Turbulence value being too low; it stems from a poor reaction between the fuel and temperature. Several attributes need to be changed to get the right reaction. First, change the Temperature Scale to 1.6. Increasing this makes the fire hotter, which visually adds more incandescence to the flame. Next, set the Buoyancy to 10. This makes the temperature rise a little more slowly than the density. In real-world terms, this helps make the smoke rise above the flames. The last temperature setting, Dissipation, makes the temperature die out; the higher the dissipation, the faster the flames die. Set it to 0.4. Use Figure 6.27 as a reference to the settings.

Figure 6.27

The Temperature
settings

▼ Temperature			
Temperature Scale	1.600		
Buoyancy	10.000		
Dissipation	0.400		
Diffusion	0.100		
Turbulence	0.100		

16. With the temperature set, the environment is ripe for a reaction. Change the Fuel
    Scale to 1.9, making it a bit more intense than the temperature to help produce a
    stronger-looking reaction. Set the Reaction Speed to 0.9. This creates a slow burn,
    giving the flame longevity and a more intense look. Figure 6.28 has the settings.

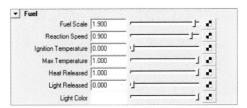

Figure 6.28

The settings for
the fuel

The simulation is run again. Figure 6.29 shows a rendered image of frame 150. Notice
that the core of the flame now has definition. The Shading Quality still needs to be
adjusted, resulting in the flame's center looking pixelated.

To check your work so far, you can compare it to `flame3.ma` on the DVD. You can also
watch `flame1.mov` on the DVD to see the flame's rendered motion.

Figure 6.29

The flame at
frame 150

17. The flame is looking good based on still frames, but the rendered motion is slow. To speed it up, set the Simulation Rate Scale to 3. Also, for added detail to the flame's motion, turn on High Detail Solve for All Grids Except Velocity. Adding High Detail Solve to the Velocity would give the flame unnatural motion. Figure 6.30 has the settings.

Figure 6.30

The settings
for the fuel

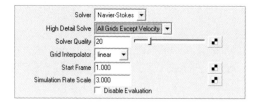

18. You can also see in flame1.mov that the flame wavers too much from side to side and shows signs of instability. Figure 6.31 shows an example of what is happening at frame 72.

Increasing the Simulation Rate Scale and the High Detail Solve settings only amplify this effect. Instead of decreasing the Turbulence, which is already low, you want to dampen the velocity. Set the Damp to 0.02. Figure 6.32 shows frame 72 after dampening the velocity.

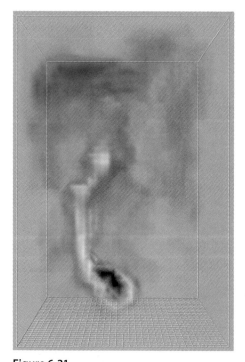

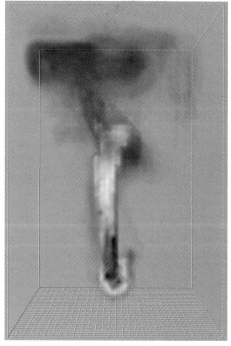

Figure 6.31
The flame wavers too much at frame 72.

Figure 6.32
A dampened frame 72

19. One last observation from the rendered animation is that the fluid is too thick when it hits the top of the container. To remedy this, change the Transparency Value to 0.6. Also set the Dropoff Shape to Y Gradient and the Edge Dropoff to 0.5. This gives the flame a good overall semitransparent effect. Figure 6.33 shows the settings.

20. Finally, increase the Shading Quality to 4 and set the Render Interpolator to Smooth to get rid of any artifacts. Figure 6.34 shows the settings, and Figure 6.35 shows frame 72 rendered.

Save the fluid fire settings as a preset. The settings will be used in the next project as a starting point. To check your work so far, you can compare it to flame4.ma on the DVD. You can also watch the finished animation, flame2.mov.

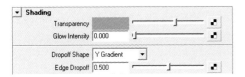

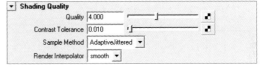

Figure 6.33
The settings for the Shading's Transparency

Figure 6.34
The Quality settings

Figure 6.35
Frame 72 rendered

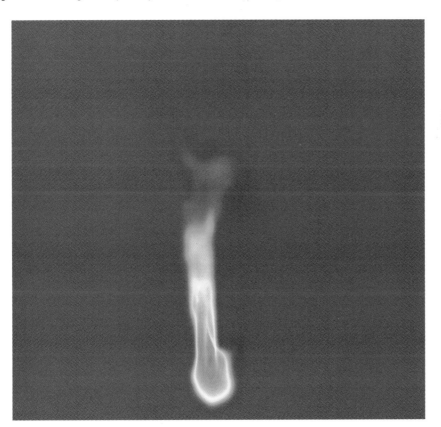

Project: House Fire Part 1

In this project, fluid fire is used to engulf a house in flames. The cabin in the F5 project from the preceding chapter is resurrected and used as the house. The house has been modified slightly from the F5 project. The roof geometry has been separated so it can fall apart. Fields are also employed to direct the fire better.

The final resolution required for burning the house is high. Some computers may not be able to handle it. It is best to work at a low resolution for as long as you can. With experience, it is possible to fine-tune the fluid's performance and look at a lowered resolution. Throughout this project, where applicable, two rendered images are provided, one using a low-resolution fluid container and the other using high resolution. Key factors are identified.

1. Open the scene file `houseFire1.ma`. The scene contains the house and plane. The material shaders on the house have been animated to fade to a dark gray to give the house the appearance of being burned. Figure 6.36 shows the setup.

2. Create a 3D fluid container. Apply the fire preset saved from the Flame project. If you didn't save the settings, you can also get them from the DVD.

3. Change the Resolution and Size to match the settings shown in Figure 6.37. The resolution is not high enough to provide sufficient detail. We will use it to get the scene ready and then increase it when we're ready.

Figure 6.36

The House Fire environment

4. Translate the container to 25 in the Y and 2.244 in the Z.

5. The house geometry will be the source of emission for the fluid fire. Select the four sections of the house—the roof, front, left, and right pieces. Hold Shift and select the container. Choose Fluid Effects → Add/Edit Contents → Emit from Object. We will use the same emitter settings from the Making Fire project. They are shown in Figure 6.38.

At this point, we need to see how the flame preset is reacting in its new world. Play the simulation and evaluate it at frame 60, as shown in Figure 6.39.

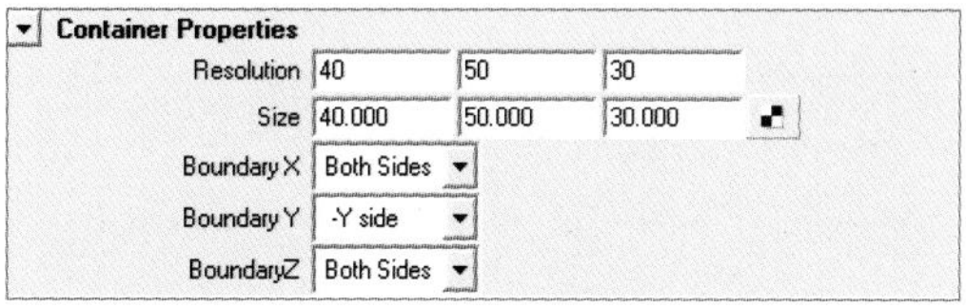

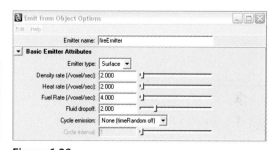

Figure 6.37

The settings for the container properties

Figure 6.38

The settings for the emitters

Figure 6.39

The flames using the fire preset at frame 60

Again, the resolution is not high enough to produce the desired detail. Before continuing, it's necessary to compare the low-resolution and the high-resolution results, to evaluate what changes need to be made. The container's resolution is set to 160, 200, and 120 for the X, Y, and Z. The results at frame 60 are shown in Figure 6.40. You can also watch the movie houseFire1.mov on the DVD.

Both the high-resolution and low-resolution results have the flames traveling too high and not enough smoke. You can also notice in the high-resolution rendering that the flames look stiff and linear. Based on these observations, we'll make some changes.

6. Change the Density's Buoyancy to 10. This decreases the overall rate at which the fluid travels. Slowing the fluid down gives the fluid more opportunity to end before it reaches the top of the container.

7. To get rid of the fire's apparent stiffness, increase the amount of Swirl to 20.

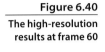

Figure 6.40

The high-resolution results at frame 60

8. The flames produced by a burning house are much larger than the flame created in the Making Fire project. Therefore, more turbulence can be added. The larger the flame, the more turbulent it will be. The flames should waver with a greater intensity, more often, and faster. Change the Turbulence settings based on Figure 6.41.

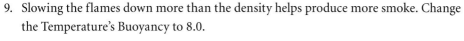

Figure 6.41

The Turbulence settings

9. Slowing the flames down more than the density helps produce more smoke. Change the Temperature's Buoyancy to 8.0.

To check your work so far, you can compare it to houseFire2.ma on the DVD.

After making the preceding adjustments, run the simulation again and compare the new results to the old. Figure 6.42 shows the low-resolution render, and Figure 6.43 shows the high-resolution render. You can also watch the high-resolution render, houseFire2.mov, on the DVD.

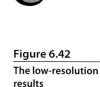

Figure 6.42

The low-resolution results

Figure 6.43

The high-resolution results

At first glance, the images don't look too different from their previously reviewed counterparts. However, looking at the high-resolution image close up, you can see some major differences. The fire has more ripples, a greater perturbation, and a different shape overall. Almost everything we set worked—except for the height of the fluid. The flame is still strong and forceful.

There are several telltale signs indicating which attributes need adjusting in the low-resolution image. The fire appears to have round dots floating around it and in it. These shapes are indicators that the fluid is moving too fast. Instead of flowing from voxel to voxel, it is skipping or jumping. You don't want to change the behavior of the fluid, only its speed.

10. The fire's strength has a lot to do with the Simulation Rate Scale. We perceive larger objects as moving slower. Cinematically speaking, the more grand an object is, the slower it moves. Change the Simulation Rate Scale to 1.6. Figure 6.44 has the low-resolution results, and Figure 6.45 shows the high-resolution version. You can also watch the high-resolution render, houseFire3.mov, on the DVD.

Figure 6.44

The low-resolution results with a Simulation Rate Scale of 1.6

11. Comparing the two, you can see that there is still not enough smoke. The flames should turn to smoke sooner. The temperature Buoyancy cannot be lowered any further without causing the fire to lose some of its natural characteristics. Instead, modify the Incandescence by having it turn to black sooner. This can be done without altering the color graph. Change the Interpolation for all of the color keys to Smooth, effectively reducing the amount of self-illumination at the beginning and end of the flame. Also move the Input Bias to −0.7. Use Figure 6.46 for reference.

12. The smoke and the flames don't look transparent enough. Increase the Transparency value to 0.7. Run the simulation again. Figure 6.47 shows the low-resolution render, and Figure 6.48 shows the high-resolution render.

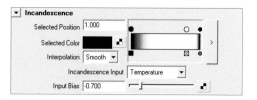

Figure 6.46

The Incandescence settings

Figure 6.47

The low-resolution results with the shading modifications

Figure 6.48

The high-resolution
results with
the shading
modifications

13. The flames rising above the house are too intense. Also, more smoke is still needed. To reduce the amount of flames and make the smoke more visible, modify the fluid's emissions. The Density is the smoke, and the Heat is the flame. Reducing the amount of heat per second brings the flames down. The fuel is also adjusted to keep the fuel-to-heat ratio. Change the settings on each emitter to match Figure 6.49.

Figure 6.49

The settings for all
of the fluid emitter's
attributes

Fluid Attributes		
Density/Voxel/Sec	2.000	
Heat/Voxel/Sec	1.500	
Fuel/Voxel/Sec	3.000	
Fluid Dropoff	2.000	
	☐ Emit Fluid Color	
Fluid Color		
	☑ Jitter	

Run the simulation again and evaluate the results. Take a look at Figure 6.50 and
Figure 6.51. You can also watch the high-resolution render, houseFire4.mov, on
the DVD.

Figure 6.50

The low-resolution
results with the new
emitter settings

Figure 6.51

The high-resolution
results with the new
emitter settings

Figure 6.51

The high-resolution results with the new emitter settings

14. The final adjustments are to the quality of the fluid. The first is the solver's quality, listed in the Dynamic Simulation attributes. The flames look a bit disconnected from each other. Increasing the solver's quality to 100 helps create a more cohesive look. Next raise the Quality to 8, in the Shading Quality attributes, smoothing the

rendered look of the fire. Compare Figure 6.52 and Figure 6.53 to the previous set of images to see the improvements.

To check your work so far, you can compare it to houseFire3.ma on the DVD. You can also watch the high-resolution render, houseFire5.mov, on the DVD.

Figure 6.52

The low-resolution results with the higher-quality settings

Figure 6.53

The high-resolution
results with
the higher-quality
settings

Project: Controlling Fire

As you learned from the previous project, fluid fire needs to be modified based on the situation and materials being burned. Fire reacts differently when it grows, creating its own wind forces. You may have noticed in the previous project that the amount of fire coming off the walls of the house is negligible compared to the amount coming off the roof. Because the house is not colliding with the flame, the fire is allowed to pass through and rise as if the house wasn't there. Turning the house into a collision object is extremely expensive. Even at the high resolution of the container, there may not be enough fidelity to calculate the collisions accurately. The alternative is to use fields to push the flames away from the house.

1. Open the scene file houseFire3.ma. The scene is the last saved file from the previous project, House Fire Part 1. The fluid fire is at its full resolution. Assign it to a layer and hide it. This enables you to move unencumbered through the scene.

Figure 6.54

Translate and scale the volume cube.

2. Select the fluid and add a Uniform field. Change the field to a volume cube.

3. Translate and scale the cube by using the values in Figure 6.54.

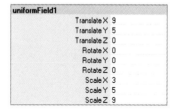

uniformField1	
Translate X	9
Translate Y	5
Translate Z	0
Rotate X	0
Rotate Y	0
Rotate Z	0
Scale X	3
Scale Y	5
Scale Z	9

4. The size and position of the volume is just big enough to push the fire out of the house and then let it go. Set the field's Magnitude to 100. Figure 6.55 shows the setup so far.

Figure 6.55

Set the Magnitude to 100 to push the flames away from the house.

Figure 6.56

Rotate and translate the duplicated volume cube.

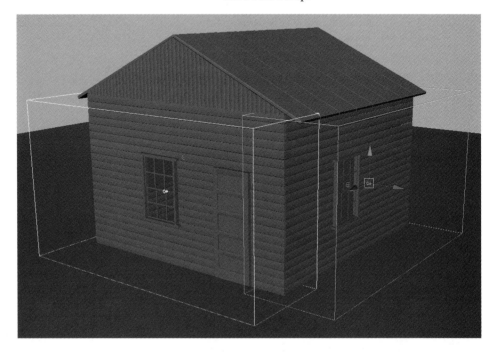

uniformField2
Translate X	0
Translate Y	5
Translate Z	9
Rotate X	0
Rotate Y	-90
Rotate Z	0

5. Duplicate the Uniform field. Rotate and translate it based on the values in Figure 6.56.

6. Select the duplicated field and the fluid fire. Choose Fields → Affect Selected Object(s). Change the direction of the field to 1 in the Z. Figure 6.57 shows the setup.

Figure 6.57

The volume cube is set to push flames in the Z direction.

Unhide the fluid and play the simulation to frame 90. You can compare your results with Figure 6.58.

Depending on the hardware of your computer, it may be necessary to Batch Render the scene instead of using a viewport. The fluid is large and expensive and could cause your machine to fail.

Figure 6.58

The rendered results of frame 90

The Uniform fields work, but only partially. The fluid is being pulled into the field and pushed out through a third of it. The influence is greatest at the center of the volume.

7. To fix the uneven distribution of flames, you need to break the fields into smaller volumes. Scale both fields to 3.0 in the Z axis. Figure 6.59 reflects the changes.

8. Create two more Uniform fields with the same size and magnitude as the existing fields. Position them along the front of the house. The fields do not have to touch. Space them so that they extend beyond the corners of the house. Use Figure 6.60 for reference.

Figure 6.59

Scale the volume fields to 3 in the Z axis.

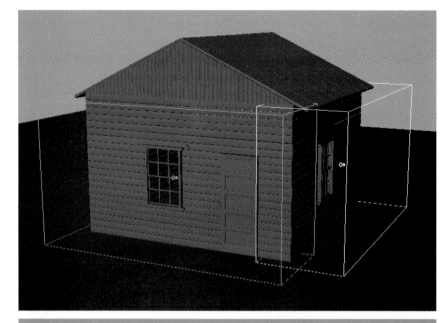

Figure 6.60

Add two more volume fields to the front of the house.

9. Change the direction of the corner fields to push the flames in the X and Z directions. The field at the left corner of the house has values of −1.0 in the X and 1.0 in the Z. The right corner has values of 1.0 in the X and 1.0 in the Z.

The house is now engulfed in flames. The smaller fields successfully pull the flames out and allow them to rise. Figure 6.61 shows the burning house at frame 90.

From the camera's view, the far side and back of the house are not seen. If the camera were to orbit around the house, you would have to add more Uniform fields to push the flames out for those sides of the house.

To check your work so far, you can compare it to houseFire4.ma on the DVD. You can also watch the high-resolution render, houseFire6.mov, on the DVD.

Figure 6.61
The final rendering of the house fire

Figure 6.62

The objects in
the scene

Project: Burn It to the Ground

Burn It to the Ground is a continuation of the House Fire project. The house is in flames. As the simulated wood burns, it should lose its stability and crumble to pieces. Using a technique similar to the one we used for destroying the house in the F5 project in the preceding chapter, we'll use nCloth to make the house collapse. We will also use an animated ramp texture to gradually cause the collapse and control the order in which the pieces of the house fall.

1. Open the scene file houseFire4.ma. Select all four pieces of the house and choose nMesh → Create nCloth, using the default settings.

2. Select each piece of the house and individually add a Transform constraint. Choose nConstraint → Transform. It is important that each piece of geometry has a separate constraint node. To make the house fall apart, we will use an animated texture. Without separate constraint nodes, the pieces would end up sharing the same texture and therefore animate in unison.

3. Rename each constraint to match the part of the house it corresponds to. Figure 6.62 shows the list of objects in the scene.

4. Go to the nucleus settings. Turn on Use Plane. Set the Plane Origin to –0.1, putting it just under the bottom of the house. Set the Space Scale to 0.304. The house is all set. When the simulation is played, the house remains perfectly still, as it should. Turn the nucleus off to prevent it from solving.

5. You can now add a ramp texture to the glue strength of each constraint. Eventually, the parameters of the ramp will be animated, causing the constraint to turn off vertex by vertex. A ramp texture is used because it is easy to animate and modify. For more exacting results, you can paint your own animated texture.

   Select the roof constraint and open Window → Hypergraph: Connections. Find and select the nComponent node. Use Figure 6.63 as reference.

Figure 6.63

Find the nCompo-
nent node in the
Hypergraph Con-
nections window.

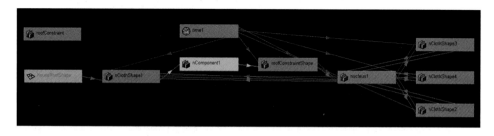

6. Open the Attribute Editor. Change the Component Type to Point, forcing the texture to be mapped on a per point basis instead of the entire object. Choose the Create Node icon for Glue Strength Map. Add a ramp texture. Figure 6.64 shows the window.

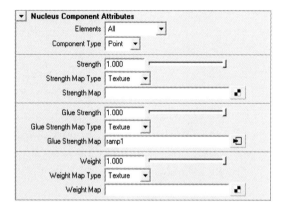

Figure 6.64

Add a ramp texture to the Glue Strength Map channel.

7. Select the ramp texture. Set the Interpolation to None. Change the color values to a black and two whites. Black represents a glue strength of zero, which turns the glue strength off. We want the roof to begin collapsing in the middle of the house and work its way out. To do this, move the black color and one white color value to 0.5. Move the second white value to 0. Use Figure 6.65 for reference.

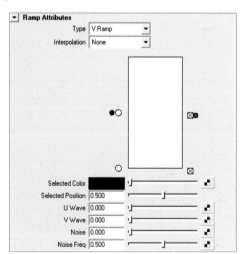

Figure 6.65

Change the ramp colors.

8. Set keys for the black value by using the numbers from Figure 6.66.

Figure 6.66

The key frames for
the black value

Keys	Time	Value	InTan Type	OutTan Type
0	1	0.5	Clamped	Clamped
1	120	0.005	Clamped	Clamped

9. Set keys for the overlapping white value by using the numbers from Figure 6.67.

Figure 6.67

The key frames for
the white value

Keys	Time	Value	InTan Type	OutTan Type
0	1	0.5	Clamped	Clamped
1	120	0.995	Clamped	Clamped

Notice that neither value is allowed to reach 0 or 1. If the color is allowed to reach either of these values, the Glue Strength becomes flooded by that value. This destroys the effect by turning the strength off or on for all of the vertices. Keeping it just shy of either end prevents this from happening.

Play the simulation and check the results. Figure 6.68 shows frame 80. The roof is collapsing as planned. To check your work so far, you can compare it to houseFire5 .ma on the DVD.

10. Add another ramp to the nComponent node for the front of the house or the front constraint. Make sure to set the Component Type to Point.

Figure 6.68

The roof collapses
accordingly.

11. Select the ramp texture. Set the Interpolation to None. Change the color values to a black and two whites. The front of the house needs to start falling apart after the roof. It should also break from the top down. To do this, set one color value to black and move it to the 1.0 position. Create a second color of white and move it to the 0.0 position.

12. You do not want the boards at the front of the house to fall in perfect order. By using the Noise and Wave attributes of the ramp, you can create an uneven pattern, breaking up the order in which the boards fall. Use Figure 6.69 for the settings.

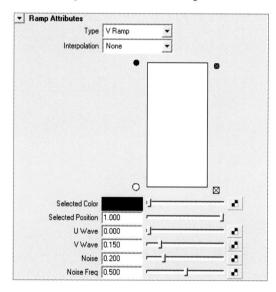

Figure 6.69

Change the ramp parameters controlling the front side of the house.

13. For the animation of the ramp, set keys for the black value, using the numbers from Figure 6.70.

Keys	Time	Value	InTan Type	OutTan Type
0	1	1	Clamped	Clamped
1	90	1	Clamped	Clamped
2	150	0.3	Clamped	Clamped

Figure 6.70

The key frames for the black value

14. The ramp for the front can also be used for the left side of the house. Drag and drop the texture into the Glue Strength Map channel of the nComponent node. Set the Component Type to Point.

To see how the house will fall apart, you can map the ramps to the color channel of the geometry's material. This is easier and faster than playing the simulation. Figure 6.71 shows an example.

Figure 6.71

The Glue Strength maps have also been applied to the geometry's color channel.

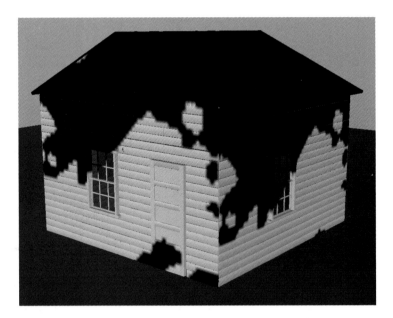

15. Add the last ramp to the right side of the house. It has the same setup as the ramp used for the front of the house, except with different wave and noise values. Use Figure 6.72 for the settings. Also, make sure to set the Component Type to Point on the nComponent node.

16. For the animation of the ramp, set keys for the black value, using the numbers from Figure 6.73.

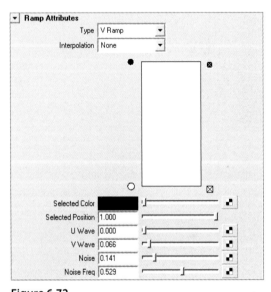

Keys				
	Time	Value	InTan Type	OutTan Type
0	140	1	Clamped	Clamped
1	200	0.5	Clamped	Clamped

Figure 6.72

Change the ramp parameters for controlling the right side of the house.

Figure 6.73

The key frames for the black value

Run the simulation to see the results. Figure 6.74 shows frame 143 of the house collapsing. To check your work so far, you can compare it to houseFire6.ma on the DVD.

To complete the burning of the house, turn the fluid back on and render the scene (Figure 6.75). You can watch the finished animation, houseFire7.mov, from the DVD.

CHAPTER 7

Explosions

There are many types of explosions. Natural explosions include those produced by volcanoes, as discussed in Chapter 4, "Volcanic Activity." Man-made explosions include bombs, both nuclear and conventional. Typically, when we think of an explosion, we envision a fiery ball. These chemical explosions are the focus of this chapter.

Creating Explosive Forces

Creating a convincing explosion is a lengthy task. Unlike the effects in previous chapters, explosions have a beginning, middle, and end. Their entire life span must be taken into account. It's not about creating a single look, but three individual looks. The explosion begins with a bright flash. As the flash settles, the remaining fire and smoke roll up into the air. In the end, the fire burns out, leaving a dissipating cloud of smoke. Take a look at Figure 7.1. It shows three explosions during various stages.

Fire and smoke have very different properties. As you learned in the preceding chapter, combining these two elements by using Maya fluids is not only possible, but necessary. A lot of heat is generated at the center of an explosion. Re-creating a bright flash with Maya fluids is best done by combining temperature and fuel. The fuel contributes to the heat and burns up at a rate you specify.

Figure 7.1

An example of the
three stages of an
explosion

Project: Explosion

The emitter you define plays a vital role in creating an explosion. Building on the flame
preset saved in Chapter 6, "Playing with Fire," you will animate a volume sphere's emission to provide the necessary burst of fluids to start the explosion. Using this existing
preset saves a lot of time, but several attributes need to be adjusted and refined. In addition, to add the level of detail that real explosions have, all three fluid textures—color,
incandescence, and opacity—are implemented.

1. Create a default 3D container. Add the flame preset. If you didn't save it from the
   previous chapter, you can find it in the Chapter 7 folder on the DVD. Assign it to the
   container.

2. Change the size and resolution of the container to match the settings in Figure 7.2.

Figure 7.2

The new settings
for the container
properties

Container Properties			
Resolution	30	60	30
Size	15.000	30.000	15.000
Boundary X	Both Sides		
Boundary Y	-Y side		
BoundaryZ	Both Sides		

3. Translate the container 15 units in the Y axis, placing it on top of Maya's default grid.

4. The dynamic simulation settings should be returned to their default values because the motion of a flame is extremely different from that of an explosion. However, as you have learned, in order to make a fluid roll like a ball of flame, you must use a High Detail Solve. In an explosion, all of the elements—fire, smoke, and soot—roll, so we will set the High Detail Solve to All Grids. Use the settings from Figure 7.3 to change the Dynamic Simulation parameters.

5. Add a default omni emitter and translate it to −13.0 in the Y axis.

6. Change the Emitter Type to Volume and its shape to Sphere. Scale the sphere uniformly to 2.2. Figure 7.4 shows the progress so far.

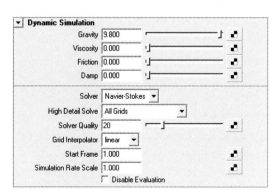

Figure 7.3
The Dynamic Simulation settings

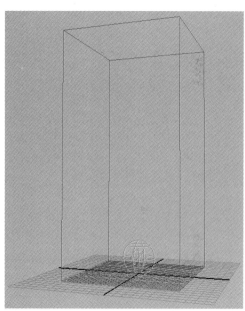

Figure 7.4
Change the emitter to a volume sphere.

7. To mimic the rapid burst of a chemical explosion, we will animate the fluid's emission starting with the Heat/Voxel/Sec attribute. Use Figure 7.5 to set the keys.

Figure 7.5
The keyframes for animating the Heat/Voxel/Sec

Keys	Time	Value	InTan Type	OutTan Type
0	10	4	Clamped	Clamped
1	11	0	Clamped	Clamped

8. Heat emission isn't the only part of the equation for getting an explosive flash. Without fuel, which is consumed in the explosion, it is difficult to rapidly decrease a fluid's temperature. Relying solely on temperature would cause the rolling flames to be just as bright as the initial flash. Emitting fuel contributes to the heat, but only as long as the fuel exists. After it burns up, the temperature returns to its defined state.

   In the previous chapter, we established a ratio of 2:1 for fuel to heat. Sticking with that ratio, use Figure 7.6 to set the keys for the Fuel/Voxel/Sec.

Figure 7.6

The keyframes for animating the Fuel/ Voxel/Sec

Keys

	Time	Value	InTan Type	OutTan Type
0	3	8	Clamped	Clamped
1	4	0	Clamped	Clamped

9. The density is the last emission to keyframe. I've saved it for last to clarify its role; in a production environment, the emissions could be done in any order. As with the fluid fire in the preceding chapter, the density provides the soot or smoke. Smoke exists throughout the life span of an explosion. As the fireball rises, it also leaves a smoke trail behind. To achieve the proper amount of smoke, we keyframe the density to emit longer than the heat and fuel. Its value is also greater to create a heavy, thick smoke. Use Figure 7.7 to set the keys for the Density/Voxel/Sec.

Figure 7.7

The keyframes for animating the Density/Voxel/Sec

Keys

	Time	Value	InTan Type	OutTan Type
0	15	10	Clamped	Clamped
1	16	0	Clamped	Clamped

Let's play the simulation to see what we have so far. Figure 7.8 shows frames 6, 15, and 35 side by side.

Figure 7.8

The progress of the three stages of an explosion

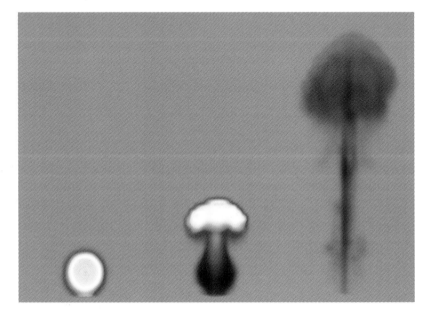

You can see the progress so far by watching the explosion1.mov on the DVD. To check your work so far, you can compare it to explosion1.ma.

10. You can now work on the content details of the fluid. We'll modify the temperature details first, as we did for the emitter. In the animation, explosion1.mov, the temperature rises quickly and loses its ball-like shape. Decreasing the Buoyancy slows down the temperature and in turn helps to keep the fireball shape. Change the Buoyancy to 5. Figure 7.9 shows the results at frame 20.

11. The temperature makes it all the way to the top of the container. It's OK for the smoke to do that as it fades away, but not for the fireball. Increase the Dissipation to 1 to make the heat fade away more rapidly. Figure 7.10 shows the results at frame 20.

12. The fireball itself is not large enough. It doesn't need to be much bigger, just a little more robust. Increasing the Diffusion disperses the temperature more readily, effectively causing it to expand. Change the Diffusion to 0.3. Adding too much Diffusion causes the heat to bleed in with the smoke, blurring any separation between the two. It also diminishes the heat's intensity, reducing needed hot spots in the fireball. Figure 7.11 shows the results at frame 20.

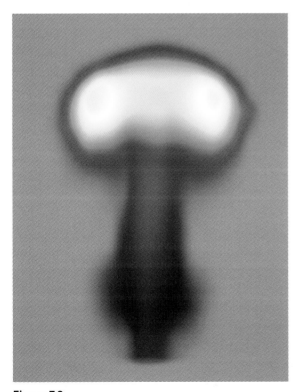

Figure 7.9

The result of the explosion with the temperature's Buoyancy set to 5

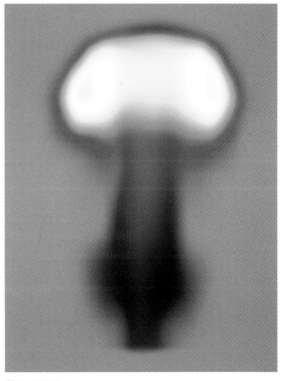

Figure 7.10

The results of the explosion with the temperature's Dissipation set to 1

Figure 7.11

The results of the
explosion with the
temperature's
Diffusion set to 0.3

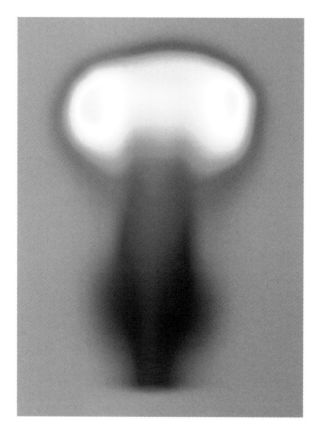

13. The last Temperature detail is Turbulence. Although explosions may seem turbulent by nature, their motion follows basic trajectories. Set the turbulence to 0.0. Use Figure 7.12 to check your settings.

Figure 7.12

The settings for the
Temperature details

Temperature		
Temperature Scale	1.600	
Buoyancy	5.000	
Dissipation	1.000	
Diffusion	0.300	
Turbulence	0.000	

14. To create the initial blast or bright flash, the fuel is made to add heat and light to the temperature while the fuel burns up. Finding the proper balance between how much heat is added and how fast the fuel burns takes some trial and error. Changing the Shaded Display to Fuel helps us visualize the reaction between the fuel and heat. The fuel should burn up just before the fireball begins its ascent, around frame 7. A Reaction Speed of 0.10 should do it.

The heat released is good with a value of 1. Next, set the Light Released high enough to provide an intense flash. A value of 1 also works well here. For the light color, use Figure 7.13. This is the same intense orange used to create the flames in Chapter 6, but with an even higher intensity.

You will need to change the Shaded Display back to As Render in order to see the added light. Figure 7.14 shows the final settings for the Fuel details, and Figure 7.15 shows frame 6 of the simulation.

15. As we know, the density provides the smoke. It needs to rise more slowly than the temperature and fuel. In fact, the density should barely move. The rising heat will carry a good amount of the fluid's density upward. To keep some of the smoke behind, the Density's Buoyancy is reduced to 0.35. In addition, we want the smoke to dissipate less and spread more easily; these are handled by the Diffusion. Use Figure 7.16 to change the settings.

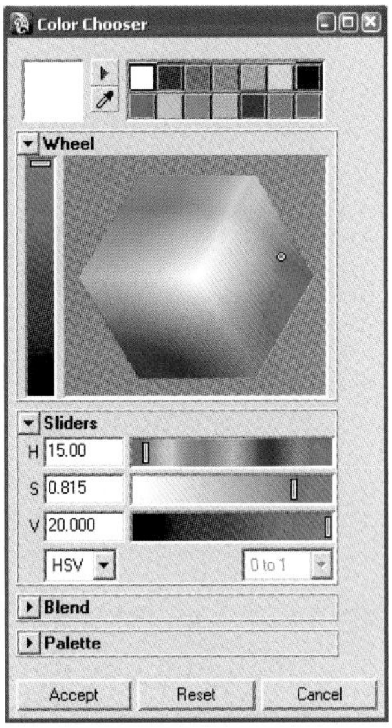

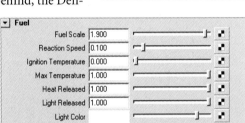

Figure 7.13

The color for the Light Released

Figure 7.14

The settings for the Fuel details

Figure 7.15

The results of the explosion with the Fuel's Reaction Speed and Heat Released altered

Figure 7.16

The settings for the
Density details

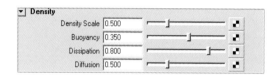

You can see the progress by watching explosion2.mov on the DVD. To check your work so far, you can compare it to explosion2.ma.

16. Reviewing the animation, we can see that the motion of the explosion looks a little too slow. Increasing the Buoyancy values for the Density and Temperature would speed up the fluid. However, as discussed in steps 10 and 15, the low Buoyancy is helping to maintain the shape of the fireball. To keep the integrity of the settings established so far and accelerate the simulation, increase the Simulation Rate Scale to 1.2.

17. Another noticeable problem we can see in the explosion2.mov animation is that the shape of the fireball starts to separate as it rises. Figure 7.17 shows an example from frame 30.

To fix this, we need to increase the fluid's thickness and its resistance to flow. The thickness is controlled by the Viscosity setting. Raise it to 0.3. Figure 7.18 shows the results at frame 30.

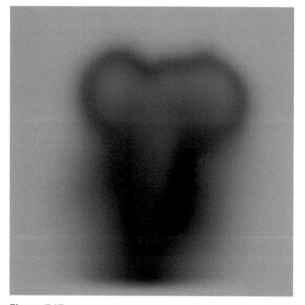

Figure 7.17

The fireball begins to separate around frame 30.

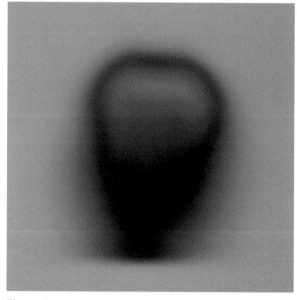

Figure 7.18

The results at frame 30 after the viscosity was increased

The Friction, the fluid's resistance to flow, contributes by slowing down the fluid, creating a stronger base for the explosion. Raise it to 0.3 as well. Take a look at Figure 7.19 to see the results at frame 30.

Figure 7.19

The results at frame 30 after the friction was increased

Figure 7.20 shows the final Dynamic Simulation settings.

18. The shading of an explosion differs greatly from our flame preset. Play the simulation to frame 30 to see the changes to the fluid immediately. The Incandescence Color graph still provides the fiery look. Like the flame, the explosion starts with a darker color to provide contrast. Because an explosion begins with intense heat, the starting color needs to be lighter. Use Figure 7.21 to establish the color at position 1.0 on the color graph.

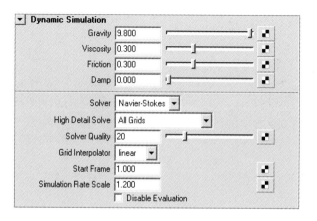

Figure 7.20

The final Dynamic Simulation settings

19. Next, slide the intense orange at position 0.8 to 0.845. Moving it closer to 1.0 reduces the transition between the colors.

20. Create a color key at the position 0.3 on the Incandescence color graph. Use Figure 7.22 to set its values.

21. Create another color key at the position 0.15 on the Incandescence color graph. Use Figure 7.23 to set its values.

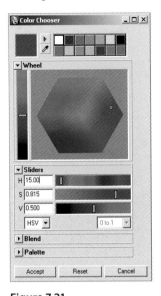

Figure 7.21

The color at position 1.0 on the Incandescence color graph

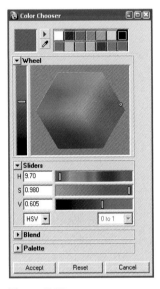

Figure 7.22

The color settings for position 0.30 on the Incandescence color graph

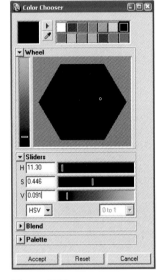

Figure 7.23

The color settings for position 0.15 on the Incandescence color graph

22. Position 0.0 does not need to be modified. The black color is perfect for the end result of the fluid or smoke. However, the dark colors leave the explosion looking too smoky. Move the Bias to 0.2 to lean the color graph toward hotter, brighter colors. Figure 7.24 shows all of the Incandescence settings.

Figure 7.24

The Incandescence settings

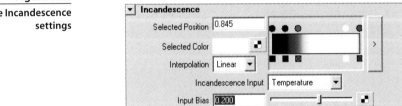

23. The Opacity is next. The Opacity is used to cut away the cool, dense portions of the fluid to reveal its hot temperature. Set the values according to Figure 7.25.

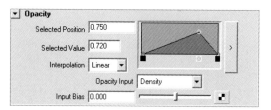

Figure 7.25

The Opacity settings

The key at position 1.0 is dropped to a value of 0.0. This controls some of the initial smoke created from the density. Its effects are not noticeable until around frame 20, after the fluid has been allowed to mature. The next keyed position, 0.750, is set to a value of 0.720. This provides the overall opacity of the explosion. The last position is the most influential. Moving the 0.0 keyed position to a position of 0.020 trims the outside edges of the explosion, giving it a crisp edge. Figure 7.26 shows frame 25 with the new Opacity settings.

Figure 7.26

Frame 25 of the sim-ulation with the new Opacity settings

24. The color settings are used to establish the color of the smoke. The smoke's color needs to change based on the temperature of the fluid and only changes a little bit. As the fluid cools, the smoke gets lighter. Set the Input to Temperature and the Input Bias to 0.045, and use Figure 7.27 to change the color for positions 0.0 and 0.2. Fig-ure 7.28 shows all of the color settings.

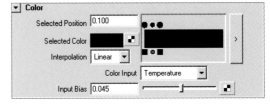

Figure 7.27

The color for the two outside positions on the color graph

Figure 7.28

The color graph settings

25. Playing through the simulation, you can see that the overall transparency of the explosion is too light. The object should be a thick, dense fireball and smoke cloud. Change the Transparency value to 0.1. Also set the Dropoff Shape to the Y Gradient with an Edge Dropoff of 0.1, to make any smoke that reaches the top of the container fade away. In addition, add 0.03 to the Glow Intensity to give the fireball an added boost of intensity. Figure 7.29 shows all of the settings. Figure 7.30 shows frame 30 with the new Transparency settings.

Figure 7.29

The Shading settings

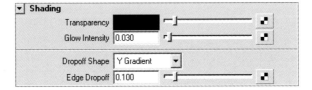

You can see the progress by watching explosion3.mov on the DVD. To check your work so far, you can compare it to explosion3.ma.

26. The explosion still looks weak. Change the emitter's Fluid Dropoff to 0.0. At 0.0, the emitter will emit from its entire surface at full strength.

27. You can now add texture to the explosion to give it its detail. Select all three texture options, Color, Opacity, and Incandescence. Change the texture type to Billow.

Billow is a computationally expensive texture to use. Perlin, with Inflection turned on, is usually a sufficient, cost-effective substitute. However, nothing is as good as the real thing. Billow provides solid detail and proper motion throughout the explosion, where Perlin fails.

28. Change the Frequency to 6 to add more contrast to the shaded elements. Figure 7.31 shows frame 25 of the simulation.

29. Take a minute to go back and examine Figure 7.1. Notice the smoke. Look at how it seems to get sucked up into the fireball. The force of the explosion creates suction as it rises into the air. To achieve this with fluids, change the Coordinate Method of the texture to Grid. Keep the Coordinate Speed at 0.2. Compare the results of Figure 7.32 with Figure 7.31.

30. Next is the motion of the texture. In the animation, the texture doesn't rise properly with the fireball. Furthermore, the fireball should evolve over time. The smoke and fire should look as if they are constantly mixing as they get higher. This effect is easily accomplished with expressions we have used in previous chapters. Add the following expressions to the Texture Time and the Y axis of the Texture Origin:

```
fluidShape1.textureTime=time*1;
fluidShape1.textureOriginY=time*-.2;
```

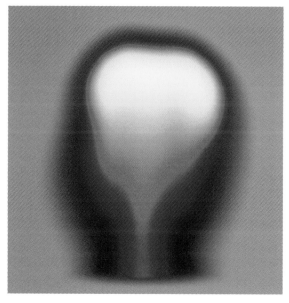

Figure 7.30

Frame 30 of the simulation with the new Transparency settings

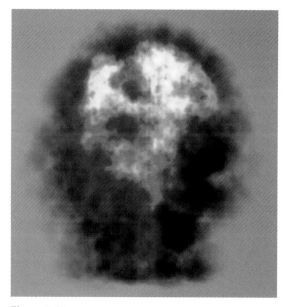

Figure 7.31

The results of the explosion using Billow to texture the Color, Opacity, and Incandescence

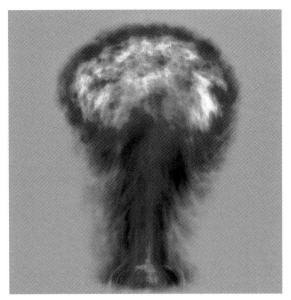

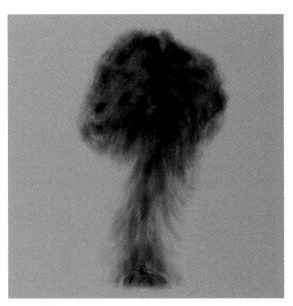

Figure 7.32

The results of the explosion at frame 40 with the Coordinate Method set to Grid

Figure 7.33

The effects of the Grid Coordinate method ruin the look of the dissipating smoke.

31. The Grid Coordinate method for the texture adds a tremendous amount of visual impact to the beginning of the explosion; however, by the end it destroys the look of the dissipating smoke. Take a look at Figure 7.33. It shows frame 55 and the strange effects of the Grid Coordinate method.

To get rid of these ill effects, we need to animate the Threshold of the texture. Increasing the Threshold raises the levels of the texture, effectively reducing the amount of contrast. Basically, it takes the blacks in the texture and turns them gray. Therefore, by adding Threshold just before the heat dissipates, you can reduce the amount of opacity, making the smoke look thick and dense. Use Figure 7.34 to keyframe the Threshold parameters.

Figure 7.34

The keys for setting the Threshold animation

Keys				
	Time	Value	InTan Type	OutTan Type
0	15	0	Clamped	Clamped
1	45	0.5	Clamped	Clamped
2	80	1	Clamped	Clamped

To check your work, you can compare it to `explosion4.ma` on the DVD. You can also watch the final simulated explosion, `explosion4.mov`.

Pyrotechnics

Explosions in film and television are highly theatrical. Fire and explosives are filmed at high speeds to slow them down, amplifying their visual impact. Most of all, pyrotechnics are well thought out, carefully staged, and anything but spontaneous.

A big part of pyrotechnics is the setup. This involves making sure the explosives are in the right spot, taking objects and prescoring them so they break apart in an expected manner, and so on. Pyrotechnics in 3D are no different. The same time and thought must be put into the scene in order to get the desired results. The next project involves blowing up a gas station. Figure 7.35 shows the gas station environment.

Figure 7.35

The gas station environment

The goal for the projects in the rest of this chapter is to demolish the gas station by using a variety of 3D pyrotechnic techniques. We are going to simulate a large explosion by using fluids. The building will be converted to nCloth and timed to explode with the fluid. The violent explosion will throw chunks of nCloth geometry into the gas pumps, knocking them over. After the pumps are gone, the fuel underneath will immediately catch fire. A column of smoke and flame will rise.

Before any of this can happen, the geometry needs to be prepped. The building is divided into two sections: the glass and the structure of the building. For film-style theatrics, we'll have the glass blow out first from the shock wave of the explosion. To do that, we'll subdivide the geometry of each piece of glass to form shapes, or shards, of glass. Using the Cut Faces tool, you can randomly add slices across the geometry. Take a look at the results in Figure 7.36. The windows and the building have been sliced with Cut Faces.

Once subdivided, all of the glass geometry is combined into a single object. Combining the nodes is not necessary. Keeping them separate gives you greater control, but for simplicity we will merge them into one object. The building elements, including the door frames, are also combined into one object for easier manipulation.

Figure 7.36

The geometry has been prescored with the Cut Faces tool.

The gas pumps are next. They were modeled as whole pieces, meaning the geometry does not flow together; they are simple cubes stacked together. The cubes were then combined into a single piece of geometry. To better understand, take a look at Figure 7.37.

Combining geometry without actually merging vertices together is a great way to control the destruction of an object. Converting the geometry to nCloth and applying a Transform constraint allows each unmerged piece to break away. Using self-collisions keeps the pieces from interpenetrating and adds greater realism. Let's get exploding!

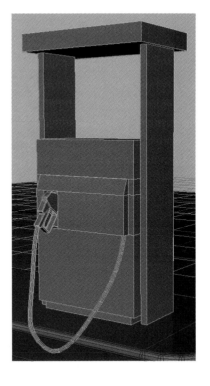

Project: Shock Wave

The first part of destroying the gas station is blowing out the glass from the doors and windows. The concept is that the explosion sends out a shock wave strong enough to destroy the glass of the building. Converting the glass geometry to nCloth and then adding a Tearable Surface constraint leaves the geometry at the mercy of any fields you apply.

1. Load the scene gasStation1.ma. The scene contains a modeled gas station with all its parts ready for devastation. The fluid explosion from the first project of this chapter is also included and hidden on a layer. It has been disabled and won't need to be activated until the next project.

2. Select the glass node. Choose nMesh → Create nCloth. Dimensions within the scene are close enough to being metric that you can leave the Solver Scale set to 1.

3. Reselect the glass node and choose nConstraint → Tearable Surface.

4. Change the Glue Strength on the Tearable Surface node to 0.0. Without any Glue Strength, the shards of glass will fly out easily.

5. Select the glass node again and add an Air field, using the Wind settings.

6. Key the Air field's Magnitude by using the settings from Figure 7.38.

Figure 7.38

The key frames for animating the Air field's Magnitude

Keys	Time	Value	InTan Type	OutTan Type
0	3	100	Clamped	Clamped
1	4	0	Clamped	Clamped

7. Set the Attenuation to 0 and turn off the Max Distance. With both the Attenuation and Max Distance off, the force of the air field will mimic an exploding force.

8. Change the Direction to 1 in the Z axis. Figure 7.39 shows the simulation at frame 10.

Figure 7.39

The glass is pushed out by the Air field.

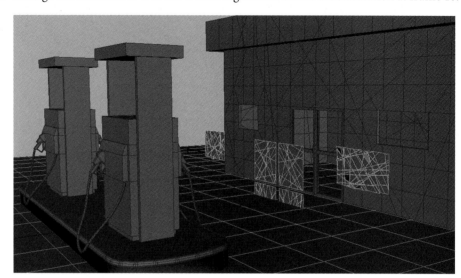

To check your work, you can compare it to gasStation2.ma on the DVD.

9. The air field provides the exploding force but will only push the glass out. It does not cause the shards to tumble in midair. Add a Turbulence field to the glass to enhance the effect.

10. Key the Turbulence field's Magnitude by using the settings from Figure 7.40.

Figure 7.40

The keyframes for animating the Turbulence field's Magnitude

Keys	Time	Value	InTan Type	OutTan Type
0	4	200	Clamped	Clamped
1	5	0	Clamped	Clamped

11. Change the Turbulence Frequency to 5, forcing the pieces of the glass node to tumble more frequently. Also set the Attenuation to 0, just as you did for the Air field. Figure 7.41 shows the progress so far.

Figure 7.41

The glass explodes and tumbles through the air.

12. The last step is to turn on Use Plane on the Nucleus node to prevent the pieces of glass from falling endlessly. Adding Friction and Bounce to the plane keeps the glass shards from sliding too much. Use Figure 7.42 for the settings.

To check your work, you can compare it to gasStation3.ma on the DVD.

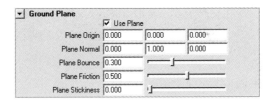

Figure 7.42

The settings for Nucleus Ground Plane

Project: Gas Station Explosion Part 1

With the windows blown out, it's time to level the rest of the building. The building will be converted to an nCloth object and blown up by using the same techniques used for the windows. The same Nucleus solver from the Shock Wave project is used here as well. It is important to note that the ground plane is turned on, and various attributes were set in the previous project to provide a realistic surface for nCloth objects to collide with. It was also established that the solver scale would remain at 1.0, to represent meters.

1. Load the scene gasStation3.ma. It picks up where the Shock Wave project left off. Select the building and choose Edit Mesh → Detach Component. Detaching components separates each and every face in geometry. It is the equivalent of adding a Tearable Surface constraint, minus nCloth.

2. Select the building and make it an nCloth object.

3. Select the building again and add a Transform constraint.

> We do not want to add a Tearable Surface constraint to the building, because we need to control the exact moment the faces blow apart. Adding a Tearable Surface constraint separates the components, but it also leaves the geometry at the mercy of the solver, resulting in the building crumbling at frame 1. To avoid this, we first separate the geometry by using Detach Component and use a Transform constraint instead of a Tearable Surface constraint.

4. Set Glue Strength on the Transform constraint to 0.01.

5. Add a Newton field with the default options. Translate the field to 2 in the Y axis and set the Attenuation to 0, eliminating any falloff of the field's power.

6. Key the Magnitude of the Newton field, using the settings from Figure 7.43. The field is animated to affect the building geometry after the glass has exploded.

Figure 7.43

The keyframes for animating the Newton field's Magnitude

Keys				
	Time	Value	InTan Type	OutTan Type
0	10	0	Clamped	Clamped
1	11	-2000	Clamped	Clamped
2	14	-2000	Clamped	Clamped
3	15	0	Clamped	Clamped

7. Play the simulation. Before the Magnitude of the Newton field has a chance to do anything, the building is already breaking apart. Check your results with Figure 7.44, which shows frame 3 of the simulation. Notice the door and window frames and the building's base.

Figure 7.44

By frame 3, the building is being destroyed.

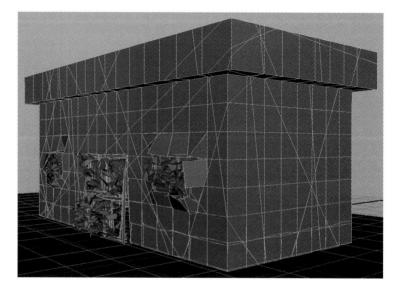

Two things are causing the building to break. The first is that the glass geometry is colliding with the building geometry. When the shards fly out, they are taking parts of the wall with them. By setting the nCloth glass to a different collision layer, we've made the building ignore the pieces. Set the nCloth glass Collision Layer to 1.0. Figure 7.45 shows the improved results of frame 3.

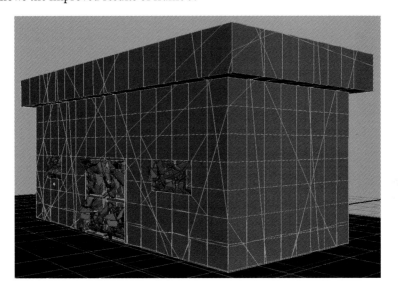

Figure 7.45

The door and window frames are now unaffected by the breaking glass.

8. The second attribute that needs to be fixed is the ground plane of the Nucleus solver. The plane and the base of the building are colliding with one another. Move the ground plane to −0.05 in the Y axis. You can now evaluate the effects of the Newton field. Play the simulation. Figure 7.46 shows the results at frame 20.

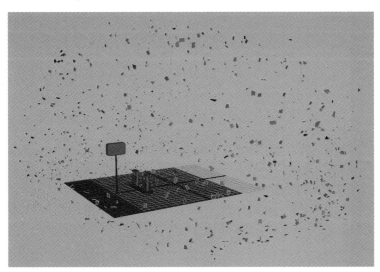

Figure 7.46

At frame 20 of the simulation, the Newton field blows the geometry apart.

9. The parts fly out with unrealistically extreme force. The Newton field's Magnitude is the culprit. However, as stated earlier, we need the parts of the gas station to knock over the gas pumps. Before trying to adjust the Magnitude of the Newton field, we will raise the mass of the nCloth building. Set the building's Mass to 10. Figure 7.47 shows the effects.

Figure 7.47

Frame 20 of the simulation with the nCloth building set to a mass of 10

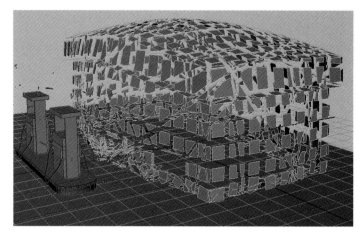

10. The parts of the building blow out with uniform precision—not very realistic. Add a Turbulence field to the building geometry, using the default settings.

11. Set the Turbulence's Frequency to 5 and set the Attenuation to 0.0.

12. Key the Magnitude of the Frequency by using the settings from Figure 7.48.

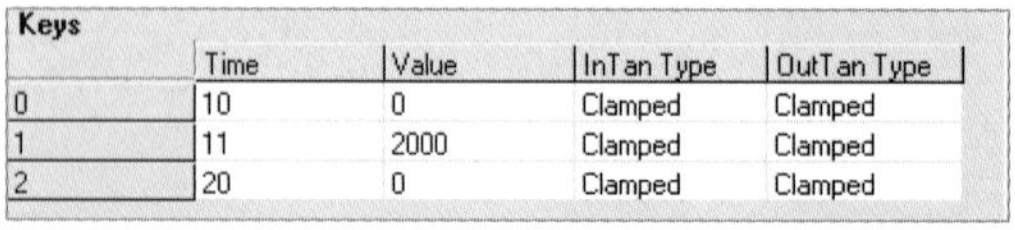

Figure 7.48

The keyframes for animating the Turbulence field's Magnitude

Keys				
	Time	Value	InTan Type	OutTan Type
0	10	0	Clamped	Clamped
1	11	2000	Clamped	Clamped
2	20	0	Clamped	Clamped

13. Play the simulation to see the effect the Turbulence field has on the nCloth pieces. Figure 7.49 shows frame 40 of the simulation.

Figure 7.49

The parts of the building spin and tumble through the air at frame 40.

The building pieces spin nicely through the air, but when they hit the ground they continue to slide along the ground plane. Change their Bounce to 0.6, Friction to 0.2, and Stickiness to 0.1 on the nCloth node. Use Figure 7.50 for reference.

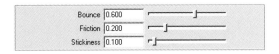

Figure 7.50

The settings used for the collisions on the nCloth building

To check your work, you can compare it to `gasStation4.ma` on the DVD.

14. With the building finished, you can now shift your attention to the gas pumps. Select both gas pumps and make them nCloth objects.

15. To prevent the pumps from penetrating the island geometry, make the island a passive collider.

16. Select the pumps again and add a Transform constraint. This keeps the unmerged parts of the geometry together. It also prevents the pieces from crumbling to the ground.

17. Set the Glue Strength on the Transform constraint to 0.003. The low Glue Strength makes the constraint easy to break.

18. Set the mass of the pumps to 0.5. The mass is low enough for the small building pieces to knock over the large parts of the gas pump and still have the pump parts look realistic when they hit the ground. Play the simulation to evaluate the results. Figure 7.51 shows the results at frame 30.

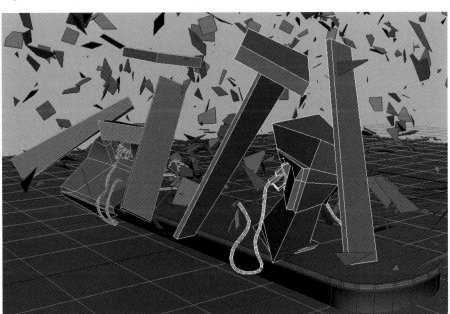

Figure 7.51

The gas pumps are knocked over at frame 30.

19. Not all parts of the gas pumps are being hit. Change the Turbulence field attached to the building to 1 to get all of the pieces.

20. The gas pumps bend and crumble too much during the explosion. By increasing the Bend and Compression Resistance, you can prevent the geometry from caving in so readily. Set the Bend Resistance to 100 and Compression Resistance to 20. Figure 7.52 shows how the new settings help keep the integrity of the geometry.

Figure 7.52

The gas pumps are knocked over again at frame 30, this time with a higher Bend Resistance.

21. The pumps receive a lot of damage during the explosion. In order to keep the damaged look, change the Restitution Angle on the gas pumps' nCloth node to 10. The Restitution Angle controls whether the geometry tries to return to its original shape after being deformed. A value of 10 means that if the geometry bends more than 10 degrees from its original shape, that geometry keeps the deformation and will not try to return to its original shape.

22. Some of the parts are having problems self-colliding. Change the Thickness to 0.01 and the Self Collide Width Scale to 1.0 for both pumps. In addition, change the Self Collision Flag to VertexEdge. Using the edges of the nCloth object for collision is more efficient for the large polygon faces used in the model of the gas pump.

23. The gas pumps need to be on a separate collision layer, like the glass. Placing them on Collision Layer 1 keeps them from colliding with any of the objects on layer 0. In particular, it prevents the pumps from having a collision conflict with the gas station island. Because the pumps sit directly on top of the island, the pumps' thickness penetrates the island, causing the pumps to get hung up on the island's geometry. Also, moving the pumps to Collision Layer 1 prevents the pumps from pushing back when the parts of the gas station collide with them. Not pushing back makes the exploding building parts more devastating to the pumps.

24. To help make sure every piece of the gas pumps is knocked over in the explosion, animate the thickness of the building. Animate it only for a few frames so its effects do not have any negative impact on the exploding parts. Increase the thickness large enough to make the parts' girth unavoidable. Use Figure 7.53 to set the keys.

Figure 7.53
Keyframe the thickness of the building.

Keys	Time	Value	InTan Type	OutTan Type
0	15	0.047	Clamped	Clamped
1	30	0.2	Clamped	Clamped
2	50	0.047	Clamped	Clamped

25. For the finishing touches, change the nCloth Friction to 3 and the Stickiness to 0.2 for both gas pumps. Increasing these values keeps the pieces of the gas pumps from sliding too far along the ground plane. Figure 7.54 shows the destruction at frame 80.

To check your work, you can compare it to gasStation5.ma on the DVD. You can also watch the movie gasStation1.mov.

Figure 7.54
The gas pumps after being knocked over by the exploding gas station

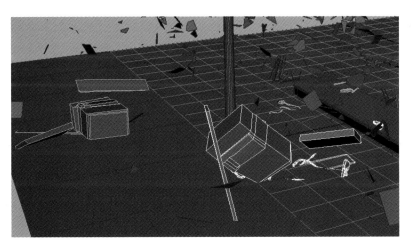

Project: Gas Station Explosion Part 2

The explosion created in the beginning of the chapter is useful for simple ground explosions. When it comes to blowing up a building or creating a multitiered fireball, several parameters need to be changed. The smoke must also be animated to get the right dissipating look. In this project, we will fine-tune the explosion by using some of the same settings and techniques used in the Plinian eruption project of Chapter 4.

1. Load the scene gasStation5.ma. It picks up where the previous project, Gas Station Explosion Part 1, left off. Before making any modifications to the fluid explosion, disable the Nucleus node. Because all of the nCloth objects share the same solver, disabling nucleus1 shuts them all down.

2. Turn on the visibility for the Explosion layer. Change the emitter from a sphere to a cube. Scale the cube to 3.5, 2, and 2.57 in the X, Y, and Z axes, respectively. The cube is scaled to roughly match the dimensions of the gas station building.

3. Because the ground work for the explosion is already done, we can jump right to refining its look. Select the fluid and open the texture options. Change the Texture Type to Space Time and the Coordinate Method to Fixed. Use Figure 7.55 for the rest of the settings. Figure 7.56 shows the explosion at frame 40.

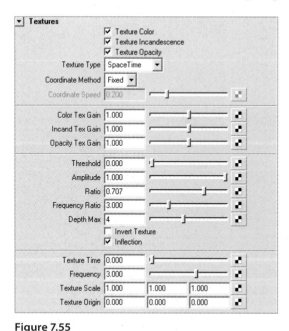

Figure 7.55
The settings for the Space Time texture

Figure 7.56
The explosion at frame 40

4. Moving from the Texture options up to the Opacity options, change the Opacity graph and Input Bias to match Figure 7.57. Set the second key to a position of 0.125. Figure 7.58 shows the explosion rendered with the new settings.

5. The explosion is predominately smoke with the new Opacity settings. However, the values give it the proper shape. Change the Incandescence graph to match Figure 7.59 to help offset some of the smoke. Change the intensity of the orange to 15 and move it to 0.7 on the graph. Figure 7.60 shows the explosion rendered with the new settings.

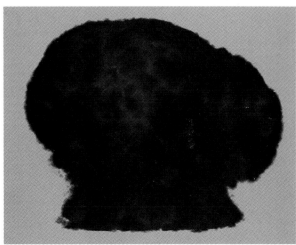

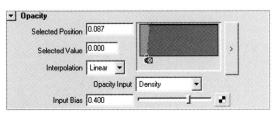

Figure 7.57
The settings for the Opacity

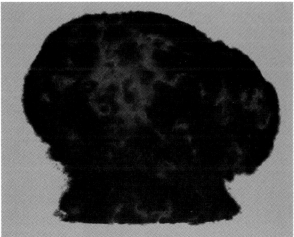

Figure 7.58
The explosion at frame 40

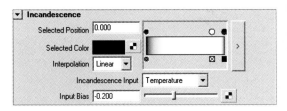

Figure 7.59
The settings for the Incandescence

Figure 7.60
The explosion at frame 40

6. The color options are next. Use Figure 7.61 to modify the settings. As shown in Figure 7.62, the change in the color options gives the explosion a richer look, creating a sharper separation between the browns and blacks.

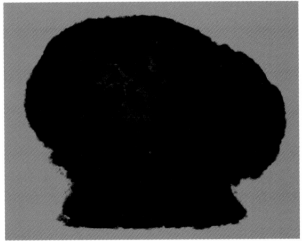

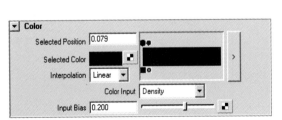

Figure 7.61

The settings for Color

Figure 7.62

The explosion at frame 40 with revised color settings

7. The last of the shading changes are to increase the Transparency to 0.250 and lower the Glow Intensity. Also set the Edge Dropoff to 0.0.

   To check your work, you can compare it to gasStation6.ma on the DVD.

8. At this point, it is obvious the emissions are unbalanced. Select the explosion emitter. Use Figure 7.63 to change the Density/Voxel/Sec keyframes and values.

Figure 7.63

The keys for setting the Density/Voxel/Sec

Keys	Time	Value	InTan Type	OutTan Type
0	8	0	Clamped	Clamped
1	9	1	Clamped	Clamped
2	20	0.1	Flat	Flat
3	60	0	Flat	Flat

9. Next, modify the Heat/Voxel/Sec, using Figure 7.64 to change the keyframes and values.

Figure 7.64

The keys for setting the Heat/Voxel/Sec

Keys	Time	Value	InTan Type	OutTan Type
0	8	0	Clamped	Clamped
1	9	2	Clamped	Clamped
2	15	2	Clamped	Clamped
3	16	0	Clamped	Clamped

10. Finally, change the Fuel/Voxel/Sec, using Figure 7.65 to change the keyframes and values.

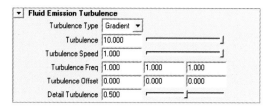

Figure 7.65

The keys for setting the Fuel/Voxel/Sec

Keys	Time	Value	InTan Type	OutTan Type
0	8	0	Clamped	Clamped
1	9	20	Clamped	Clamped
2	11	20	Clamped	Clamped
3	13	0	Clamped	Clamped

11. The emitter is large. In order to disrupt the uniform look when the fluid is initially emitted, add Turbulence at the point of emission. Use Figure 7.66 for the settings.

Figure 7.66

The emission's Turbulence settings

Fluid Emission Turbulence

Turbulence Type	Gradient		
Turbulence	10.000		
Turbulence Speed	1.000		
Turbulence Freq	1.000	1.000	1.000
Turbulence Offset	0.000	0.000	0.000
Detail Turbulence	0.500		

Emitter turbulence does not affect the motion of the fluid. It only randomizes how the fluid comes out of the emitter. This randomness helps disrupt the shape of the explosion, giving the fluid a rougher appearance. Figure 7.67 shows the explosion at frame 70.

Figure 7.67

The explosion at frame 70 with new emission settings

To check your work, you can compare it to gasStation7.ma on the DVD. You can also watch the movie gasStation2.mov.

12. Reviewing the simulation reveals a lot of things that need to be adjusted. For starters, the explosion is moving too slowly. Change the Simulation Rate Scale to 3. At such a high speed, the fluid will need to be damped slightly to keep the velocities under control. Add 0.03 to the Damp parameter. In addition, the Friction and Viscosity need to be set to 0.

13. After adjusting the emission, it is apparent that the fuel is not burning fast enough. Change the fuel's Reaction Speed to 0.3. In addition, because of the size of the explosion emitter, we no longer need to have the fuel release light. Change the Light Released to 0.0. Use Figure 7.68 to check your settings.

Figure 7.68

The Fuel settings

14. Another evaluation of the simulation, gasStation3.mov, reveals that the temperature overpowers the density, as shown in Figure 7.69.

Figure 7.69

The explosion at frame 30 with new emission settings

Change the Density settings to those shown in Figure 7.70.

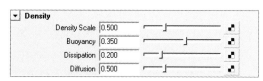

Figure 7.70
The Density settings

15. Change the Temperature settings to match those in Figure 7.71.

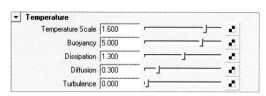

Figure 7.71
The Temperature settings

To check your work, you can compare it to gasStation8.ma on the DVD. You can also watch the movie gasStation4.mov.

16. The explosion is hitting the sides of the container. The container needs to be bigger. To accommodate the size and girth of the explosion, change the Container Properties settings to match those in Figure 7.72.

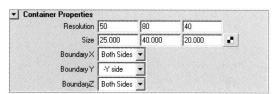

Figure 7.72
The new container properties

17. Resizing the container moves the base lower than the grid plane. Unparent the emitter from the container and translate the container to 20.0 in the Y axis.

18. The explosion is looking good but it lacks an initial destructive outburst. To achieve this, add a Newton field, using the default parameters.

19. Change the Newton field to a volume torus. Scale the torus uniformly to 2.2.

20. Transform the Newton field's position and orientation by using the values from Figure 7.73.

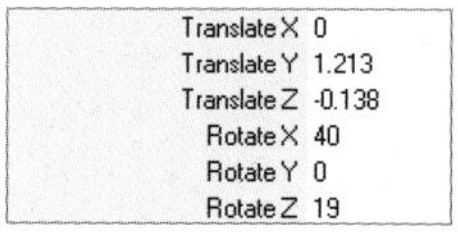

21. Set the Attenuation to 0 and use Figure 7.74 to animate the Magnitude.

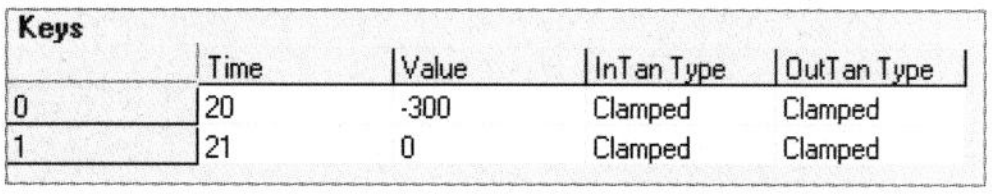

Figure 7.73
Translate and rotate the Newton field.

Translate X	0
Translate Y	1.213
Translate Z	-0.138
Rotate X	40
Rotate Y	0
Rotate Z	19

Figure 7.74
Animate the Newton field's Magnitude.

Keys

	Time	Value	InTan Type	OutTan Type
0	20	-300	Clamped	Clamped
1	21	0	Clamped	Clamped

The simulation now explodes with the appropriate amount of force. Take a look at Figure 7.75. It shows frame 30 of the simulation.

Figure 7.75

Frame 30 of the simulation

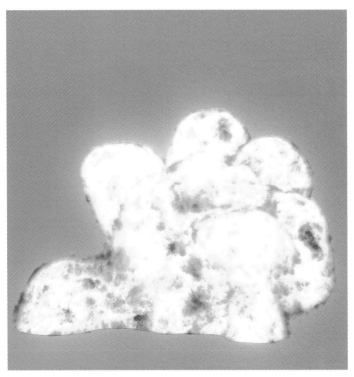

 To check your work, you can compare it to gasStation9.ma on the DVD. You can also watch the movie gasStation5.mov.

The explosion is almost done. The only thing left to do is refine the animation, which we'll do in the remaining steps of this project.

22. Add the following expression to the Texture time. This makes the texture evolve over time.

    ```
    explosionShape.textureTime=time*.12
    ```

23. The density's Buoyancy is making the smoke move too slowly. Increasing the Buoyancy only adds to the Temperature, making the entire fireball move too fast. One value over the course of the simulation will not suffice. Instead you need to animate the Buoyancy to slowly increase. As the temperature dies off, the density's buoyancy increases. Use Figure 7.76 to animate the density.

Figure 7.76

The Density Buoy- ancy keyframes

Keys	Time	Value	InTan Type	OutTan Type
0	10	0	Clamped	Clamped
1	40	3	Clamped	Clamped

Take a look at Figure 7.77. It shows frame 60 of the simulation. The smoke is not dissipating properly. It is heavily textured, when it should look soft and diffused.

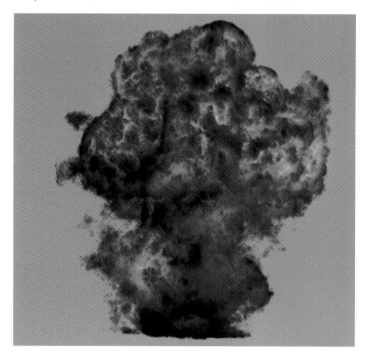

Figure 7.77

Frame 60 of the simulation reveals that the smoke has too much texture.

24. Animate the texture's Frequency as shown in Figure 7.78 to make the smoke look softer toward the end of the simulation.

Figure 7.78

The texture's Frequency keyframes

Keys	Time	Value	InTan Type	OutTan Type
0	10	3	Clamped	Clamped
1	200	1	Clamped	Clamped

25. Animating the texture's Frequency has also made the smoke disappear prematurely. To get it back, animate the first Opacity key, which is at a value of 0.0. Use Figure 7.79 to keyframe the position of the first value.

Figure 7.79

Keyframe the position of the value at 0.0.

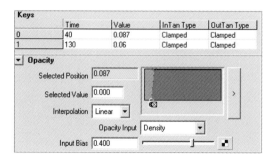

Keys	Time	Value	InTan Type	OutTan Type
0	40	0.087	Clamped	Clamped
1	130	0.06	Clamped	Clamped

▼ Opacity

Selected Position	0.087
Selected Value	0.000
Interpolation	Linear ▼
Opacity Input	Density ▼
Input Bias	0.400

> To make the smoke linger for a longer time, animate the key at value 0.0 from its original position to 0.0. The closer it gets to 0.0, the more the smoke remains.

26. The smoke looks weak toward the end of the simulation. Animate the Threshold to make it appear denser. Use Figure 7.80 for reference.

Figure 7.80

The Texture's Threshold key frames

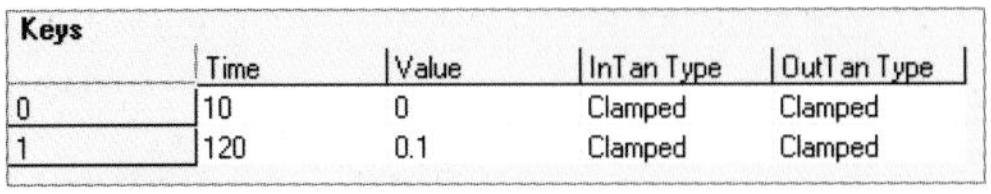

Keys	Time	Value	InTan Type	OutTan Type
0	10	0	Clamped	Clamped
1	120	0.1	Clamped	Clamped

27. One last review of the explosion reveals that the fluid is hitting the edges of the container. Increase the container's size by using the settings in Figure 7.81. You also need to reposition the container. Translate it to 4.5 in the X axis and 25 in the Y axis. Figure 7.82 shows the final explosion at frame 40.

Figure 7.81

The new container properties

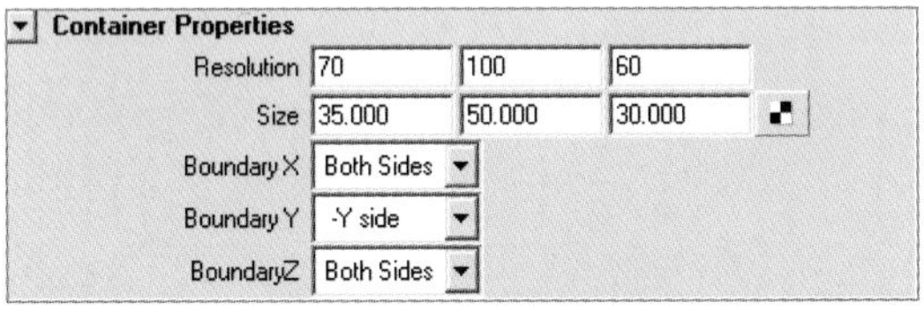

Container Properties			
Resolution	70	100	60
Size	35.000	50.000	30.000
Boundary X	Both Sides		
Boundary Y	-Y side		
Boundary Z	Both Sides		

To check your work, you can compare it to gasStation10.ma on the DVD. You can also watch the movie gasStation6.mov.

Figure 7.82

The final look of the explosion at frame 40

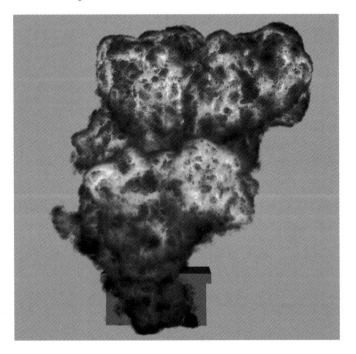

Project: Fire Columns

Not much is left of the gas station. With the fuel pumps leveled, the gasoline is let loose. In this project, the gas from the fuel pumps immediately ignites, sending a column of fire into the air. Using the explosion created in the previous project as a base, you will add a new emitter and modify the fluid explosion to explode continuously instead of in one rapid burst.

1. Load the scene gasStation10.ma. It picks up where the previous project, Gas Station Explosion Part 2, left off. Create a default 3D container.

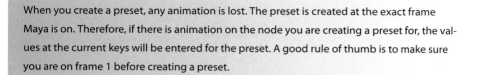

2. Create a preset from the explosion fluid in the scene and apply it to the new 3D container.

> When you create a preset, any animation is lost. The preset is created at the exact frame Maya is on. Therefore, if there is animation on the node you are creating a preset for, the values at the current keys will be entered for the preset. A good rule of thumb is to make sure you are on frame 1 before creating a preset.

3. Change the Container Properties settings to match those seen in Figure 7.83.

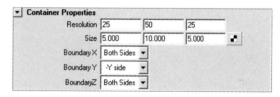

Figure 7.83

The settings for the container properties

4. Position the container on the ground, underneath pump1. Translate it to 2, 5, and 7 in the X, Y, and Z axes, respectively.

5. Create a volume sphere emitter and move it to –4.95 in the Y axis. The emitter sits inside of the island geometry. Scale it uniformly to 0.45.

6. Use Figure 7.84 to establish the voxels per second and turbulence for the sphere emitter.

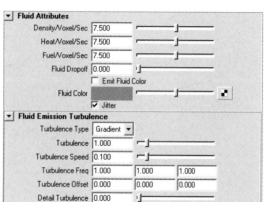

Figure 7.84

The settings for the volume sphere emitter

The emissions are relatively strong. By rapidly pushing out a lot of fluid, you create a steady stream of fire. The turbulence alternates the emissions to give the flame more contrast. Figure 7.85 shows frame 60 of the progress so far.

Figure 7.85

Frame 60 of the simulation

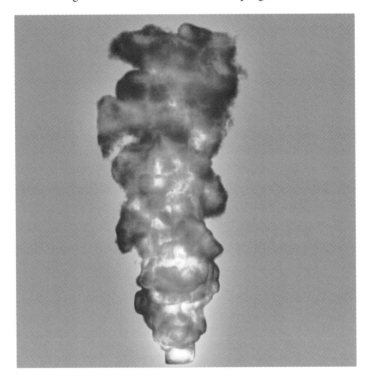

 To check your work, you can compare it to gasStation11.ma on the DVD.

7. With the emission high, Temperature Buoyancy can be lowered to 1. This also allows the smoke to climb faster than the heat, getting it to rise above the top of the flame column. Most important, set the Diffusion to 0. This stops the fluid from gradually entering into other voxels. The effect is hard, crisp detail. Use Figure 7.86 to check your settings.

Figure 7.86

The settings for the Temperature details

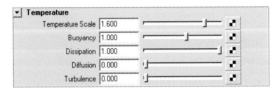

8. Remove the Diffusion from the Density also. In addition, change the Dissipation to 0.75 to have the fluid disappear rapidly. Use Figure 7.87 to check your settings.

Figure 7.87

The settings for the
Density details

Density		
Density Scale	0.500	
Buoyancy	3.000	
Dissipation	0.750	
Diffusion	0.000	

9. Increase the Swirl under the Velocity details to 10, increasing the amount of roll in the column of flame. The simulation is played and evaluated. Take a look at frame 60 in Figure 7.88.

Figure 7.88

Frame 60 of the
flame column
simulation

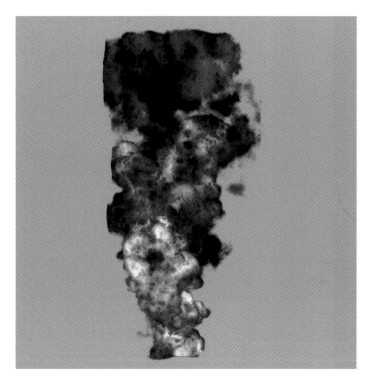

10. To make the top of the fluid come down and decrease its speed, increase Damping to 0.2. Figure 7.89 shows the results.

11. The presets do not retain animation. Add the following modified expressions back to the Texture Time and Texture Origin Y axis. The expressions were altered to make the texture move faster, keeping in sync with the rest of the fluid.

    ```
    flameColumnShape.textureTime=time*.5
    flameColumnShape.textureOriginY=time*-.25
    ```

12. The speed of the fluid demands more detail from the texture. Increase the Frequency to 8. Figure 7.90 shows the improved results of frame 60.

Figure 7.89
The rendered results of frame 60 with Damping increased

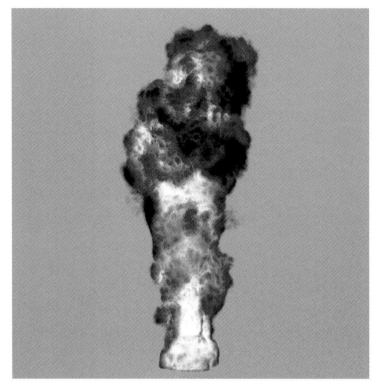

Figure 7.90
The results of the flame column at frame 60 with Frequency increased

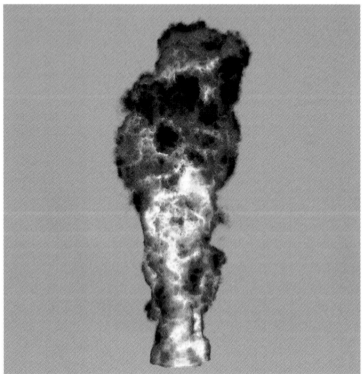

13. The flame should have more detail at its base than at the top. A simple way to achieve this is to implode the texture. Change the Implode value to −0.2. Take a look at the final results in Figure 7.91.

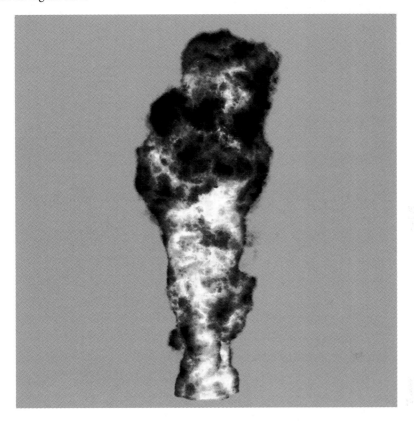

Figure 7.91

The final results of the flame column at frame 60

Presets can now be made of the flame column and its emitter to duplicate the effect for the second pump. I'll leave that up to you. To check your work, you can compare it to gasStation12.ma on the DVD. You can also watch the movie gasStation7.mov.

The gas station has met its fiery doom. All of the elements are turned on. The flame columns were integrated by keyframing their start times to correspond with their animation. When the pumps are knocked over, they emit huge fireballs and then continue to burn. The scene is rendered by using a single ray-traced directional light and having Final Gather turned on. Check out the results in Figure 7.92 and Figure 7.93.

To check your work, you can compare it to gasStation13.ma on the DVD. You can also watch the movie gasStation8.mov.

Figure 7.92

The rendered
results of frame 45

Figure 7.93

The rendered results of frame 130

CHAPTER 8

Floods

Water is the holy grail of simulated effects. Every aspect of creating it is a complex and difficult hurdle. You can divide the generation of water into three parts. First you have the body of water. Within it, you can have thousands of currents, sloshing in unison and against each other. Second is water's ability to break away and then come back together. It can be poured, splashed, or sprayed. Third is its complex shading. Water is highly reflective, transparent, and volumetric, all within the same object. Any one of these aspects is difficult to deal with, let alone all at once.

Water

Water is complex to deal with, whether you are pouring a glass of it or flooding a city street. Whenever water is involved, it needs to be handled on a case-by-case basis because of its ability to increase or decrease in volume. In this chapter, you are going to focus on only large amounts of fast-moving water.

Water doesn't have a preexisting condition or default state, unlike the phenomena we've addressed in previous simulations. Tornadoes, for instance, have a funnel cloud. There is a distinct shape. Although it can change, the funnel is a base shape from which to start. Even fire, evolving as it burns, still has an identifiable, consistent shape. Water does not. It can be at rest, sitting inside a cup, or it can be in constant motion, flowing as a river. Either way, you have to get it there. What makes water so different is that it cannot be handled as a single effect. Every action and reaction water has is like a new effect. It is always sloshing, splashing, or filling something.

It is hard to know where to start when creating a flood. You must emit enough nParticles with the right radius to create a solid-looking body of water, while still maintaining the ability to create small secondary splashing. There is a definitive trade-off between the overall look of the water and the appearance of individual water droplets. Ideally, your flood would have 100,000 nParticles being emitted every second, making the size of each nParticle almost irrelevant. Hardware and technical limitations prevent this. You must work within the confines of your hardware and find an acceptable alternative.

Several things happen to water as it moves over a rough surface, such as a city street or sandy beach, that work in our favor. When water comes crashing down—for example, as a wave on the beach—it does so in layers. Each successive layer rapidly loses speed as another layer piles over the top of it. Take a look at Figure 8.1. You can see the wave peaking and falling over onto itself. Look at the incredible amount of fine detail.

The motion of the water continues. When a wave breaks, it loses momentum. The water behind the wave rolls over the water of the crashed wave. Eventually, it too makes contact with the ground, slowing down and letting another layer of water overtake it. The process is repeated over and over again. Figure 8.2 shows multiple layers of water pushing up on the beach.

Figure 8.1

The wave begins to topple and fall over onto itself.

Figure 8.2

Layers of water push up on the beach.

Water's rising and falling works in our favor by allowing us to define fast-moving nParticles and slow-moving nParticles. The faster the nParticles go, the smaller their size, creating small drops and splash effects. The nParticles increase in size as they slow down, spreading and filling areas to make the water look whole.

The biggest challenge with water is how computationally expensive it is. Realistic water requires a lot of nParticles. Getting the right motion is possible with relatively few nParticles, but having it look like a solid volume of water takes a lot more.

City Flood

Watching massive amounts of water flood a busy metropolitan area is always a spectacular effect and a staple of disaster movies. The visual impact is tremendous. It is only fitting to finish this book with biblical-sized destruction.

This chapter presents a single scenario of flooding a city street. It will take three projects to finish the effect.

In the first project, you use nParticles to flood the city street. Titled Water Volume, the project is a computationally expensive endeavor. In order for the flood to be believable, thousands of nParticles must be used. As a result, the final simulation is brief, roughly 3 to 4 seconds in length.

The next project, Making Waves, concentrates on the motion of the water. The water is in a turbulent, flowing state. Every nParticle must have a mind of its own but still be willing to follow the crowd. In the last project, Rendering Water, we'll render the final outcome. The look of the water is finalized by converting the nParticles to polygons.

Project: Water Volume

A large amount of water is required to flood a city. In this project, you create a volume emitter and emit wave after wave of nParticle water down a street. Before that can happen, we need to make sure we have appropriate collision objects in place for the water to crash into. The only attribute that has been set on the collision surface is Bounce, which has been set to 0.6. In addition, the Nucleus solver's Space Scale has been set to 0.304 to match the scale of the scene.

1. Open the scene file `waterVolume1.ma`. The scene contains a city with several buildings, sidewalks, and streets. Figure 8.3 shows the environment.

   Each element of the environment has been placed on a separate referenced layer. In addition, a low-resolution model has been created to represent the city. Named city-Collision, it is used as a passive collider for the nParticles to collide against, replacing the need to use the actual city geometry. Figure 8.4 shows the reduced mesh.

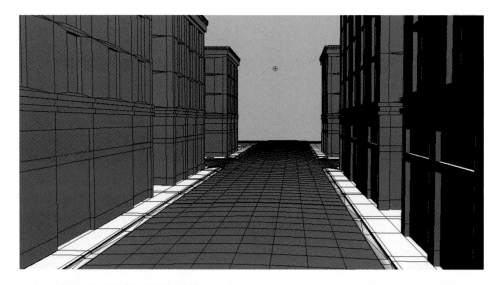

Translate X	-33
Translate Y	9
Translate Z	-228
Rotate X	0
Rotate Y	0
Rotate Z	0
Scale X	18
Scale Y	3
Scale Z	1

2. Create a water-emitting nParticle Volume Cube emitter.

3. Translate and scale the emitter by using the settings shown in Figure 8.5. The emitter is moved to the beginning of the street.

4. Start with a small emission rate to see how the water reacts in the environment. Set the Rate to 200 on the Volume Cube emitter. Figure 8.6 shows the results at frame 100.

5. The nParticles are being influenced only by gravity at this point and have no motion of their own. Before you get them moving, increase the nParticles' Radius to 3. This value is large for the scene, but it helps us see what is going on. We will fine-tune the radius later.

6. To get the nParticles moving, change the emitter's Directional Speed to 30 and the Random Speed to 10. A quick preview of the simulation reveals the nParticles being emitted in the wrong direction. Figure 8.7 shows the results at frame 40.

7. Set the emitter's direction to 1.0 in the Z axis and 0.0 in the X axis. Play the simulation. The nParticles progress down the street, colliding with the buildings. Figure 8.8 shows the results at frame 60.

To check your work so far, you can compare it to waterVolume2.ma on the DVD.

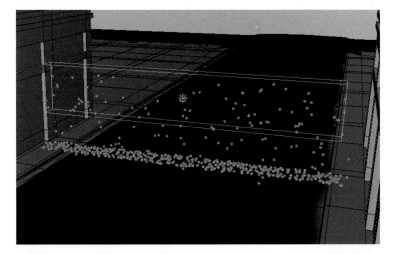

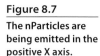

Figure 8.6

The nParticles fall to the ground in a pool under the emitter.

Figure 8.7

The nParticles are being emitted in the positive X axis.

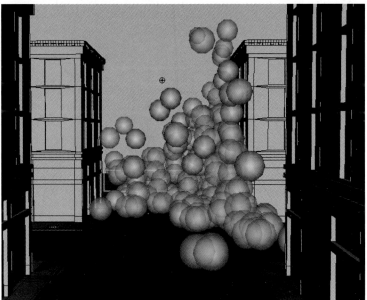

8. The nParticles are reacting well so far. Turn on Self Collision. The nParticles quickly deflect off each other, shooting in multiple directions. Figure 8.9 shows the effect from frame 35. The bouncing is caused mainly by the large radius we set in step 5.

9. Change the nParticle Radius to 1. This is still a high value. Reducing the nParticles' Radius incrementally helps to evaluate the simulation before we need to increase the emission rate in order to fill the street. Take a look at frame 60 and how the nParticles respond to their new radius in Figure 8.10.

10. With the decreased radius comes an increase in the number of particles needed to fill the street. Change the emitter's Rate to 600. Figure 8.11 has the results at frame 60.

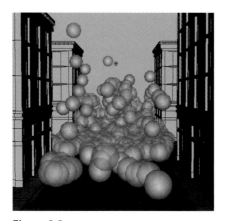

Figure 8.8

The nParticles bounce and collide with their surroundings as they travel down the street.

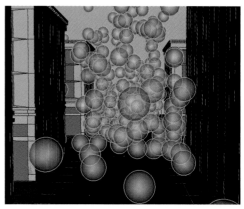

Figure 8.9

Self-collision causes the nParticles to shoot off in different directions.

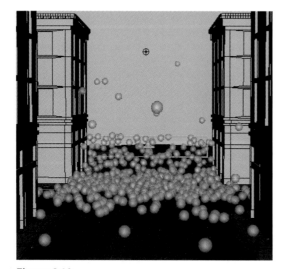

Figure 8.10

The nParticles flow down the street in an organized fashion.

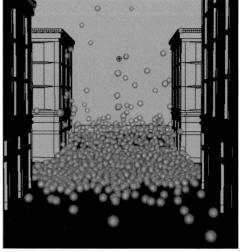

Figure 8.11

The nParticles fill the street.

11. The nParticles are not as close together as they should be. If they are spread too far apart, gaps will appear in the final look of the water. To bring the nParticles closer together, change the Collide Width scale to 0.7. Figure 8.12 has the results at frame 60.

12. When the nParticles are first emitted, they hit the ground with a dull thud. To make them more reactive and rebound a little, set the nParticle Bounce to 0.3 and the passive collider Bounce to 0.6. When the two objects collide, these two values are added together for the reaction. When water hits a surface at high speed, it breaks apart into a splash. Having each nParticle split into more nParticles would be extremely expensive and too difficult. Adding Bounce to both the nParticle and passive collider helps give the illusion of the water breaking apart. By the end of the simulation, you will be emitting enough nParticles to make this effect look convincing.

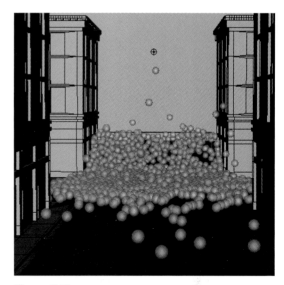

Figure 8.12
The decreased Collision Width Scale helps bring the nParticles closer together.

To check your work so far, you can compare it to waterVolume3.ma on the DVD. You can also watch waterVolume1.mov to see the water's rendered motion.

Water Turbulence

Taking water out of its element, for example, removing ocean water and flooding a city street with it, means the rules change. The laws of physics are still the driving force, but getting the water to crash and splash must be artificially provoked. In the ocean, winds cause waves. Moving or flowing water has a lot of turbulence. Water molecules, minerals, and other matter in the water contribute to its diverse motion. Water turbulence is primarily caused by objects surrounding the water. In a large-scale, cinematic flood, the water needs to deliver a relentless pounding. There needs to be streams of water crashing together from every direction, twisting and churning to deliver the maximum amount of destruction.

Project: Making Waves

In the first project, Water Volume, you created a flowing body of water through a city street. The motion of the water was linear and lacked cinematic excitement. This project picks up where the Water Volume project left off and adds turbulence to the flow of water. Two fields help us add realistic motion to the water.

1. Open the scene file waterVolume3.ma. The scene picks up where the project Water Volume left off. Select the nParticle node and then choose Fields → Vortex. The Vortex

field is ideal for getting water to tumble. However, it is not effective when applied to the nParticles as a whole. It needs to be attached to each nParticle, giving them the ability to influence the nParticles around them.

Select the nParticle node and the Vortex field and choose Fields → Use Selected as Source of Field. The Vortex field becomes a child of the nParticle node. Each nParticle now travels with its own Vortex field.

2. In addition to attaching the vortex to the nParticles, you must turn on Apply to Each Vertex on the Field node. This can be done through the Channel Box or under the Special Effects section in the Attribute Editor. Turning it on activates the field for each vertex, or in this case, each nParticle.

3. The Vortex field won't have much of an effect just yet. Change the attributes shown in Figure 8.13 to give the field the necessary force.

Figure 8.13

The Vortex field settings

▼	**Vortex Field Attributes**			
	Magnitude	20.000		
	Attenuation	2.000		
	Axis	1.000	0.000	0.000
▼	**Distance**			
	✔ Use Max Distance			
	Max Distance	7.000		

Play the simulation to see the results. The nParticles start to roll upon emission. The rolling effect forces the nParticles into the ground, causing them to bounce. Figure 8.14 shows the results at frame 60.

Figure 8.14

The nParticles roll upon emission.

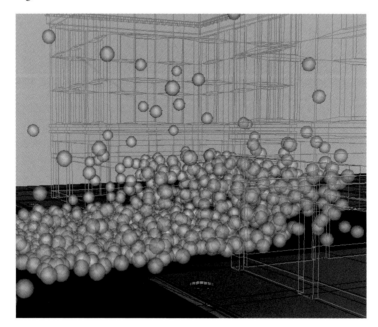

4. The nParticles are churning too much. You do not want to reduce the amount of influence the Vortex field has on the nParticles; you only want to gain some control. By reducing the Conserve attribute, or intensity of dynamic forces acting on the nParticles, you can get them to calm down. Select the nParticles and change the Conserve setting to 0.97. Figure 8.15 shows frame 60 of the simulation. The nParticles are more tightly packed, making the rolling effect more noticeable.

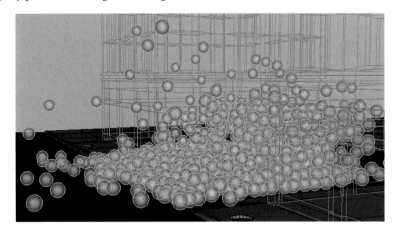

Figure 8.15

The nParticles move in a more controlled fashion with Conserve slightly lowered.

5. The nParticles are emitted with a lot of force, but their speed dies quickly, especially with the reduced Conserve setting. If this were a real situation, and the oceans were overflowing into the streets, the force of the ocean's tides would continually propel the water along for miles. Because we are taking the water out of context and it has no real source driving it, we need to add a Uniform field to move the nParticles along. You are, in effect, creating your own current.

   Select the nParticles and choose Fields → Uniform. As with the Vortex field, you want to add the Uniform field to each nParticle. Select the nParticle and the Uniform field. Choose Fields → Use Selected as Source of Field. The Uniform field becomes a child of the nParticle node. You must also set Apply Per Vertex to On.

6. Change the Uniform field's settings to match Figure 8.16.

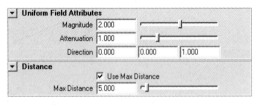

Figure 8.16

The settings for the Uniform field

To check your work so far, you can compare it to `makingWaves1.ma` on the DVD. You can also watch `makingWaves1.mov` to see the water in motion.

7. As discussed at the beginning of the chapter, the various nParticles' radii should change based on each nParticle's speed. Fast-moving nParticles are smaller than slower-moving nParticles. The current Radius of the nParticles is 1. This is a good average radius. Ideally, you want to have the faster nParticles be half as large, and the slower nParticles twice as large. This gives you a range of 0.5 to 2. The easiest way to achieve this range is to set the Radius of the nParticle to its maximum size and then use the Radius Scale to reduce it.

   Open the attributes of the nParticles. Change the Radius to 2 and use the settings shown in Figure 8.17. The Input Max is high to help achieve a smooth transition from the fast nParticles' small size to their larger slow size.

8. To better visualize what is happening, set the Color Input for the nParticles to Radius. Change the color to match the differences in fast- and slow-moving water. Use Figure 8.18 for reference.

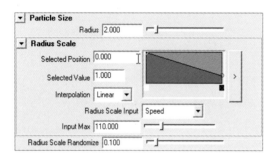

Figure 8.17
The Radius settings

Figure 8.18
The Color settings

9. Change the Opacity to 1 to get rid of the transparency on the nParticles. This change will make the motion of the nParticles easier to see.

10. It's time to increase the emitter rate to 5000. With this many nParticles, you need to lower the Collide Width Scale. Lowering it to 0.15 makes the nParticles overlap and flow more uniformly. It also prevents them from being pinched between the two buildings. Figure 8.19 shows the result at frame 30.

To check your work so far, you can compare it to makingWaves2.ma on the DVD. You can also watch makingWaves2.mov to see the water in motion.

11. The water's motion is almost complete. To get the layered effect of water crashing onto itself, as discussed at the beginning of this chapter, you increase the friction of the ground and nParticles. Adding friction to the water and the objects it collides against can cause a substantial amount of turbulence in the water.

   Water also has a way of adhering to surfaces and cohering to itself. Adding stickiness to the water gives it the ability to cling to objects. Use Figure 8.20 for the nParticle's Collision settings.

Figure 8.19

The emitter is emitting 5000 nParticles at frame 30.

12. Next, set the Friction on the city collision object. Use Figure 8.21 to confirm the Collision settings on the city collision object.

13. To no surprise, the water now moves much more slowly than before the Friction and Stickiness were added. To compensate, increase the Uniform field's Magnitude to 2.

14. The Liquid Simulation Properties are undoubtedly the most important attributes to control. Fortunately, the defaults are good, and only one of the four settings needs to be adjusted. The Liquid Radius Scale controls the amount of overlap between the nParticles. Increasing the Liquid Radius Scale to 2 or higher clumps the water together and gives the simulation a grander effect. For example, Figure 8.22 shows frame 40 using a Liquid Radius Scale of 2. Compare it to Figure 8.23, which uses a Liquid Radius Scale of 4. Use a value of 4 for the final Liquid Radius Scale.

To check your work, compare it to makingWaves3.ma on the DVD. You can also watch makingWaves3.mov to see the water in motion.

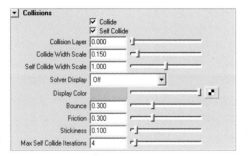

Figure 8.20

The nParticle's Collision settings

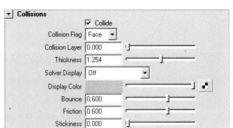

Figure 8.21

The Collision settings for the city collision object

Figure 8.22

The nParticles with
the Liquid Radius
Scale set to 2

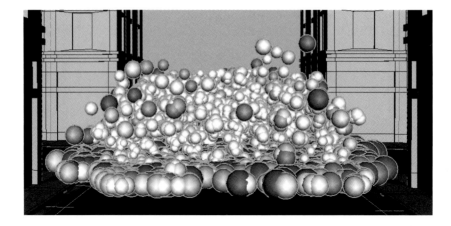

Figure 8.23

The nParticles with
the Liquid Radius
Scale set to 4

Project: Rendering Water

The nParticles only provide the motion. A critical step in making water look realistic is to convert the nParticles to polygons, which are essential in getting the water to have a cohesive look. In addition, you gain an extra attribute, Motion Streak, which extends the length of the geometry based on the nParticles' speed. Furthermore, converting the nParticles to geometry expands your shading abilities.

To texture water properly, you need to have a shader that can be influenced by nParticle attributes. Currently, no such shader exists in Maya, and nParticle data cannot be passed through a Particle Sampler node because meshes do not support that type of connection. Therefore, the advantage of being able to shade your geometry becomes limited. For clear water, a blinn shader with transparency and reflectivity works nicely. However for a flood of dirty ocean water, transparency would destroy the effect.

1. Open the scene file `makingWaves3.ma`. The scene picks up where the Making Waves project left off. Advance the simulation to frame 10. You want only a few nParticles in the scene before converting them to geometry. Select the nParticle and choose Modify → Convert → nParticle to Polygon. Hide the nParticles to see the results. The geometry does not exist yet. The nParticles Output Mesh settings need to be modified.

2. Select the nParticle and open the Output Mesh attribute settings. The first setting to modify is the Blobby Radius Scale. Increase the Blobby Radius Scale to 10. The Blobby Radius scales each nParticle internally and then uses that size to determine the shape of the geometry. It does not affect the nParticles' radius directly; it affects only how the nParticles are converted to polygons. You want the Blobby Radius Scale to be as large as you want the volume of water to be. A good way to figure this out is to adjust the scale until it surrounds the largest nParticle. You can also think of the Blobby Radius Scale as shrink wrap surrounding the nParticles. Figure 8.24 shows the results.

> When testing the nParticle output mesh, it is best to hide the geometry and advance the simulation while viewing the nParticles. At the desired frame, you can then turn the nParticles off and the output mesh on. It will take several minutes to a half hour for the mesh to update, depending on your settings and computer's speed.

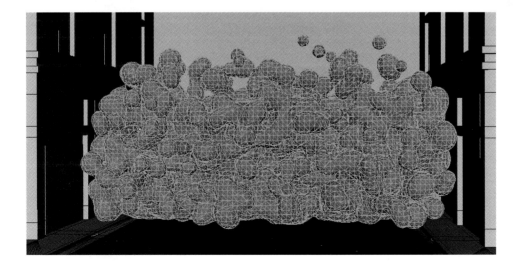

Figure 8.24

Set to 10, the Blobby Radius Scale encompasses the nParticles.

3. Next, modify the method used to tessellate the output mesh. Change the Mesh Method to Quads and increase the Smoothing to 2. Maya calculates Quads the quickest by creating uniformly spaced meshes. The clean quad geometry is not always desirable, especially when creating rough or turbulent-looking surfaces; however, speed is more important at this point. Take a look at Figure 8.25. It shows a screen capture of the quad geometry with the Mesh Smoothing Iterations set to 2. Compare it to Figure 8.26, which shows the geometry with the most expensive method, Acute Tetrahedra. For this project, use Quads for your Mesh Method.

Increasing the Smoothing to a value greater than 2 is typically not required. Because you are using geometry instead of nParticles, you can use Maya's mesh operations on it. For instance, adding a smooth node calculates faster and has a better algorithm to give the geometry a finished look.

Figure 8.25

The Mesh Method is set to Quads.

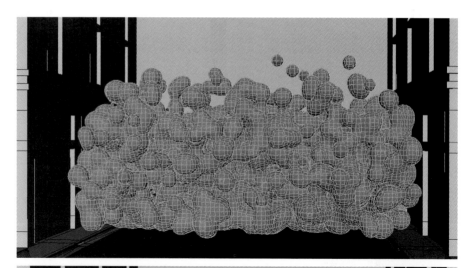

Figure 8.26

The Mesh Method is set to Acute Tetrahedra.

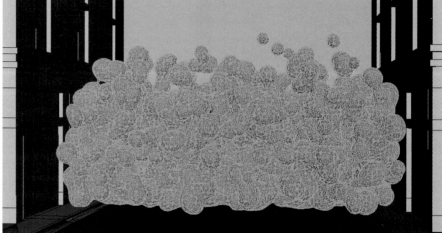

4. The Mesh Triangle Size, simply put, controls the size of the triangles in the polygon mesh. The smaller they are, the more detail you are capable of creating. (Warning! Smaller triangles mean higher-resolution meshes.) Your goal for the Mesh Triangle Size is to keep its value as high as possible. Although low values increase accuracy, they come at a price—a price so high your computer might not be able to pay for it. It is very easy to end up with millions of triangles in your mesh. Set the value to 0.6. Figure 8.27 shows the results.

5. A great advantage to converting nParticles to polygons is the availability of Motion Streak, which stretches the nParticle based on its speed and distance over one time step. The result elongates the mesh associated with each streaking nParticle. Change the Motion Streak to 2. Figure 8.28 shows the results.

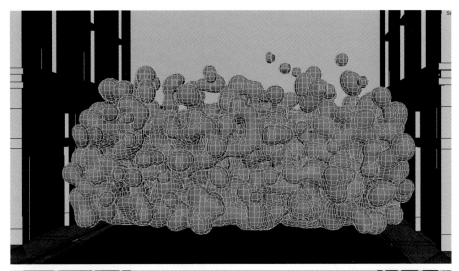

Figure 8.27

The Mesh Triangle Size is set to 0.6.

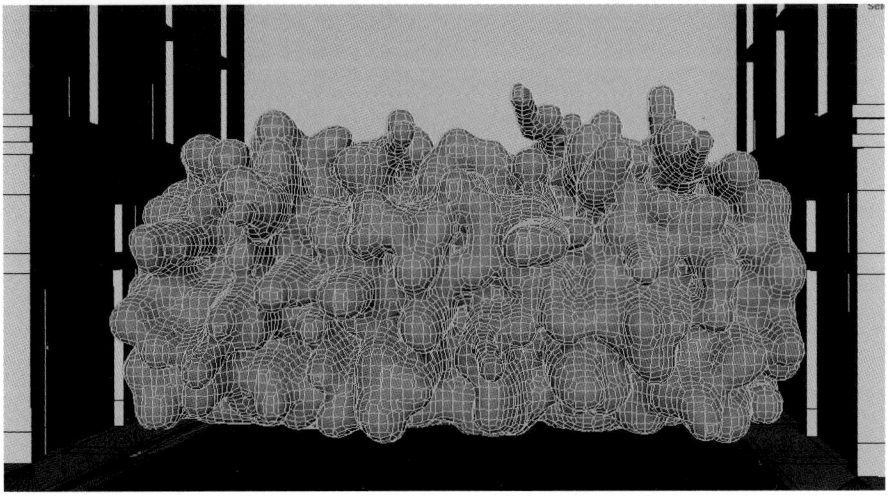

Figure 8.28

The Motion Streak has been changed to 2.

Figure 8.29

The output mesh
with a Threshold
of 0.6

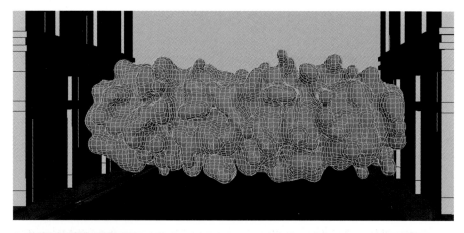

Figure 8.30

The output mesh
with a Threshold
of 0.8

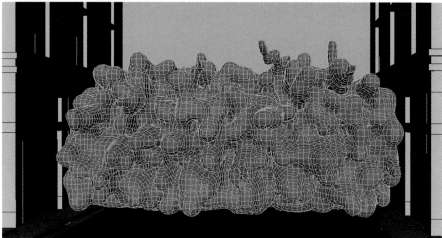

6. Next, modify the Threshold. This controls the blending between nParticles. The nParticles need to blend with each other enough to create stringy bits of fluid as they get tossed around and pull away from the main body of water. Set the Threshold to 0.8. Raising the Threshold also reduces the volume of each nParticle. The effects are most noticeable when the nParticles start to separate from one another. Take a look at Figure 8.29. It shows frame 6 with a Threshold of 0.6. Compare that to Figure 8.30, where the Threshold has been set to 0.8. Notice the highest peak as it separates. With the Threshold set to 0.8, the mesh looks tighter.

7. The Max Res does not produce any visible effects at this point. However, this seemingly innocuous attribute plays a huge role in the simulation. If Max Res is not properly set, the polygon mesh will seemingly disintegrate during your simulation. The nParticles' output mesh is solved by using a voxel grid similar to Fluids. The voxel grid dynamically changes size in order to compensate for the increasing size of the output mesh. The Max Triangle Resolution puts a cap on how big the voxel grid can get. If the grid size exceeds the set Max Triangle Resolution, the triangles are increased to compensate. If the triangle size increases too much in terms of other settings such as Blobby Scale Radius, the mesh appears to disintegrate (because the triangles become too large for the other settings). Set the Max Res to 500. Take a look at the mesh at frame 50 (Figure 8.31) to see the progress so far.

8. The size of the nParticles' radius is producing large globules. For the final simulation, the emitting nParticles setting is increased to 10,000. Although increasing the number of nParticles makes simulating more difficult, it helps reduce the size of the splashing geometry while maintaining the look of a large volume of water. Because the quantity of the nParticles increased, you need to decrease the Radius. Change the Radius to 1.8 and cache the nParticles. At frame 50, you'll see the results shown in Figure 8.32.

Figure 8.31

The results of the mesh at frame 50.

Figure 8.32

The results of the mesh at frame 50 with 10,000 nParticles and a Radius of 1.8

9. To further refine the look of the geometry, you can alter the size of the Radius and Radius Scale settings after the nParticles have been simulated. Use Figure 8.33 for the new Radius and Radius Scale settings. The two graph values are 0.4 for the first key and 0.68 for the last key. Figure 8.34 shows the new mesh.

Figure 8.33

The settings for the Radius and Radius Scale

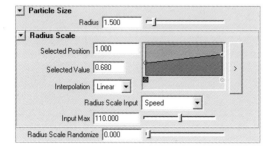

10. As mentioned at the beginning of the project, correctly shading the water is not possible in the current version of Maya. A decent work-around, albeit not perfect, is to add an ocean shader to the geometry. Create your own or use the preset, muddy-Water, from the DVD. The key to developing your own look via an Ocean Shader is to set the scale. A scale value between 8 and 15 should do the trick. Figure 8.35 shows the rendered results at frame 50 with the muddyWater ocean preset.

To check your work, compare it to renderingWater1.ma on the DVD. You can also watch renderingWater1.mov to see the water in motion.

Figure 8.34
The results of the mesh at frame 50 with the new Radius settings

Figure 8.35
The results at frame 50 with the water shader applied

About the Companion DVD

IN THIS APPENDIX:

- **What you'll find on the DVD**
- **System requirements**
- **Using the DVD**
- **Troubleshooting**
- **Customer care**

What You'll Find on the DVD

You will find all the files for completing the tutorials and understanding concepts in this book in the Chapter Files directory on the DVD. You can access the incrementally saved Maya scene files, all of the figures shown in the book, and the incrementally created movies of each project.

Each chapter directory is divided into subdirectories so you can easily find the files. Figures from the book are located in the Figures directory, QuickTime movies in the Movies directory, and so on. Note that the content for each chapter varies, so some chapters will have more materials than others.

All of the Maya scene files are called out in the text of the book. Use these to confirm your settings or test new ideas. The figures are useful to scrutinize detail that doesn't show up in print. Some can also be used for reference, to match color and shapes.

We discourage you from working with Maya project files directly from the DVD. Maya scenes link to external files such as texture maps and dynamic caches, so it's better to copy the entire project for each chapter to your local drive, including the empty folders, to ensure that the example scenes function properly.

System Requirements

To fully use all of the files on the DVD, you will need to be running Maya 2010 or Maya 2009 Unlimited (the software is *not* included on the DVD).

> There is no Maya software provided on the DVD. You need to already have a copy of Maya software to use the files on the DVD.

Make sure your computer meets the minimum system requirements shown in the following list. If your computer doesn't match up to these requirements, you may have problems using the files on the companion DVD.

- A PC running Microsoft Windows XP (SP2 or higher) or Windows Vista
- A Macintosh running Apple OS X 10.5.2 or later
- An Internet connection
- A CD/DVD-ROM drive
- Apple QuickTime 7.0 or later (Download the latest version from www.quicktime.com.)

For the latest information on system requirements for Maya, go to www.autodesk.com/maya. Although you can find specific hardware recommendations on these web pages, there is some general information that will help you determine whether you're already set up to run Maya: You need a fast processor, a minimum 2GB of RAM, and a *workstation graphics card* for the best compatibility (rather than a consumer-grade gaming video card).

Using the DVD

To access the files from the DVD, follow these steps:

1. Insert the DVD into your computer's DVD-ROM drive. The license agreement appears.

> Windows users: The interface won't launch if you have Autorun disabled. In that case, click Start → Run (for Windows Vista, Start → All Programs → Accessories → Run). In the dialog box that appears, type **D:\Start.exe**. (Replace *D* with the proper letter if your DVD drive uses a different letter. If you don't know the letter, see how your DVD drive is listed under My Computer.) Click OK.

2. Read through the license agreement, and then click the Accept button if you want to use the DVD.

The DVD interface appears. The interface allows you to access the content with just one or two clicks.

Alternately, you can access the files at the root directory of your computer and copy them to your hard drive from there.

Mac users: The DVD icon will appear on your desktop; double-click the icon to open the DVD and then navigate to the files you want.

Troubleshooting

Wiley has attempted to provide programs that work on most computers with the minimum system requirements. Alas, your computer may differ, and some programs may not work properly for some reason.

The two likeliest problems are that you don't have enough memory (RAM) for the programs you want to use, or you have other programs running that are affecting the installation or running of a program. If you get an error message such as "Not enough memory" or "Setup cannot continue," try one or more of the following suggestions and then try using the software again:

Turn off any antivirus software running on your computer. Installation programs sometimes mimic virus activity and may make your computer incorrectly believe that it's being infected by a virus.

Close all running programs. The more programs you have running, the less memory is available to other programs. Installation programs typically update files and programs; so if you keep other programs running, installation may not work properly.

Have your local computer store add more RAM to your computer. This is, admittedly, a drastic and somewhat expensive step. However, adding more memory can really help the speed of your computer and allow more programs to run at the same time.

Customer Care

If you have trouble with the book's companion DVD-ROM, please call the Wiley Product Technical Support phone number at (800) 762-2974. Outside the United States, call +1(317) 572-3994. You can also contact Wiley Product Technical Support at http://sybex.custhelp.com. John Wiley & Sons will provide technical support only for installation and other general quality-control items. For technical support on the applications themselves, consult the program's vendor or author.

To place additional orders or to request information about other Wiley products, please call (877) 762-2974.

Please check the book's website, www.sybex.com/go/MayaStudioProjectsDynamics, where we'll post additional content and updates that supplement this book should the need arise.

Index

Note to the Reader: Throughout this index **boldfaced** page numbers indicate primary discussions of a topic. *Italicized* page numbers indicate illustrations.

W

wall clouds, 103
water
　characteristics, **221–223**
　city floods, **223–227**, *224–227*
　rendering, **232–238**, *233–239*
　and sinkholes, 56–57, 61, *62*
　turbulence, **227–231**, *228–232*
waves, 222, *222*
　ramps, 175
　shock, **195–197**, *196–197*
　simulating, **227–231**, *228–232*
wind and Wind settings
　shock waves, 195
　tornadoes, **125–132**, *126–131*
Wind Field Generation setting, 130, *130*
wrecking ball effect, **50–56**, *50–55*

X

X axis
　containers, 24–25, *25*
　smoke columns, 74
XYZ resolution, 116, *116*

Y

Y axis for containers, 24–25, *25*
Y Resolution setting, 28, *29*
Y Size setting, 28, *29*
Y Velocity Scale setting, 94

Z

Z axis for smoke columns, 74